OPERATIONS OF THE MOUNTED TROOPS OF THE EGYPTIAN EXPEDITIONARY FORCE

Gosling Press

Copyright © W. J. Foster, J. G. Browne, Rex Osborne

This edition Copyright Gosling Press 2023

All rights reserved.

ISBN: 978-1-874351-22-1 (Hardback)
ISBN: 978-1-874351-23-8 (Paperback)

Introduction

The E.E.F. came into being in March 1916 from the remnants of the British troops from Gallipoli and the troops already in Egypt although it lost ten of its fourteen infantry divisions to other theatres in quick order. The multinational force of Australians, New Zealanders, Indians and British Territorial troops became a strategic reserve for the British Army

The principal task of the E.E.F. in spring 1916 was the defence of the Suez Canal, a key communications link of the British Empire. To this end, large parts of the E.E.F. were engaged in building and occupying a series of interlocking defensive posts to the east of the Canal. From taking over the E.E.F., Murray had been keen to push the defensive line out into Sinai, gradually advancing it towards the Egypt-Palestine border, allowing him to defend Egypt with fewer troops and freeing up manpower to be used on other fronts. As the E.E.F. advanced along the northern edge of Sinai it pushed out a railway, a wire netting road and water pipeline behind it to ensure its logistical support. At Romani on 4 August 1916, the E.E.F. conducted a successful defensive battle that was followed by a faltering pursuit of the Ottomans across northern Sinai in the second half of 1916. This culminated in the destruction of the El Arish garrison at the battle of Magdhaba on 23 December, and then the capture of the border post defences at Rafah on 9 January 1917.

After the failure of two attempts to take Gaza, General Murray was replaced in June 1917 by General Allenby who put in place a major reorganisation creating three Corps – two infantry and a Desert Mounted Corps. With the increase in troop numbers and artillery resources the E.E.F. broke through the Gaza-Beersheba line at the third Battle of Gaza 31 October to 7 November and during the following month pushed the Ottoman Army northward.

On reaching a line just north of Jaffa the advance moved eastwards and Jerusalem was occupied on 9 December.

During the spring of 1918, the E.E.F.'s operations expanded into the Jordan valley to the east. There were also two attempts to reach Amman to cut the railway line south to the Hejaz to support the Arab revolt. During this period, because of the constant demand for troops on the Western Front as a result of the battles of 1916-17, nearly three-quarters of the British Soldiers were replaced by Indian troops. Many of these new Indian troops had no combat experience, so much of the summer of 1918 was spent training them and integrating them into the E.E.F.'s formations.

The E.E.F. then launched a major offensive against the Ottoman Army, which had suffered significantly from disease and shortage of men and equipment. Allenby used his infantry in September 1918 to open a gap in the coastal plain north of Jaffa through which he poured his mounted troops. In a short space of time, the cavalry had encircled the majority of the Ottoman Army in Palestine capturing over 75,000. On 1 October, The Australian Light Horse entered Damascus. The Ottomans signed an armistice on 31 October

This fascinating book was originally published as a series of ten articles in the *Cavalry Journal* between 1921 and 1923. The articles were an attempt to bring together learning form what was probably the last major cavalry campaign. Unfortunately, the *Cavalry Journal* exerted little or no editorial control over the authors who each wrote sections leading at times to some confusion

Abbreviations & Acronyms

Many, perhaps most, perhaps all of these will be known to most readers but there may be some that are unfamiliar so I have thought it may be useful to include 'explanations' of the Abbreviations & Acronyms that are to be found in the text from both the authors and the original officers in the campaign.

A.I.F	Australian Imperial Force. Formed in late 1914 it was the main Australian Expeditionary force throughout the War,
A.L.H.	Australian Light Horse. Organized before World War 1 as mounted infantry. In 1914 the Regiments were already in organized brigades.
A.M.G.	Australian Machine Gun. Often attached to the A.L.H. Brigades
A.P.M.	Assistant Provost Marshal. Responsible for prisoners (as well as discipline).
ANZAC	Australian and New Zealand Army Corps, formed in Egypt in December 1914. Used throughout the First World War, the term has since passed from an abbreviation into a true acronym.
Ausdiv.	Australian Mounted Division.
B.G.G.S.	Brigadier General General Staff.
C.I.H.	21st Horse (Central Indian Horse). A Regular Army Regiment of the Indian Army
C.R.A.	Commander Royal Artillery. Still a current abbreviation in the British Army the C.R.A. is the commander in theatre not a separate rank.
E.E.F	Egyptian Expeditionary Force. The official title for the British Army formation operating in Sinai, Syria and Palestine in the First World War.
Descorps	Desert Mounted Corps. Combining the Army's mounted units, including the Imperial Camel Corps.
G.H.Q.	General Headquarters. Army headquarters
G.O.C.	General Officer Commanding. Commander-in-Chief in theatre
H.A.C.	Honourable Artillery Company. The senior

	Regiment of the British Army, in 1914 an artillery unit
I.C.C.	Imperial Camel Corps. Formed in December 1916 in the Middle East it eventual comprised four battalions, one each from Britain and New Zealand and two from Australia.
I.S.	Imperial Service. One regiment each from the Indian Princely States of <u>Jodhpur</u>, <u>Hyderabad</u>, <u>Mysore</u>, <u>Patiala</u> and <u>Alwar</u> (together with other states supplying smaller numbers) formed the Imperial Service Brigade of three regiments with units serving in rotation, but the Brigade was never more than three regiments at any time.
L.A.M.	Light Artillery Mountain
L.A.M.B.	Light Artillery Mountain Battery
L.G.S.	Limbered General Service (wagon). Horse drawn wagon, which provided much of the logistical transport for the British Army during the First World War on all fronts
M.G.S.	Machine Gun Squadron
N.Z.M.R.	New Zealand Mounted Rifles
R.A.F.	Royal Air Force. Created 1 April 1918 from the R.F.C. and the Royal Naval Air Service (see below)
R.F.C.	Royal Flying Corps. Created 13 April 1912 as the air arm of the British Army. On 1 April 1918 it was merged with the Royal Naval Air Service to become the Royal Air Force
R.G.A.	Royal Garrison Artillery. Formed in 1899, initially to man garrisons and not to take the field. During the First World War it was often responsible for the field deployment of the Heavy Artillery. It was merged into the Royal Artillery (sometimes called the R.F.A. – Royal Foot Artillery) in 1924.
R.H.A.	Royal Horse Artillery. Responsible for the more mobile artillery that accompanied cavalry units.
Yeodiv	Yeomanry Mounted Division

OPERATIONS OF THE MOUNTED TROOPS OF THE EGYPTIAN EXPEDITIONARY FORCE

LIEUT-COLONEL W. J. Foster, C.B., C.M.G., D.S.O.
LIEUT-COLONEL J. G. Browne, C.M.G., D.S.O.
LIEUT-COLONEL Rex Osborne, D.S.O., M.C.

Edited by John Wilson

FOREWORD

In the October 1920 number of the *Cavalry Journal* a few examples of the long distance patrols in the Sinai Desert were given, and it is now proposed to give, in brief outline, the doings of the mounted arm from their jumping-off place, at Kantara, on the Suez Canal, to the final overthrow of the Turkish forces in Syria[1]. It is a story of an indispensable arm, of brilliant leadership, and of men but for whose moral and fine horse mastership the campaign could not have been. They were amazing times and embrace the conquering of a hundred miles of desert; the building of the iron road and all that it implied; the conquest of Palestine and the desperate fighting in the hills north of Jerusalem; the grim relentless determination with which the cavalry held the Jordan valley throughout a summer of intense heat and blinding dust, despite the fact that the natives never thought of staying there during that period; the brilliant leading of troops at night across mountain country, where often only goat tracks existed; the daring raids in the Moab country, despite intense cold and rain; the realisation of the cavalryman's dream, when on that bright September morning in 1918 the Cavalry Corps burst through the gap made by XXI Corps between Tabsor and the sea and, riding hard and straight, overwhelmed the Turkish armies and, finally, the brilliant staff work in that classic pursuit by two columns on widely divergent roads, which caused the two columns to arrive at the objective, over hundreds of miles of country, after several hard fought actions, within almost a minute of each other.

---

[1] In collaboration with Lieutenant-Colonel J. G. Browne, C.M.G., D.S.O., 14th (King's) Hussars, who served as G.S.O.1 of the ANZAC Mounted Division, throughout the operations described. After the Armistice, a historical section under Lieutenant-Colonel W. J. Foster was formed in connection with the A.I.F., E.E.F.
Much accurate information was thus obtained from officers who took part in the various actions, and many valuable sketches and panoramas were received, some of which are included, by permission, in this account

There are today a few critics whose minds seem all obsessed by the standpoint of warfare on the Western Front. It should hardly be necessary to remind them that the British officer's horizon is not limited by the doings in one particular theatre of war, however great that struggle may have been, and, although the development of the world war has added to the numbers of weapons employed, it has not replaced those of former days.

When the world theatre of war is examined, not only does it demonstrate the tremendous possibilities of the cavalry, under dashing and intelligent leadership, and gives to the true cavalryman a vast encouragement, but it shows beyond doubt that today the Empire needs the best cavalry that can be produced. The campaign in the East is rich with examples of cavalry work in the desert, on the plains and in the hills, in thickly and sparsely populated lands and in cooperation with infantry and the air force.

He who serves the Empire today must be prepared to do so in all climes and under widely varying conditions.

It is for those who may be called upon to soldier outside Europe that these notes have been written, in the hope that they may be of use to them.

Contents

		Page
	Introduction	i
	Abbreviations & Acronyms	iii
	Foreward	v
1	The Sinai Campaign.	1
2	First Moves Eastward	7
3	Difficulties Of The Country	10
4	Commencement Of The Desert Campaign	15
5	Patrolling The Desert	20
6	Period May-July, 1916 Operations In The Wadi Um Muksheib	24
7	Operations Prior To The Battle Of Romani	27
8	The Battle of Romani	42
9	Raid on Bir El Mazar, Extension of The Railway Eastwards and Final Preparations for the Clearance of The Sinai Peninsula.	63
10	Action at Magdhaba.	71
11	Action At Rafa, 9 January 1917	75
12	Period Prior To The Operations For The First	86

Attack On Gaza

13	The First Battle of Gaza	93
14	The Second Battle of Gaza. Preparations For The Battle.	102
15	The Asluj-Auja Expedition and The Period of Minor Enterprises, May 1917	113
16	Phase III	117
17	Operations North-East Of Beersheba	151
18	Pursuit And Battle	168
19	Phase IV. The Advance Into The Judean Mountains	183
20	Phase IV, Operations Across Jordan	200
21	The Es Salt Raid	211
22	Phase V Consideration, In July 1918, Of Offensive Operations On A Grand Scale.	231
23	The Final Plan	245
24	Phase V Preliminary Operations	265
25	Phase V	285
26	Phase V Part 2	303
27	Exploiting Success	313

List of Illustrations

	Page
Sketch Map A	2
Panorama A Sinai Peninsula	4
Panorama B Romani	28
Panorama D Wellington Ridge looking South	34
Panorama E Mount Royston northward to the railway Line	36
Panorama F View showing centre of outpost line Held by 3rd A.L.H. Regt	40
Plan of Romani Position	43
Sketch Map of the battle of Bir El Abd	57
Sketch Map of the main attack	60
Plan Showing Distance in Miles from Camps to Bir El Abd	64
Sketch map showing troop movements, night 20–21 December 1916	69
Sketch Map G Map El Magdhaba	72
Sketch map H Rafa	76
View of battlefield of Rafa from NZ Mounted Rifle Brigade HQ	77
Plan of attack as actually carried out at Rafa	80
Map to show where operations took place from start of First Gaza	87
Positions 26 March 1917	90
Map showing Turkish line facing SW	102
Map showing part of the Second Battle of Gaza	105
Map showing the Raid on the Asluj-Auja Railway	112
Plate VI The second offensive, capture of Beersheba	126
Plate VII Capture of Beersheba	141
Plate VIII Yeomanry mounted attack on Huj Nov 1917	163
Plate IX Plan of position at El Mughar	172
Plate X Jerusalem operations	191
Plate XI Capture of Jerusalem	196
Map B	201
Operations in and beyond the Jordan Valley	210
Map C	232
Plate XIII The Battles of Megiddo and Sharon	234
Plate XIV British dispositions as shown by enemy intelligence	239
Plate XV Situation night of 18 September 1918	240

Plate XVI Disposition of troops during operations against Semakh, 25 September 1918 — 304
Plate XVIb Capture of Damascus — 306
Plate XVII Map showing main lines of communication, July 1917 — 314

1. THE SINAI CAMPAIGN.

An enemy force moving from Palestine against the Suez Canal and Egypt had to cross a comparatively waterless desert for a distance of over a hundred miles. There were two main routes by which invading armies might approach from Palestine. The first, or northern route, the Darb el Sultani, the oldest road in the world, ran roughly parallel with the Mediterranean, through Rafa, el Arish, Bir el Abd and Qatia to Kantara. The second, or centre route, ran from el Auja, through Jifjaffa and the Wadi Muksheib to Serapeum. There was also a third route, through Nekhl. The first was the bettered watered route, there being a considerable oasis area stretching from Qatia to Bir el Abd, in which any number of troops could concentrate within striking distance of the canal. On the second route, the only large water supply was at Moiya Harab, 45 miles east of Serapeum, where it was stored in very large ancient rock cisterns, supplemented after a good rainfall by a small lake on the Wadi Muksheib. On the third route, water was considered insufficient to maintain any large force. Such an enemy force would, moreover, be operating far from its base, with long lines of communication. The northern route was, to a certain extent, vulnerable from the sea. The second route is safeguarded from interruption by the desert it traverses and the long distance it is from the coast.

On the outbreak of war, the garrison of Egypt was reinforced by troops sent out from England, India and Australia. The Suez Canal, through which vast numbers of troops were passing, was of vital importance as a main line of communication to the Allies.

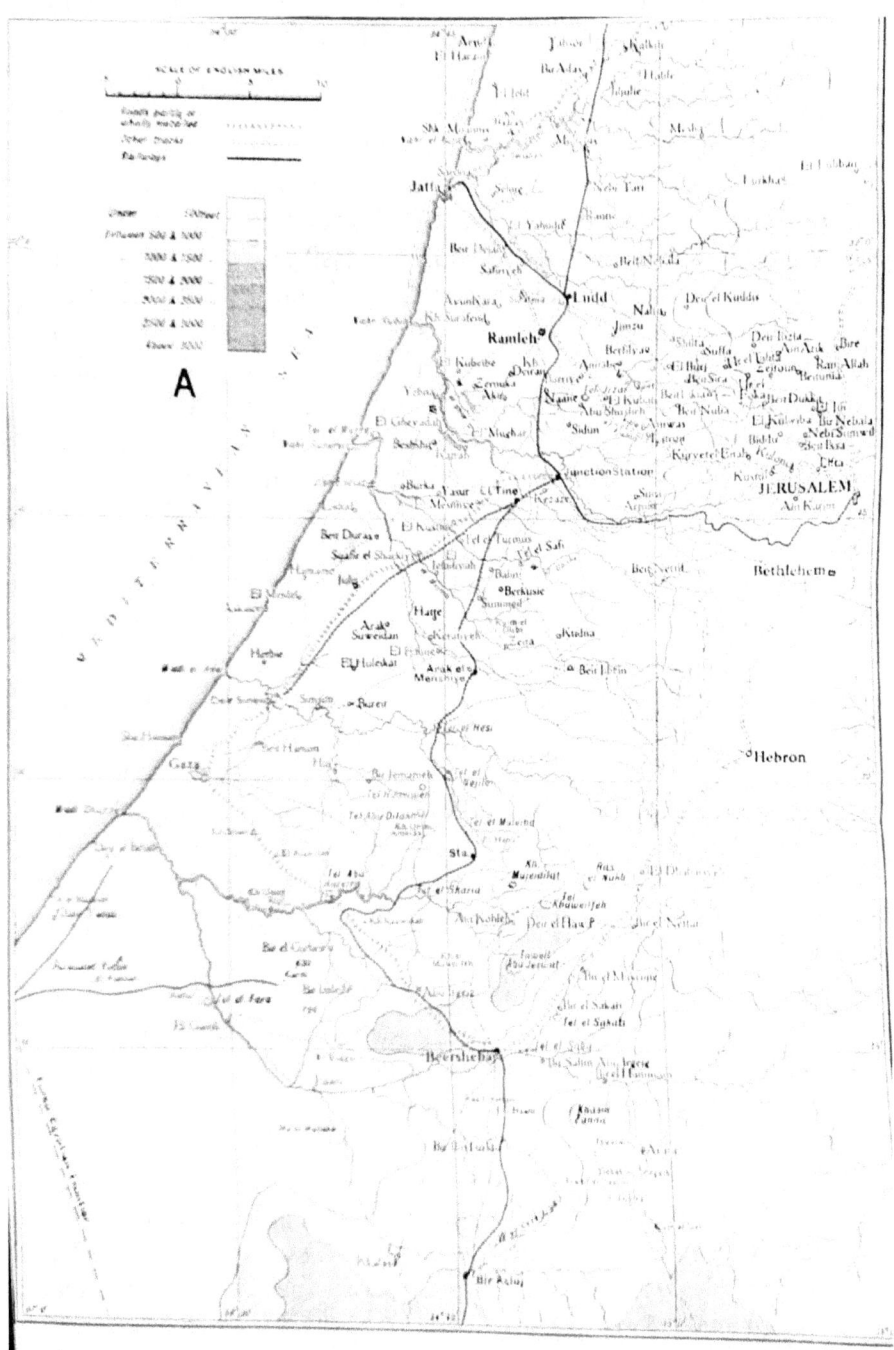

On 5 November 1914, Turkey threw in her lot with the Central Powers, probably induced by the possibility of the restoration of her supremacy in Egypt. With Turkey's open threat to invade Egypt, the protection of the canal and of Egypt became a matter of urgency. The policy of defence adopted was that of making the line of the canal the line of resistance. A large portion of the lower lying desert to the northeast of the canal was flooded, so as to render approach by that direction impossible. Warships took up stations in the canal itself, while naval launches took over the duty of guarding the Bitter Lakes. The troops detailed for the defence of the canal itself were entrenched on the western side, with reserves concentrated at points of tactical importance. It was thought that the difficulties of crossing the desert would make approach by the Turks well nigh impossible. Whether the Germans ever intended to pay the price for Turkish alliance, by sending a strong enough force to make the invasion practicable is doubtful. The Turkish rank and file were led to believe that a serious invasion was intended. The primary object was to detain as large a British force as possible in Egypt and possibly, a secondary object, to render the canal temporarily impassable. There were rumours in Syria that, when their army crossed the canal, the disaffected population in Egypt would rise. Whatever may have been the object, Turkey made an attempt in February 1915. As a preliminary move, the railway in Syria was put in hand, and by January 1915, the Turks had formed advanced posts at el Auja, on the frontier, and also at El Kossaima and el Arish.

The promised attack materialised in February 1915. The Turks came by the central route, being no doubt influenced in this direction by the possibilities of raids on the northern route. It was of course conceivable that a raid via the Wadi el Arish might temporarily dislocate communications; but only mounted troops could have done this. Such difficulties as transport by sea and a landing at el Arish, or a long march along the coast and water difficulties as well, made such an attempt by us most improbable. However, as regards the second route, the very points that safeguard it from its greatest difficulties as a route by which to attack the canal.

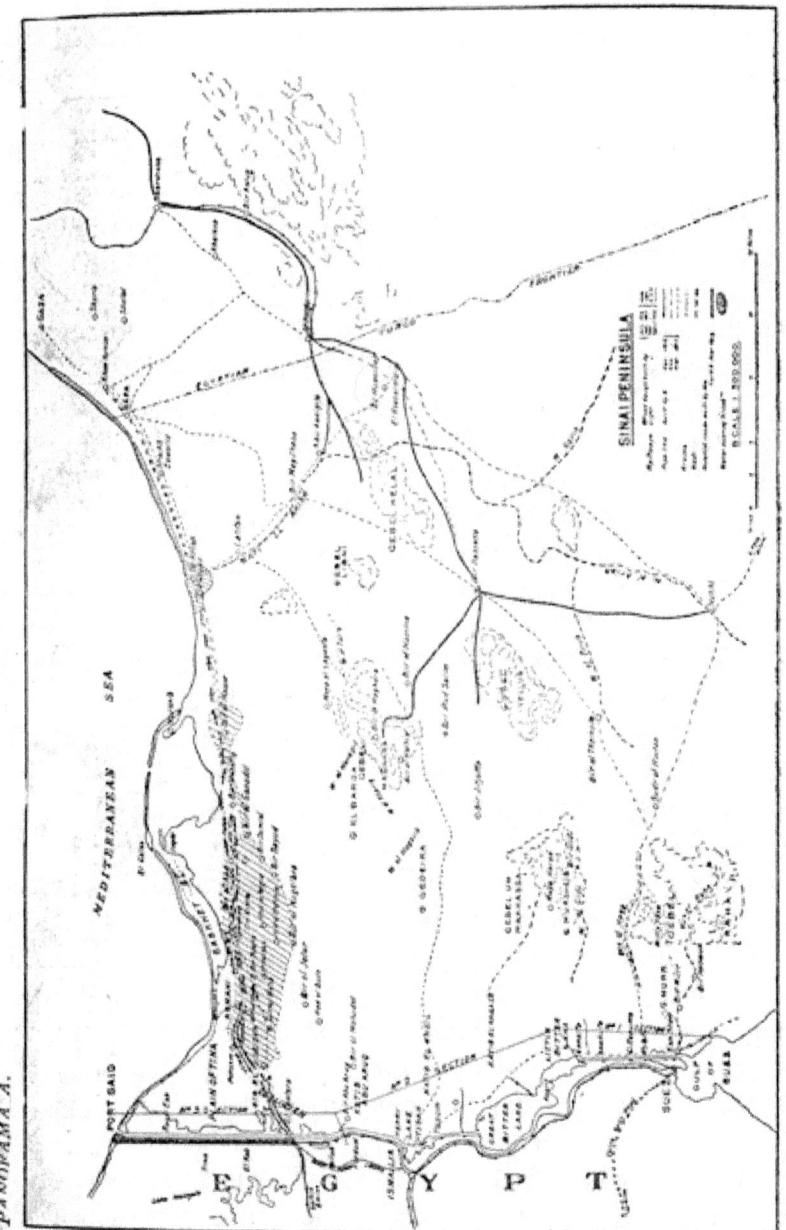

The Turk, although he managed to reach the canal and actually placed pontoons in the canal, was driven back with some loss. He finally withdrew and marched back to Palestine, which, we are told, he reached in a most pitiable condition. This was the only time that a formed body of the enemy succeeded in reaching the canal. The result, however, had shown that it was possible to achieve the almost impossible.

After the evacuation of Gallipoli, most of the forces there were withdrawn directly or indirectly to Egypt, and subsequently again met the Turk in the advance into Palestine. The situation in the Sinai Peninsula early in 1916 was obscure. Although the Turkish means of communication in Southern Syria and Sinai, commenced with a view to another attack on the canal, were in a backward state, it was known he had a force of 250,000 men or more available for such an attack.

In the light of over a year's experience of actual war, views on the military situation had altered. In the first place, we had been disillusioned as to the impossibility of crossing the desert. The Turks had announced that what they had effected was only a reconnaissance. In any case, they had shown us that, backed by the resources of the Central Powers, there would be no insuperable obstacles to their bringing a large and fully equipped army across the desert. In the second place, the problems of defending the Canal and Egypt were not identical. While the canal formed an excellent obstacle, difficult to negotiate when stoutly defended, and so a capital defensive line for the protection of Egypt, yet this line was inadequate for the protection of the canal itself or for securing the immunity of the passing ships. It was also realised that some other line must be found for the protection of the canal itself. In 1915, while the defences were on the western bank, small parties of the Turks approached the eastern bank. On more than one occasion in the summer of 1915, they placed mines in the fairway of the canal. It would have been possible, therefore, to have interfered seriously with the working of the canal and the passage of shipping. A defensive line across the actual desert may be all very well in wartime, but to keep a garrison on such a line always would be well nigh impossible. It appeared that sooner or later the best line for the defence of the canal lay in the fertile country beyond the eastern desert- Palestine.

Finally, it had been brought home that the worst form of defence is passive defence.

2. FIRST MOVES EASTWARD

In accordance with the policy of defending the Suez Canal upon a line farther east, decided upon about October 1915, a scheme of defence had been prepared, certain works constructed, railways, pipe lines and roads commenced in the various sections of the canal defences, which had been divided into three sections.

Troops were being concentrated in the three sections of the canal defences. The work on the defences was backward and a part of the front defence line was first occupied by the 2nd Australian Division about 4 February 1916. The situation did not give any great cause for anxiety, as there were no signs of any immediate advance by the enemy from his advanced posts, now at El Kossaima and Bir Hassana. The defences were, however, hastened on with all speed, in order that the paramount importance of organising the offensive defence could be achieved. Hence, all troops returning from the peninsula were employed as far as possible on the canal.

Practically nothing had been done towards the organisation of mobile forces. Any advance by the enemy, owing to the season, had to be commenced by the middle of March. The collection of a large number of riding and transport camels was at once undertaken and the Australian Light Horse Brigades and the New Zealand Mounted Rifle Brigade were rapidly reequipped and horsed. One brigade (1st Australian Light Horse Brigade) was sent off at once to prevent raids on the Nile Valley by the Senoussi from the desert area west of Egypt, to prevent the stirring up of the native tribes that were favourably inclined towards the enemy, and also to prevent unrest in this area among disaffected or nervous elements of the population. These duties were successfully accomplished and passed off without incident.

In the meantime, the situation on the eastern front became easier. The decisive defeat of the Turkish Army at Erzerum by the Russians, on 16 February, crushed the Turkish hopes of a conquest of Egypt, and necessitated a withdrawal of a considerable number of troops from the Egyptian Front. The garrisons of Syria were gradually reduced until it was estimated that not more than 60,000 were available for an attack on Egypt, consequently the withdrawal of troops in March and April for embarkation to France had no immediate effect on the campaign. The work of completing the front line defences (some 80 miles) was pushed forward rapidly, in spite of the difficulties of the *khamseen* storms, which blew during the whole of March. Trenches were continuously filled with sand. Wire entanglements would be found at the end of a dust storm to have disappeared entirely, being some two to three feet under the sand. The work was successfully accomplished. At times, the heat was overpowering. Sometimes, when the wind was carrying with it so much of the desert that the sun was hidden by dust clouds, the temperature went up to 115 and 120 degrees. Lips cracked and the daily scanty allowance of water did not relieve parched throats for an hour. The allowance of water for all purposes was never more than a gallon a day, and very often less. Pipelines and roads were pushed on, but for some time all water had to be brought in *fantasses* on camels for a distance of over nine miles. *Fantasses* are small iron receptacles and hold from 10 to 15 gallons each. Two usually make a load for a camel. The troops, notwithstanding the greatest discomforts of continuous dust and flies, worked day and night and completed the trenches in a remarkably short period.

During this period a small reconnaissance, which was sent out from No.2 Section of the defences to ascertain the attitude of the local Bedouins and to obtain information regarding the water supply at Moiya Harab in the Wadi Muksheib and at El Kassif, covered a distance of 72 miles, over a waterless and barren area, in 37 hours (including halts), demonstrating very early in the campaign the use of cavalry for long distance patrols.

Formation of the ANZAC Mounted Division.
On 16 March 1916, the Australian and New Zealand Mounted Division was formed, under Major-General H. G. Chauvel, C.B., C.M.G.,[2] and consisted of the 1st, 2nd and 3rd Australian Light Horse Brigades and the New Zealand Mounted Rifle Brigade. No Dominion Horse Artillery was available, so the Ayrshire, Inverness, Somerset and Leicester Territorial Horse Artillery batteries were attached to the Division, and remained with it throughout. During the second week of April, the Division moved to Salhia and came into No.3 Section canal defences. It is interesting to note that Salhia was Napoleon's jumping-off place when he started on his invasion of Syria. The Imperial Camel Corps was also formed about this time, from volunteers from the Yeomanry, Australian and New Zealand infantry and also from the Light Horse and New Zealand Mounted Rifles.

The system of entrenched posts, covering practically the whole length of the canal and on an average seven miles east of it, was naturally very expensive in troops and, as all the infantry that could be spared were urgently required in France, some more economical system had to be adopted. It was therefore decided to occupy the Qatia-Abd oasis area, empty the water at Moiya Harab (thus rendering the second route useless) and keep sufficient troops in the vicinity of Suez to ward off any raid in that direction, while holding the rest of the defences, except those at Kantara, lightly.

---

[2] Afterwards Lieutenant-General Sir H. G. Chauvel, G.C.M.G., K.C.B., commanding the Desert Mounted Corps

3. DIFFICULTIES OF THE COUNTRY

In order to understand thoroughly the campaign in the Sinai Peninsula, it is necessary to grasp the difficulties under which troops, particularly the mounted troops, worked for nine months. The three big factors were water, sand, and the palm hods or plantations.

The problem of water supply had always presented a difficulty to armies crossing this waterless desert. There are a certain number of reservoirs or cisterns[3] that held up water during the rains. Water for animals is plentiful in certain areas, particularly in the Qatia area, the Zugba Peninsula and in the hods along the beach near el Arish. In most places within easy reach of the coast, water could be got at a few feet, and large sumps were made. In very few instances only was water so obtained fit for human consumption. Testing parties were always with the advanced troops. Water containing less than 50 parts of salt in 100,000 could, after chlorination, be issued. Wells containing less than 50 parts of salt were, however, few and far between. Water for the troops had to be brought by the pipeline and supplies by the railway, hence it was a matter of great difficulty to maintain a mobile column for any length of time at any distance from the railhead. The nature of the soft sand prevented the use of wheeled transport to any extent, and even then, it could only be used in a very limited way on the main tracks. First line transport consisted of camels, while camel convoys took the place of the divisional train. The progress of the campaign, therefore, became regulated by the speed with which the railway could be opened up. Material

---

[3] Cisterns are bottle shaped and dug into the ground to depths varying from 20 to 30 feet, with diameters up to 15 feet.

for the railway and the pipeline was the most serious obstacle, and at times considerable delay ensued owing to its non-arrival. At first, the horses would not drink the water, particularly coming off fresh water. The water was brackish and contained a large percentage of alkaline matter. Horses, unless very thirsty, would not touch water that contained more than 150 parts of salt. Drinking water in the Sinai, unless chlorinated, was dangerous. Most of the wells are in the palm hods and are used by the Bedouins. They are usually filthy and always required cleaning. A few wells like these occasionally relieved the pressure on the pipeline, but, in the main, water brought by the pipeline alone could be depended on. From the pipeline, it was brought in *fantasses* to the troops.

The problem of drinking water was always an anxiety and limited the activity of the mounted troops at any great distance from the railhead. The water for animals was, as a rule, easily obtainable once a camp was formed, but in the long distance patrols carried out by the mounted troops off the beaten palm tree areas (coastal area), horses had to do without water until the return to camp.

The wells in the hods were unsuitable. The best wells, as a rule, were found under the high sand dunes. The construction of them was often a difficulty, owing to the pressure of sand and, until a suitable well lining was brought up, trouble was always occurring in keeping them open. Where water was found at depths of under six feet, big sumps were dug. In the early days, it was found necessary to construct wells in the reconnoitred areas, and special protective detachments for this purpose were sent out from time to time. A supply of water for the horses was then usually ensured for small bodies. A good deal of the difficulty was later overcome by the employment of the 'spearpoint'. The spear point was in effect a small boring plant, and consisted of a triangle, pulleys, large pipe in sections and weight, et cetera. The pipe was driven in until water was reached and the smaller pipe for the pump then inserted, when the larger pipe was withdrawn. The whole gear could be easily packed on a half limber, together with pumps. It could also be carried on the pack animal. It was quick and easy to put down, and solved a lot of the water difficulties, provided that the water was not more than 20 feet from the surface. Later when el Arish was occupied, all the water was confined to the beach and very little inland. The only exceptions inland were at certain places down the Wadi el Arish, particularly at Magdhaba, where a plentiful supply was available. Even at el Arish, some 90 miles from the canal, the troops were still dependent on the pipeline for their water supply.

The carriage of water in tanks on the backs of camels, a method used by us locally for supplying troops between water dumps and the headquarters of units, proved successful here thousands of years ago. Further progress was made when supplies were transported in tank trucks along the railway. However, a bolder adaptation of modern science was reached when it was decided to lay a piped supply of water from the Nile. Purity had to be considered as well as adequacy of supply. A peculiar danger had to be guarded against, the *bilhaziosos*. This disease is conveyed by a parasitic worm found in the waters of the Nile, and affects not only those who drink the water but also those who bathe in it or merely wash, consequently no troops were allowed to touch it unless it had been previously treated.

The supply east of the canal was restricted and only one gallon per man per day for all purposes allowed. Large waterworks were put up at Kantara, water drawn in from the sweet water canal, mixed with alum and pumped through settling tanks with filters. When it had passed through these, it was pumped underneath the Suez Canal into reservoirs on the eastern bank. Here it was chlorinated and hence the water, now fit for all purposes, was pushed forward to its destination. There being no gradient to assist the natural flow of the water, it had to be pumped forward by successive stages. The first stage was Romani. When working at its greatest length there were 17 in all. At times during the advance, the railway had to be called in to aid with water tanks. Ultimately, when the infantry settled down to protracted trench warfare, before Gaza, this pipeline was delivering a constant flow of water to the trenches, distant some couple of hundreds of miles from the banks of the Nile.

Beyond a little rough grazing in isolated parts for camels, no vegetation existed in Sinai, and so, throughout the period, the horses never had an opportunity of grazing.

The general run of the sand dunes is from south-east to north-west, and steep on the north side. The march from north to south is, therefore, considerably lengthened. The soft sand is tiring to the horses, which often in parts sank down to the hocks. Leading horses, as is usual on a night march, is frequently impossible when the soft areas have to be traversed.

Very often, the only route possible was to slide down the side of dunes at angles as steep as one in one. It was hopeless to attempt climbing them, and deviations of over a mile had constantly to be made.

On dark, moonless nights, the sense of direction of the most acute was sorely tried. Patrols off the beaten tracks had the greatest difficulty in finding their way. The hot season, May to August, was most trying; at times the continual glare, the abnormal distances, unusual means of transport (often none), sand storms, the mirage, and the awful heat tried troops to the utmost limit, and only troops whose physique and morale were of the highest order could have stood the strain.

The horses stood the strain well. Beyond battle casualties there were few evacuations. Even though the standard of horse mastership was high, only horses that had been carefully selected as the right type could have lasted. A poor type horse seldom lasted more than one patrol, hence the greatest care had to be exercised in sending forward remounts. The Australian remount always stood his test and rarely failed.

The heavy sand cut down the marching powers of our infantry to one-third of the normal; but the sand did not prove so much an obstacle to the enemy. He was usually barefooted, got over it easily, and silently, and at night was difficult to locate.
The horseman, on the other hand, always makes a noise,

especially when horses are worried by sand flies. The sand always gives a well defined track, and in this respect was equally disadvantageous to the enemy as to us.

The palm hods were of tactical value for concealment, especially at Qatia, but the sand surrounding them would show up the tracks leading into them. They were hot in summer, and damp and cold in winter.

Vehicles were given up early in the campaign and, beyond a few limbers, sand carts for the ambulances and cable wagons, camel transport was wholly depended on. Considerable difficulty was at first experienced with the artillery in the heavy sand. Sand tyres (an iron tyre some six to eight inches wide) partly overcame the trouble, except in the soft sand country. It was not until the pedrails had been adopted that the 18pdr could keep up with a column, using eight horses per gun, two wheel, three centre, and three lead. The pedrail consisted of stout blocks of wood about a foot square and two and a half inches thick held on the tyres by chains. Sand sledges for carrying the wounded were also found preferable to the camel *cacolets*, which is a sort of canvas arrangement on both sides of a camel for carrying either sitting or laying down cases. The evacuation of the wounded was always a serious anxiety.

The railway was broad gauge and commenced at Kantara. It eventually became the trunk line between Egypt and Palestine, and later with Syria and beyond. In the days of trench warfare before Gaza, in 1917, it transported freight heavily laden with ammunition and stores, troop trains conveying officers and men in open trucks, hospital trains, and a sleeping car express running nightly in each direction. In its conception, it was just a military railway, laid with but little preparation across the sands of the desert. To this railway, however, was largely due the success of the campaign.

4. COMMENCEMENT OF THE DESERT CAMPAIGN

The 5th Mounted Brigade were operating in the Qatia oasis and patrolling as far as Bir el Nuss and Hodum Ugba. In this district, the last within striking distance of the Suez Canal where there is sufficient water to allow the concentration of a large body of troops, preliminaries to the accomplishment of the ultimate aim, the permanent occupation of the well-watered zone radiating 15 miles east and south-east, were begun. Bir el Abd, 45 miles from the canal, was reconnoitred by a squadron of the Gloucestershire Hussars on the 2 April and found occupied. A further reconnaissance on the 9 April, by the Worcestershire Yeomanry, found the enemy in considerable strength in possession of a ridge north-east of Bir el Abd. The enemy were driven eastwards, but owing to the heavy soft sand, no shock action was possible, and the squadron was compelled to return to Qatia.

Aeroplane reconnaissance had reported small enemy forces at Hassana and Nekhl, with a fairly strong force at el Arish.

In the meantime, the railway had been pushed forward to Pelusium. A force of approximately 2,500 enemy, with some guns, was now at Bir el Abd. On the 22 April the Flying Corps reported small bodies of the enemy troops at Bir el Bayud, 15 miles east-south-east of Qatia and Bir el Mageibra, 10 miles south-east of Qatia.

The disposition of troops in No. 3 Section on 21 April was as follows:

Worcestershire Yeomanry   Qatia
Warwickshire Yeomanry   Hamisah
(less one squadron)

5th Mounted Brigade Headquarters and Gloucestershire Yeomanry	Romani
156th Brigade, 52nd Division	Pelusium (railhead)
Detachment 5th Bn Royal Scots Fusiliers	Dueidar
52nd Division (less one brigade)	Kantara
ANZAC Mounted Division (less two brigades)	Salhia (some 20 miles west of Kantara, or approximately 65 miles from Bir el Abd)

On 21 April, one squadron of the Worcestershire Yeomanry moved into bivouac at Oghratina, seven miles east-north-east of Qatia, to cover an R.E. party (50 dismounted men) detailed to prepare wells. On 22 April, another squadron of the regiment proceeded to Oghratina. This place was within 10 miles of Bir el Abd, and it was intended that these two squadrons, if attacked in force, should retire on Qatia, thence, if necessary, on Romani. It is questionable, in view of the overwhelming enemy force within striking distance, whether the officer commanding these two squadrons would have been able to hold off the enemy long enough to enable him to get his dismounted party away ; the chances were less if attacked at night. As it turned out, the enemy, favoured by a dense fog, attacked Oghratina at dawn on 23 April. The first encounter took place at 05:30. By 07:00, the enemy bad surrounded Oghratina on all sides and escape for the dismounted party was beyond hope. The garrison of the post practically died to a man. A squadron of the 6th Light Horse Regiment reached Oghratina two days later, and the scene on the battlefield, yeomen and Turkish dead lying together, proved beyond doubt that not only had the yeomen put up a great and gallant fight, but, rather than surrender, had died almost to a man. Only three badly wounded men were left to tell the story. Two of these subsequently died. As the squadron had no means of transporting the wounded, the men carried them in relays on their backs to Romani, some 10 miles over the soft sand.

At 09:30, this column then attacked Qatia, which was finally taken about 14:00. In the meantime, another enemy column, of about 1,000, moving up from the south, attacked Dueidar at 06:30, but the garrison, reinforced by two companies from Hill 70, counter-attacked at 12:30 and forced the enemy to withdraw. The Turkish columns after this raid fell back on Bir el Abd and Bir el Bayud. After Qatia had fallen a portion of the 5th Mounted Brigade, which had made desperate efforts to rescue the force at Qatia, withdrew partly to Romani, and the remainder of the brigade to Dueidar, and subsequently the whole brigade to Kantara.

In view of the possibility of attack on these isolated posts in the Qatia area, the 5th Australian Light Horse Regiment had left Salhiaat at 06.00 on 22 April and bivouacked at Kantara on the night of 22–23 April. The regiment was not sent forward from Kantara until 13:00, a delay of half a day, although 14 miles from the nearest enemy, who were then retiring southeast. The regiment, however, managed to get in touch with the Turkish column before dusk and inflicted material damage on it.

The remainder of the 2nd Australian Light Horse Brigade left Salhia at 13:00 on 23 April. The first intimation that the ANZAC Division received was at 17:30, when orders were given for the remainder to move to Kantara as rapidly as possible. The whole division (less guns) left at 19:00, and marching all night reached Kantara at 04:00 on the 24 April.

Thus commenced one of the most interesting campaigns in history, for, although the occupation of the oasis was at first undertaken as a purely defensive measure, there is no doubt that the defeat of the Turks at Romani in August, 1916, led to the further advance on el Arish and the clearing out of the Turks from Egyptian territory, and the subsequent victories at Magdhaba and Rafa opened the way for the invasion of Palestine. These Australian and New Zealand horsemen and Territorial horse gunners were to form the nucleus of one of the largest bodies of horse that had ever operated under one commander since the days of Darius and, with their comrades from Great Britain and India, not only maintained the traditions of cavalry but added to them.

At 09:00 on 24 April, the 2nd Australian Light Horse Brigade (less 5th A.L.H. Regiment) left Hill 70 for Pelusium railhead. The column had hardly started when information was received that a large force of the enemy was reported by the Flying Corps moving on the railhead. The brigade at once increased the pace, and notwithstanding the heavy going (soft sand) maintained a speed of six miles until within two miles of the railhead, when the advanced patrols reported 'all quiet'. The enemy column reported turned out to be some 400 Egyptian Labour Corps, who had been working on the railway track between Pelusium and Romani, and no rations having been delivered to them during the excitement of 23rd, they had decided to come in and see about it.

The brigade bivouacked there that night and, moving at 05:00 on the 25 April, occupied Romani at 09:00. Strong patrols were pushed out to locate the enemy, who now had retired to Bir el Abd. The remainder of the Mounted Division remained at Hill 40. One regiment of the New Zealand Brigade moved up to Pelusium on the 26 April. The 5th Mounted Brigade was withdrawn to Kantara.

Owing to the difficulties of supply, it was apparently not possible to move the division earlier to Kantara; hence, it could hardly be considered within supporting distance of the force occupying the Qatia oasis when the enemy made his raid. The division thus had to move 32 miles over very soft sandy country before it could reach even the nearest advanced defensive post at Dueidar, and this meant the loss of at least 24 hours, which was of paramount importance.

The 2nd Light Horse Brigade (6th and 7th Regiments at Romani and the 5th Regiment at Dueidar) remained in the oasis, patrolling the Qatia district and the country to the south, which was quickly cleared of the enemy's outposts. When the enemy was known to be in close proximity the troops patrolled about 14 miles out, where they remained until dark and then returned to camp. Throughout the campaign units in the front area had everything in readiness to move straight out so as to take the enemy on in the open should he advance.

In No.2 Section of the Defence Zone, a very successful reconnaissance to Jifjaffa was carried out on 11 and 13 April, by a detachment from the 3rdLight Horse Brigade. The force, commanded by Major W. H. Scott, D.S.O., 9th Light Horse Regiment, consisted of one squadron 9th L.H. Regiment with detachments from the 8th L.H. Regiment, Bikanir Camel Corps, Engineers and Camel Transport Corps. A pack wireless detachment also accompanied the force.

The objective was 52 miles from the starting point, and a jumping-off place for the attack, eight miles south-west of objective, was reached at 02:30 on 12 April. From here, the attack was made by three troops upon theenemy'spositionat09:00. The enemy, cut off in their attempted retreat, by the right flanking party of the attack, stood on one of the hills above the wells and lost 16 men killed and 15 men wounded before surrendering. One Austrian Lieutenant of engineers and 33 other prisoners were captured, our casualties being one man and one horse killed. The destruction of the enemy's camp was thoroughly carried out, a quantity of correspondence was taken, and the elaborate well-boring plant, which had been at work for five months, was completely demolished.

The raid is of particular interest as being the first carried out by the cavalry against the enemy in Sinai. The distance, though long, and the time allowed to reach the objective short, proved that the cavalry could be efficiently used in desert warfare. The actual distance covered by the raiding party was over 120 miles in less than three and a half days.

5. PATROLLING THE DESERT

From the end of April, continuous patrolling within a radius of 20 miles from Romani and Dueidar was maintained, but the nearest enemy outpost was Bir el Abd, and he very rarely ventured beyond it. Efforts were made early in May to flood the Bardawil Lake, by means of a canal cut in from the sea, as a partial barrier against an enemy advance, but the depression being only eight inches deep no appreciable amount of water was let in.

Value of Cavalry for Long Distance Patrolling.
Raids at frequent intervals were made on the enemy's advanced outposts. Although the Turk had materially increased his numbers in Sinai, doubtless with a view of detaining troops in Egypt, there were indications that he was drawing in his advanced posts. The Turk early found that his posts within 30, and, later in September, 45 miles, notwithstanding the heavy sand and heat, were within striking distance of the ANZAC mounted troops at Romani.

During May, several successful reconnaissances were made. At first only one brigade was kept in the forward area, but from the middle of May onwards two brigades were always kept there (Romani and et Maler) and divided the patrol work, which had become increasingly heavy. The various oases were always visited by strong patrols, which rounded up any small enemy parties within reach. Later the leakage of information by Bedouins became apparent and, while they were allowed to remain unmolested, the possibility of surprising any of the Turkish outposts was out of the question.

The native population comprises some 17 minor tribes of nomadic Arabs or Bedouins, numbering in the whole peninsula perhaps 10,000 adult males, with possibly 25,000 women and children. Over these tribes, the nominal sheikhs have but little control and the tribesmen are in most matters a law unto themselves. The Bedouin moves over the desert silently and in the soft sand country can easily outdistance a column. It was also known that a majority, though not actively hostile, were favourable to the Turk, and often gave him warning of our approach in sufficient time to allow him to escape. In that heavy country, it was not possible to capture the Turk if he had been warned in time to allow his getting even a start of only a thousand yards. After several unsuccessful attempts to round up Turkish patrols known to have been warned the Bedouins were taken in hand also, and, thus robbed of his most accurate means of information, the chances of minor enterprises became brighter, and the enemy outposts' patrols often fell an easy prey.

In the early periods, the long distance reconnaissance was always made in strength, a whole brigade often being employed, and seldom less than a regiment. The methods we worked on were:
(a) an objective was selected and either that alone was visited or we struck at two or three objectives at the same time.
(b) no party sent out was less than a squadron for each place.
(c) at least a regiment was ready to back up the party carrying out the reconnaissance.
(d) the operation was always timed to hit the objective at dawn. The march was therefore always at night and so avoided heat and being seen by the enemy. It was the policy adopted to employ these larger bodies, and it certainly had the advantage of getting everyone to know the country by day and night, and accustomed the horses to move in the sand and to drink the water. Had our intelligence of the enemy's movements been more accurate in those days it would perhaps have been more advantageous to have adopted more frequent reconnaissances with smaller bodies. In the long distance raids, the column always moved at night and struck at dawn. By day, any element of surprise was impossible and the night work was always cooler and less fatiguing. Maps issued were on a scale of 1:125,000, accurate enough as regards location of places but of little use otherwise. The sandy desert features of the country were monotonous in their regularity, and often the only way of locating one's position was by the old

telegraph line from Kantara to el Arish. Many a weary column returning, after working to the south, heaved a sigh of relief when the line appeared in sight.

Necessity for Thorough Compass Knowledge.
Compass work at times was alone possible. There are no outstanding features to guide one – just sand dune after sand dune – and the difficulties of getting to an obscure post some 30 miles away, and marked only by a few palm trees, were great. Often the palm trees were in a depression and could not be seen until within a hundred yards. The lie of the sand dunes made a direct march impossible. The direction had to be carefully plotted, especially for night work, distances on each bearing carefully noted and, as the march went on, careful calculations had to be made for the various deviations, and the column brought back again on the direction as soon as the dune country allowed. Seldom, however, was a unit late in getting to its destination. One particular instance is noteworthy of a unit moving all night in a dense fog over unknown dune country, surrounding its objective, some 29 miles away, and capturing the garrison by dawn.

By day, the hazy mirage effects also proved an added obstacle. Often no pace faster than a walk was possible for hours, and the heat in some of the return journeys so great that the men could not even touch their water bottles, and the rifle barrels became so hot that men's hands were often blistered. Some of the distances covered by these patrols are of interest. The starting point was either Romani or Et Maler.

Salmana	48 miles in	30 hours.
Bayud	60 ,,	32 ,,
Ge'eila	44 ,,	24 ,,
Mageibra	34 ,,	24 ,,
Bir el Abd	40 ,,	24 ,,

A good deal of the work was carried out in conjunction with aeroplanes and according to intelligence from agents. The enemy used his aeroplanes to a limited extent and relied a great deal on Bedouins as spies.

The reconnaissance to Bayud, 60 miles in 32 hours, was probably the most strenuous during the desert period. On arrival, it was found that the bird had flown, and after burning a few stores, the regiment (6th Australian Light Horse) turned for home. In moving back, they had a particularly bad time. It was a day of intense heat: the temperature in the tents at Romani was over 120 degrees Fahr. A very hot wind began at 09:00 and continued until 16:00. The glare on the sand was almost blinding. The steel on the equipment became so hot as to be almost unbearable. The track back to Qatia, the nearest adequate supply of water for the horses, ran over what was probably the worst soft sand dune country in the peninsula. Altogether, there were 160 cases of heat exhaustion, of whom 70 had to be evacuated to hospital.

In spite of the awful heat, the men, in order to save their horses, led them for the first 10 miles into the palm hods at Hod el Metiana. On reaching there, many of the men literally collapsed. It is perhaps one of the finest examples of good horse mastership that can be given.

6. PERIOD MAY-JULY, 1916 OPERATIONS IN THE WADI UM MUKSHEIB

On 10 June a detachment from the 3rd Light Horse Brigade, consisting of
Two squadrons 9th Light Horse Regiment,
10th Light Horse Regiment,
Four Machine Guns,
8th and 10th Light Horse Regiments,
Detachment 14th Army Troops Company,
Detachment Royal Engineers, and a Wireless Section,

left Serapeum railhead, No. 2 Section, for the Wadium Muksheib, 40 miles southeast of Ismailia. The camel convoy for the above, some 650 camels, left under escort on the night 9–10 June, and were overtaken on the night of the 10th by the column. The object was to drain the rock cisterns and pools with a view to preventing the enemy using them as an area of concentration for a raid on the Suez Canal. The rock cisterns were not destroyed as they were of great value to the Bedouins. The water was siphoned out of the cisterns. The work was completed on the 12th, and the column returned to Serapeum on the 14th. Some five million gallons of water were disposed of, the party working continuously until completion. In the case of the pools, a hole was cut in the water-holding layer of clay and the water ran through into the ground below. A further reconnaissance was made on the 18th to complete the draining of the pools and thus closed to the Turk any possible advance by the central route.

No.3 Section.
Towards the end of May, the infantry (52nd Division) began its concentration in the Romani-Mahemdia area. Throughout June

and July, while the cavalry kept the forward area clear, the infantry constructed a series of strong redoubts from Katib Gannit to Mahemdia, and the railway was completed to Romani (see sketch Battle of Romani).On 1 June, the 1st Light Horse Brigade camp at Romani was bombed by an enemy aeroplane, probably in retaliation for a very successful raid carried out by the New Zealand Mounted Rifle Brigade on 30–31 May, when they cut up a Turkish post at Salmana. The casualties in the bombing were 1 officer and 7 other ranks killed, and 3 officers and 19 other ranks wounded.

Operations in No.3 Section, July 1916.
More than half the month of July had passed without any important occurrence. The usual reconnaissances were continued. On 17 July, however, enemy aircraft was active in the Romani-Dueidar area. On the 18th, a patrol came into contact with a camel patrol of 15Turks near Oghratina. A few shots were exchanged with the patrol, which then retired rapidly eastwards. Up until this date, there had been no considerably body of Turkish troops farther west than Bir el Mazar, some 40 miles east of Oghratina, where for some time there had been a camp of between 1,500 and 2,000.

The dispositions of the mounted troops on the 18 July were .as follow:

Headquarters ANZAC Mounted Division Divisional Troops (less Field Squadron and R.H.A. Batteries)	Hill 40
Leicester Battery	Hill 40
Divisional Wheeled Transport	Kantara
Field Squadron	Kantara
Somerset Battery	Kantara
New Zealand Mounted Rifle Brigade (less Wellington M.R. Regiment)	Hill 70
5th Mounted Brigade (attached to N.Z.M.R. Brigade and in process of reorganisation)	Kantara
3rdLight Horse Brigade, No. 2 Section	Canal Defences
Inverness Battery No. 2 Section	Canal Defences
1st Light Horse Brigade	Romani

2nd Light Horse Brigade (less 5th L.H. Regiment but with
Wellington M.R. Regiment attached)   Ft Maler
5th Light Horse Regiment   Dueidar

Dispositions of Other Troops.

52nd Division	Occupying the Romani-Mahemdia position.
42nd Division	Kantara, with detachments at Gilban, Dueidar and Hill 70
53rd Division 3rd Light Horse Brigade 11th and 12th Light Horse Regiments City of London Yeomanry Three Dismounted Double Squadrons Bikanir Camel Corps Part of Imperial Camel Brigade	No. 2 Section. Based principally on Ismailia and Serapeum

7. OPERATIONS PRIOR TO THE BATTLE OF ROMANI

The situation suddenly changed on 29 July, when an evening reconnaissance by the Flying Corps revealed the fact that a large force of the enemy had moved westwards from el Arish and established itself on the line Bir el Abd-Bir Jamiel-Bir Bayud. Their numbers were estimated to be between 8,000 and 9,000, of which from 3,000 to 4,000 were at Bir el Abd and the remainder divided between the other two places. A peculiar incident had been noticed at Oghratina by the patrol on the 18 July, when it had been driven back by the enemy camel men. On the old battlefield of 23 April, a number of tins had been noticed, arranged on some systematic pattern, and there was reason to believe that the enemy worked out his trench sites in advance, so that work could be begun on them without delay on arrival of his troops.

The 2nd Light Horse Brigade, when moving out from et Maleron the 29 July, had intended sweeping all the country north of the Oghratina-Birel Abd telegraph line, with a view to clearing the area of all Bedouins, an influx of whom had been reported. There were also rumours of an intended enemy advance, and it was partly owing to this and partly to ascertain that the country to the east was clear during the sweeping operations of the 2nd Light Horse Brigade, that a special reconnaissance, with Brig.-General E. W. C. Chaytor, C.B., C.M.G., commanding the New Zealand Mounted Rifle Brigade, had been asked for by the General Officer of the ANZAC Mounted Division.

PANORAMA B.

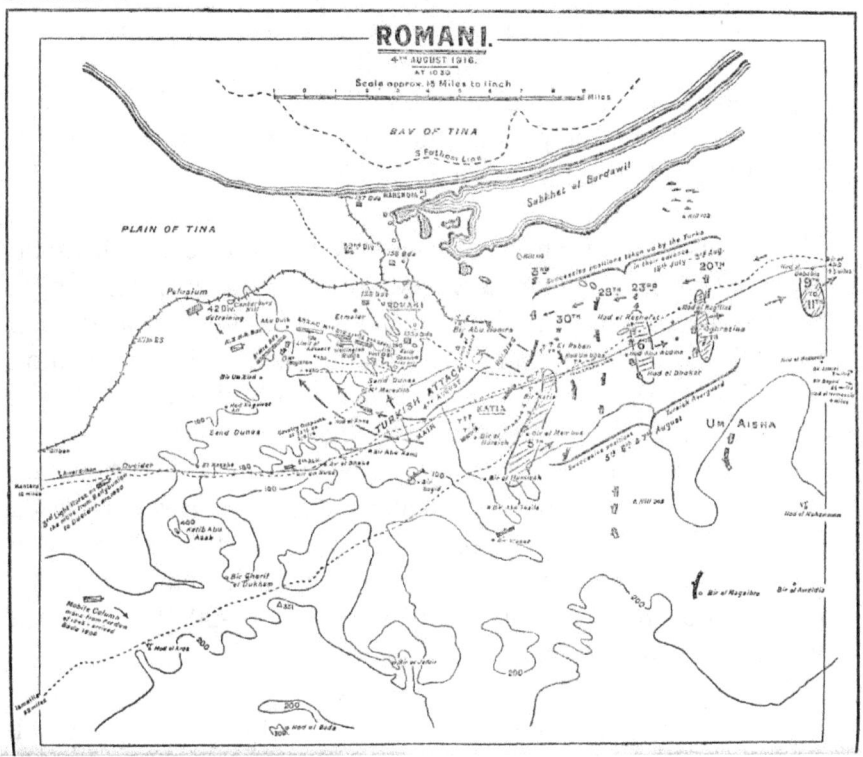

The 2nd Light Horse Brigade had just reached Qatia when the aeroplane report was received by the Divisional Headquarters at Romani at 17:30 to the following effect:

> July 19th, 16:00 – 3,000 men and 2,000 camels with from 200 to 300 large shelters at Bayud. Also three rows of trenches facing west. At Bir el Abel from 3,000 to 3,500 men, 2,000 camels, 200 to 300 large shelters, 20 to 30 bell tents, 1 large black hut and 3 circular trenches.

This estimate of numbers later turned out to be very accurate. Immediately on receipt of it, General Officer Commanding ANZAC Mounted Division ordered the following action:

> The 2nd Light Horse Brigade to remain at Qatia, putting out a strong outpost line. At 03:00 on 20th to send patrols, of

two troops each, to Bir el Hamisah, Hill 245, Hodes Sagia and Oghratina. 5th Light Horse to send patrols, one troop each, to Hod el Aras, Bir Gharif, El Dukhan and Bir ed Dhaba, leaving Dueidar at 03:00 on 20th, 1st Light Horse Brigade to send patrols, one troop each, to Hill no. 110 and Bir ed Dhaba, leaving camp at 03:00 on 20th.

The patrols were to remain out until orders were sent to them, but in the event of an enemy advance, to withdraw gradually on the brigade, keeping touch with the enemy. The brigades at Romani and Hill 70 were to stand to at 03:00 on 20 July. In addition, patrolling of the pipeline from Romani to Hill 70 was at once undertaken. Both the railway and the pipeline were open to enterprises by the enemy agents, as were also the telephone and telegraph line between Romani and the Section Headquarters at Kantara. If these went communications could still be kept up by cable via Port Said, but the water might easily have become a very serious matter. During the night of 19–20, the Ayrshire Battery arrived at Romani.

Nothing occurred during the night of 19–20, but at 04:45, patrols from the 2nd Light Horse Brigade met the enemy in the neighbourhood of Oghratina and made progress until Hod Abu Rodha was reached, where their advance was held up. Patrols to other points, except Sagia, found all clear, but the patrol to Hodes Sagia reported some 150 camel men about two miles south of Oghratina.

Policy Adopted.
At 06:45 on the 20th orders were received from the section as to the future action of the mounted troops. Touch was to be kept with the enemy, but, in view of the operations that were to follow, the men and the horses were to be kept as fresh as possible. No action likely to bring on an engagement at present was to be undertaken. This, of course was only following out all the previous policy, which was, if the enemy appeared, he was to be drawn on and made to fight as near Romani as possible – if possible among the sand hills to the south and south-west of the

Romani position (see panoramic sketches C, D, E and F outpost line). On no account was any action to be brought on so far away that infantry would have to march over the heavy sand to join in. Should the enemy, however, make a heavy attack against the southern flank of Romani-Mahemdia position, the role of the Australian and New Zealand Mounted Division was to act vigorously against the enemy and delay his advance until the 52nd Division had extended its right flank to cover the railway. The mounted division was responsible for maintaining close touch with the 52nd Division throughout and was to act vigorously against the southern flank so as to crush the hostile attack between the two divisions. On no account was the enemy to penetrate through a gap between the two divisions. In considering this policy it must be borne in mind that, although the Australian and New Zealand Mounted Division consisted of four mounted brigades, only two, the 1st and 2nd, were under its immediate command. The 3rd Light Horse Brigade was still in No. 2 Section, based on Serapeum, while the New Zealand Mounted Rifle Brigade was at Hill 70 and became for the time being, to all intents and purposes, Section troops. The action of the mounted troops in delaying and retarding the enemy advance and endeavouring to bring him to battle south-west of Romani, within striking distance of our infantry, was governed by certain local conditions which had a decisive influence on the policy. The heavy sand cut down the marching powers of the infantry out of all proportion, produced weariness and hence troops were unfit to attack at the end of it. Only a limited supply of water was available for drinking, and probably the infantry, if called on to march, would have to be content in that broiling heat with one water bottle per diem. Thirst would be the natural consequence and men would be driven to drink from the native wells, probably with disastrous results. Heat acting in conjunction with the other two factors would, and later did (in the march of the 42nd Division from Pelusium to Qatia on 7 August), have an overpowering adverse effect on the marching powers of the infantry. These points were given their proper weight, and action taken accordingly. They had, however, a very grave effect on the two front mounted brigades. A third brigade, which would have relieved matters, was asked for but was refused, and it was not until 09:00 on 5 August, after the Turk had made his decisive but unsuccessful attack, and had fallen back to a prepared position at Qatia, that all the mounted brigades, widely separated, were put under the command of the General Officer Commanding Australian and New Zealand Mounted Division and ordered to take up a vigorous pursuit. The immediate result of the order was that the two brigades had very little time to rest, especially as it was of vital importance that the Turk should be continually harassed, particularly at night. The procedure adopted meant that a brigade left its camp at Romani at 02:00, moved six miles to Qatia and thence, getting touch before daylight, operated against the enemy during the day and moved back to Romani after nightfall. Officers' patrols were left out during the night. Each of the brigades did this on alternate days. The principle of the general withdrawal of the cavalry after dusk, necessitated wholly by the water supply, when the enemy became aware of it, allowed him to carry out his moves in practical security. It is doubtful whether the enemy was aware for the first 10 days of the cavalry withdrawal west of Qatia at night.

Thus, the 1st and 2nd Light Horse Brigades bore the burden and heat of the day from 19 July onwards. They took the brunt of the Battle of Romani, and when the time came to take up a bold and vigorous pursuit, only these two brigades, whose endurance had already been tested to the uttermost, were in the hands of the cavalry commander. The lesson taught, however, was that cavalry can picket the enemy and keep a close observation on all his movements while avoiding being drawn into an engagement.

By 07:42, it was certain that the enemy was in strength at Oghratina and digging in. The patrol at Hill 245 reported at 09:00 a body of troops six miles to the south-east. The enemy at Oghratina still showed signs of coming on. He was digging hard but his patrols were active. Later it was ascertained that he was entrenching a position from Hod Negiliat to the south-east. Apparently, a gun emplacement was being made, and that a strong line was in course of construction was evident. About this time the aeroplane reconnaissance, which had been over Bir Bayud and Bir Jamiel, reported that the enemy had either concealed his force or moved in some other direction. Here the value of the palm hod country from a tactical point of view came in. It was evident from after events that the enemy had moved into the palm groves in the Hod el Hassania area and the Um Aisha district and thence appeared again. All that was known temporarily was that the enemy about Bayud and Jamiel had vanished. At first, his forces at Oghratina seemed weakened, but patrols early found his strength. By midday it was obvious that a movement was in progress towards Mageibra, and an enemy post was reported established two and a half miles south-east of Hill 245. At 12:55, the patrol at Hill 245 captured some prisoners, from whom it was discovered that the force in front of us was the Turkish 3rd Division, consisting of 31st, 32nd and 39th Regiments, with mountain guns, heavy artillery and special machine gun companies. The artillery was manned by the Turks, Germans and Austrians, and there were Germans with all the machinegun companies. The prisoners also stated that a general attack on Romani was intended. It was quite plain, from their badly blistered feet, that the enemy's columns had come a long way. Prisoners also stated that there were other echelons following behind these advanced troops at a distance of one day's march. The information was confirmed in all essentials by the complete knowledge subsequently obtained of the attacking force, except that the prisoners all exaggerated the number of troops that were following behind. The whole force consisted of the 3rd Turkish Division, with eight machine gun companies, officered and partly manned by the Germans, mountain artillery and some batteries of 4-inch and 6-inch howitzers and anti-aircraft guns, manned chiefly by Austrians, with a body of Arab camelry. It was commanded by Colonel Kress Von Kressentein, a German in Turkish employ, and the German personnel of the machinegun units, heavy artillery, wireless sections, field hospitals and supply section had been organised in Germany as a special formation for operations with the Turkish forces. The force was in fine physical condition and admirably equipped.

At 17:30, our patrols reported that the enemy was moving on

Qatia. Their guns came into action west of Oghratina at 18:19. The battery with the 2nd Light Horse Brigade came into action at 18:45, and shelled their camps at Oghratina with effect. The 6th Light Horse Regiment attacked the enemy's northern flank from the direction of Hodel Negiliat and drove it in on that place. About this time, the enemy's advanced troops withdrew. An aeroplane message reported that the enemy was in strength about Mageibra. His numbers were estimated at from 2,000 to 3,000 and about 1,000 camels. They were also reported to be digging in rapidly. The 2nd Light Horse withdrew after dark to Romani. It had been arranged that the horses should be watered at Qatia, but the water here soon ran out, necessitating the watering of the majority at Romani. As an enemy advance on Qatia might deny the use of the water there at any time the construction of wells sufficient for one mounted brigade was at once put in hand in the valley just north of Mount Meredith. From here, the outpost brigade could operate east of Qatia, watering both morning and evening. The position of the wells was concealed from the front. Large working parties were sent out daily from No. 2 Section, cleaning out the old wells at different points to the east and southeast, in order to provide an adequate supply of water for a force operating from there.

From the night 21–22 July onwards the following scheme for watching the enemy by night, the only possible one without completely exhausting the men and horses of the two brigades, was adopted. The brigade on outpost, on withdrawing, left out three officers' patrols, who were to keep as close to the enemy as possible and watch his movements during the night. The brigade taking up the outpost work next day left camp at 1.30 and marched to the wells in the sand dune half a mile south of Katib Gannit. Here the brigade waited until 03:00 and then moved on Qatia, taking up the observation of the enemy from the officers' patrols, which then returned to the camp in Romani or Et Maler. The brigade resting in camp had to provide an outpost line covering et Maler and send patrols to Bod ed Dhaba, linking up with the 5th Light Horse Regiment from Dueidar, and later to Hill 110.

The tour of duty for the two brigades was as follows :
A Brigade.
(1) Left camp at 01:30 on X day and marched to a point two miles south of camp.
(2) Waited there till 03:00 on X day.
(3) Then moved on Qatia and took on the work of observation and reconnaissance for X day.
(4) Withdrew after dark on X day, leaving out officers' patrols.
(5) Returned to camp about 21:00 on X day.
(6) The officers' patrols remained on duty for night X-Y day and were relieved by B Brigade before dawn on Y day.

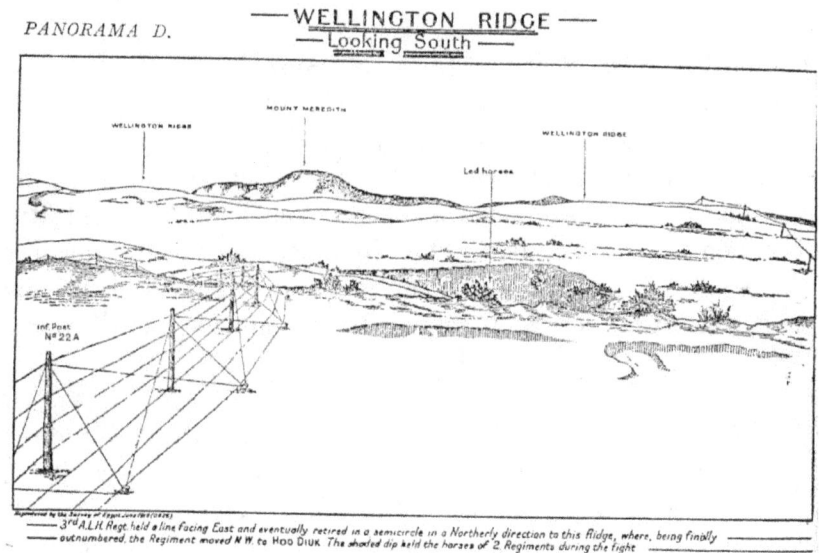

B Brigade.
Left camp at 01:30 on Y Day.
Each brigade therefore was on duty from 01:30 on X day to 21:00 on X day, or eighteen-and-a-half hours; offduty21:00 on X day to 01:30 on Z day, or 28 and a-half hours, but providing certain outpost duties and patrols.

The necessity of constructing defensive works on Wellington

Ridge and turned north on et Maler had been urged. To the south and west of the mounted camps, no works existed. It had been the accepted theory that a Turkish attack on the Romani position would be from the south and south-west. Works in this direction would have made an effective barrier, and the construction and occupation of them by the infantry would have relieved the resting brigade from outpost duty at Romani and left them comparatively fresh to carry out their legitimate role of picketing and harassing the enemy.

Beyond some patrol encounters, the day passed quietly. Some prisoners were taken near Hodes Sagia. They stated that they had left Bir el Abd on 21 July and there were still four battalions and 10 guns there.

Formation of the Section Mounted Troops.
A temporary command, known as the 'Section Mounted Troops,' was formed under Brigadier-General E. W. C. Chaytor, and came under the direct orders of No.3 Section. The troops forming this command were the Canterbury and Auckland Mounted Rifle Regiments, 5th Australian Light Horse Regiment, two squadrons Warwick Yeomanry, one squadron Gloucester Yeomanry, one squadron Worcester Yeomanry, with the Somerset and Leicester Batteries R.H.A.

On 27 July, a mobile column was formed in No. 2 Section, to operate against the enemy's left flank and left rear, in the neighbourhood of Mageibra and Bayud. It consisted of the 4th Australian Light Horse Regiment, City of London Yeomanry, and four companies of the Imperial Camel Corps. It was concentrated at Ferdan Railhead, where it remained until 4 August, when it moved to Bada.

Position of the Turkish Force.
It was now evident that the enemy had no immediate intention of a raid upon the Qatia district, but was preparing to establish himself firmly in the Um Aisha district, so as to block our advance towards el Arish, and possibly to protect his own

communications between Syria and the Hedjaz, and to prevent us from denying to him the whole of the Qatia area, the only district within which he could collect and maintain any considerable force within striking distance of the Suez Canal. It is possible that he might have intended to strike at the canal defences farther west, but with a cavalry and an infantry division on his flank, it did not seem probable. Later it became evident that he intended to seize Romani, consolidate himself there and at Qatia and, with the arrival of reinforcements, attack the Suez Canal.

To attack the Turk on his Oghratina-Mageibra line forthwith with infantry was impracticable, since 15 miles of desert separated our main positions from those of the enemy, and it was necessary that any force to advance across this tract to the attack on a strong enemy position should be equipped with camel transport on a complete scale. The force in No. 3 Section, therefore, was for a time compelled to remain on the tactical defensive.

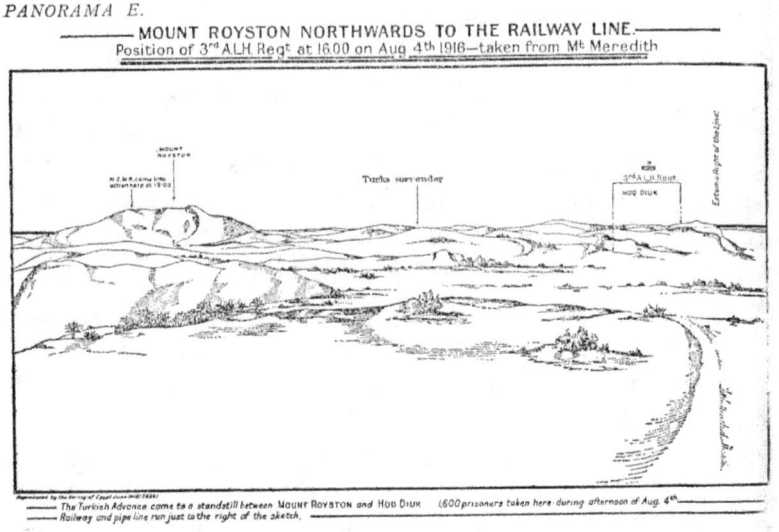

PANORAMA E.
MOUNT ROYSTON NORTHWARDS TO THE RAILWAY LINE.
Position of 3rd A.L.H. Regt at 16.00 on Aug 4th 1916—taken from Mt Meredith

The Turkish Advance came to a standstill between Mount Royston and Hod Diuk. 1600 prisoners taken here during afternoon of Aug. 4th.
Railway and pipe line run just to the right of the sketch.

It was the intention of the higher command that all formations should be ready to take the field by 1 August, and attack the enemy in force about 13 August. By strenuous endeavours, the organisation of the essential camel transport and the completion of the infantry units on a mobile scale was accomplished by 3 August.

Frequent patrol encounters and continued harassing of the enemy's line marked this period. The enemy still continued to entrench himself on the Oghratina-Mageibra line, occasionally pushing forward patrols towards us, particularly in the southern sector. These patrols were invariably driven in and resulted usually in a few prisoners being taken. On 25th, some old tents were pitched in Qatia. Some shelters were put up and a few trenches dug, with the idea of leading the enemy to believe that we were occupying Qatia permanently in some strength. The 5th Light Horse Regiment, operating from Dueidar, also placed a few tents in scattered hods to the south-east and patrols visiting them early at night and just before dawn placed lighted candles in them to give the impression that these hods were occupied. From some enemy diaries captured later it was found that the means adopted had the desired effect.

From the night of 27–28 July until 3 August, the enemy gradually pushed his line forward. Enterprises at night against any enemy patrols were carried out, but in all cases, it was found that the enemy had only strong posts out a short distance from his firing line. They established the fact, however, that the enemy kept his force very much together at night, and avoided any risk of our cutting out isolated or small posts. During the whole of these operations, the enemy rarely exposed a small body to the chance of capture. One noteworthy exception occurred at 16:00 on 28 July. Some 50 Turks had pushed forward in front of their entrenched line and entered Hod um Ugba. The Wellington Mounted Rifle Regiment (then attached to the 2nd Light Horse Brigade) saw their opportunity, worked up to the hod, and suddenly charging mounted into the hod, drove the enemy out, killing 16 and taking 8 prisoners and some camels. The regiment lost 2 men killed and 1 wounded.

The enemy was now within striking distance of Romani, and it had further been reported by agents and prisoners that the attack was to take place during the feast of Bairam. This ended on the 4 August. It was also evident now that we could concentrate against him as his line of attack was fairly well defined. It appeared certain that he would attack the Romani position and that, while holding us in that position, he would throw his main attack against the Qatia-Gannit-et Maler line in a north-westerly line, with the object of forcing back our entrenched line before troops could be brought against him from the west and north-west.

If the enemy was to attack he must do so soon or we would have our concentration complete, and in that case be far too strong for him. It certainly was more to the enemy's advantage to get us to move out and attack him in the Qatia area, but probably, being now so far ahead of his base, feeding was getting difficult. From subsequent information, it was known that he thought, or at any rate published in his orders, that we were weaker than we actually were. He certainly made a grave miscalculation in the position of the cavalry covering et Maler from the south. It seemed certain that the attack would come, probably at once; as for its probable direction, from the position at Qatia, the enemy could strike at Romani from the east or the south, or at Dueidar.

Though he might have trusted to destroying the infantry posts with gun fire and attacking from the east, it would have taken a long time. The south of the position from the infantry post no.21 Wellington Ridge would be able to shoot into the camp at 800 yards range. Moreover, this ridge completely dominated the whole place, but it was considered too far out for the infantry to hold.

Plan Of The Romani Position
A move on Dueidar was possible, and from there it would be quite easy to cut the railway line in the neighbourhood of Gilban and to move north against Romani, with the idea of capturing the troops at that place. There were two factors against this: first, he was not strong enough to keep his ranks guarded while doing so; and, secondly, it meant a long march through heavy sand to

Dueidar and certainly a move of part of his force south of Katib abu Asab.

Action of The Mounted Troops in Case of an Attack From The South-West

The possibility of the attack from the south-west had been often considered and it had been decided that, if the enemy did attack that way, the mounted division should engage him and, without becoming seriously involved, withdraw slowly before him, with the left flank on the infantry post No. 21, and drawing the enemy into the heavy sand dune country, south of the et Maler camps. If the enemy attacked that way, as now seemed probable, it was plain that he would try to assemble his forces as near as possible to the et Maler position before dawn, as any move by daylight would be well under observation. To stop this the General Officer Commanding Australian and New Zealand Mounted Division decided to hold an outpost line from the night 3–4 August onwards, from Hod el Enna (inclusive) on the right, to the infantry posts south of Katib Gannit (exclusive) on the left. This line was reconnoitred by 10:00, and the 1st Light Horse Brigade detailed to take up the position that night (see panorama C).

In the meantime, the 2nd Light Horse Brigade, at 08:00 on 3 August, found the enemy holding the ridge north of Bir el Hamisah strongly. About the same time, the Section Mounted Troops reported that the enemy, 2,000 strong, was at Bir Waset and moving on Bir Nagid. The troops, Auckland Mounted Rifle Regiment, at Bir Nagid remained in observation. A prisoner was taken there but could not be questioned, as there was no interpreter. By means of signs, however, he explained that the attack was to come that night when troops would be asleep, and he also indicated that the route by which they would come was from the south on Romani. It was arranged that this squadron should have a post at Bir abu Raml, and that the cavalry outpost line that night would keep connection with it by patrols at frequent intervals during the night. At 12:10, large bodies of the enemy were reported moving towards Er Rabah. The aeroplanes also reported teams of horses hauling guns towards Hod el

Reshafat, and a considerable movement was noticed towards Bid abu Theila. They were also reported placing a gun on the ridge north-east of Er Rabah. In the evening, the enemy's line had been located as follows:

> From a point two miles east of Hill 110 to a point bearing 168 degrees from Hill 110 through Bir Qatia, thence to a point just south of Bir Nagid.

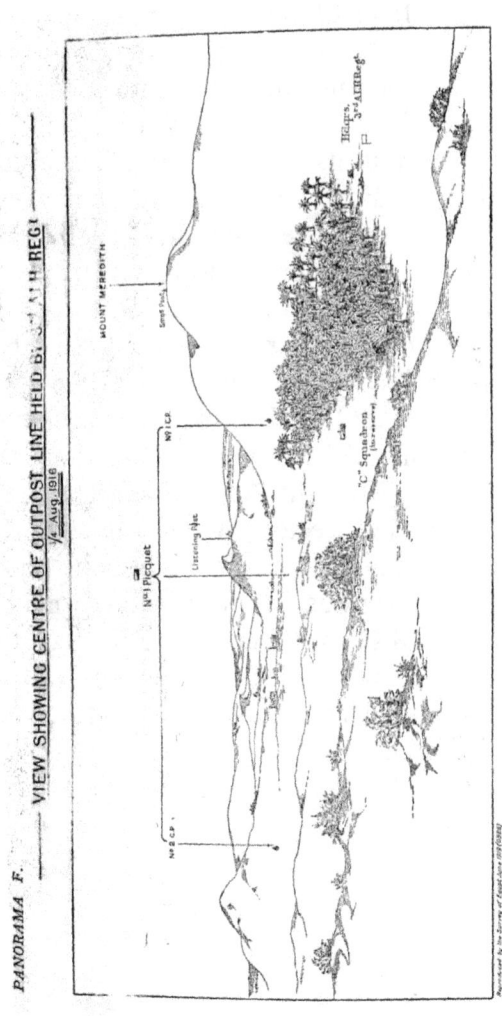

The detailed arrangements for the night 3–4 August were:
> The 2nd Light Horse Brigade to leave out the usual officers' patrols and withdraw to the et Maler camp. The 1st Light Horse Brigade to put out an outpost line after dark, running from Katib Gannit (exclusive) to Hod el Enna (inclusive) towards Qatia (as already described on 21 July). Two regiments to hold this line of three miles, with one regiment in reserve at Romani, being about half a mile from headquarters of the brigade and about two miles from the southernmost flank of the line.

Complete telephonic arrangements were made to link up all units. The arrangements for next day, if all was quiet, were for the reserve regiment to join its brigade at 03:00, the brigade then to move forward and gain touch with the enemy at 04:00. One battery R.H.A. was to move with the brigade. The 5th Light Horse Regiment was under orders to leave Dueidar at 00:30 and reconnoitre Nagid at dawn, the object being to locate the enemy's left flank and to find out, if possible, his strength; any serious engagement was to be avoided. The outpost line got into position and reported all quiet at 21:30 (see panorama sketch A). The 2nd Light Horse Regiment held the right sector Hod el Enna (inclusive) to Mount Meredith (exclusive). The 3rd Light Horse Regiment held the left sector Mount Meredith (inclusive) to infantry post No. 21 (exclusive). The right flank reported at 22:00 that the advanced post was in touch with a small party of the enemy. At 22:02, a light was reported at Qatia. It was exposed four times, for 10 seconds each time, then ceased. By 23:30, there seemed to be a general feeling as to a movement of the enemy along the whole of the outpost line, and the Battle of Romani began, the first shots being fired at 23:50.

8. THE BATTLE OF ROMANI

A few minutes before midnight, 3–4 August 1916, the 1st Light Horse Brigade reported that some 30 men had approached Hod el Enna. East of that place, a larger party of about 500 could just be distinguished. The reserve regiment (1st Light Horse) was ordered to turn out and join its brigade. At midnight, heavy firing broke out along the whole of the outpost line and columns of the enemy were reported both at Hod el Enna and at Mount Meredith. The 2nd Light Horse Brigade, in bivouac at et Maler, turned out and remained ready to move just outside its lines. Matters were stationary in front of the outpost line for about 45 minutes and then it became apparent that the enemy was in great strength opposite Hod el Enna and Mount Meredith. At 00:45, one squadron went forward from the reserve regiment to reinforce the line near Mount Meredith, two troops going north and two south of the hill. This move apparently checked the enemy, and the situation with him was probably as follows :

The enemy's plans were based on finding his line of approach clear until he was near the southern side of the et Maler. His orders and plans subsequently captured showed this. When, therefore, his columns struck, in the dark, the unexpected line of the 1st Light Horse Brigade, it was taken merely for some weak posts and, failing to thrust it aside, his columns halted to report – and to recast plans.

Delaying Action by the 1st Light Horse Brigade.
Dawn was about 05:00. At any rate up to 02:15, nothing went on except continuous, though not very heavy, firing. Apparently, the order then was to attack whatever was in front, as at this hour the firing increased along the line, and the enemy commenced to press hard our troops at Hod el Enna and Mount Meredith.

At 02:30, a bayonet charge was made by the enemy at Mount Meredith, but was broken up by the 3rd Light Horse Regiment. The 2nd Light Horse Regiment, at Hod el Enna, was now attacked by greatly superior enemy forces, and was being gradually pressed back. Further pressure was now being made on Mount Meredith and the 3rd Light Horse Regiment was compelled to give ground. Another squadron was sent to reinforce them, but the enemy, whose strength was now about 8,000,

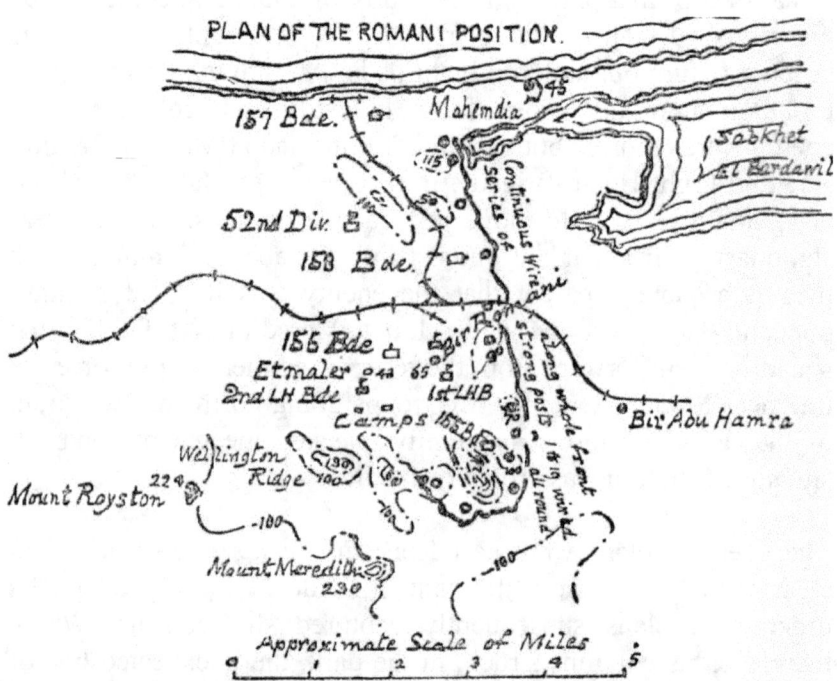

continued to press. The brigade, pivoting on its left, fell back slowly, fighting bitterly and contesting practically every inch of the country, delaying the enemy's advance by holding on behind the sand dunes and tussocks with which the country is covered. At 03:20, a little information came in from another source. The detachment of the Auckland Mounted Rifles at Bir abu Raml had sent a patrol out under a non-commissioned officer directly the enemy was seen. The N.C.O. encountered the enemy advancing, almost at once, and, leaving the rest of the patrol to watch, sent back to Bir abu Raml to warn the rest of the party there, but the enemy had already passed through the place, gathering the party with them. The N.C.O. found himself with Turks on all sides of him. He moved near enough to gather the information that there were two columns at this point, between Bir el Dhaba and Bir abu Raml, moving north-west. He then rode quickly down one column until he struck a gap in the transport columns, went through, and then made off with his information, apparently unobserved. He managed to get to Pelusium, five miles north-west of Romani, and got his information through.

Meantime, the 1st Light Horse Brigade was falling back gradually on the et Maler camp, not so much on account of the direct enemy pressure on their front, as the fact that strong bodies of the enemy were outflanking their right, passing through Hod el Enna, and so north-west. The attacks on Mount Meredith were gaining ground slowly as well. The last squadron of the reserve regiment was put in at 03:35, to strengthen the right flank. The outflanking movement continued, and by about 04:00 the brigade was forced back on the right to the southern slopes of Wellington Ridge, and on the left to the next sand hills north of Mount Meredith, leaving the hill itself in the hands of the Turks, who at once lined the crest and brought machine guns into action. So far, the 1st Light Horse Brigade had withstood the onslaught of about one Turkish Division. The 2nd Light Horse Brigade was brought up at 04:25. It had not been put in previously, as it was still too dark, nor was it advisable to get it involved in a contest in the sand dunes, where it would be impossible to pick up the situation till dawn. This brigade had been standing by, ready to be put in if the situation had become desperate, but the gallant stand made by the 1st Light Horse Brigade obviated this necessity.

The enemy was now sweeping the ridges with heavy machine gun fire, and, under cover of it, pushing forward behind the tussocks and sand. Just as it was light enough to see (04:30), a large body of Turks, who had been collecting behind the western slopes of Mount Meredith, suddenly arose and charged over the crest of the hill and into a depression only 300 or 400 yards in front of the 1st Light Horse Regiment. The situation on the right was, however, the most dangerous, and the G.O.C. Australian and New Zealand Mounted Division ordered the 2nd Light Horse Brigade to extend the line from the right of the 1st Light Horse Brigade to the west. The 6th and 7th Light Horse Regiments took up this line, with the Wellington Mounted Rifle Regiment in reserve.

Just before 05:00, the enemy's guns came into action for the first time, firing shrapnel on Wellington Ridge and searching the ground in rear. Enemy aeroplanes appeared at this hour and bombed the camps, but effected little damage.

Meanwhile, the enemy's outflanking move continued, and at 05:15, it was evident that Wellington Ridge would soon become untenable. Hostile aeroplanes were very active with bombs in the neighbourhood of the Divisional Headquarters. It was also evident that the enemy had committed his troops to a decisive attack. The enemy's heavy guns opened at this time on the infantry posts east of Romani and the hills north of Katib Gannit. The enemy had also deployed some troops towards Abu Hamra, but contented himself on the east with a purely holding attack . The enemy who had occupied Mount Meredith now lined the crest of that hill, and from there were sweeping the crest of Wellington Ridge with machine guns. About 06:00, the Leicester Battery R.H.A. came into action near et Maler and drove the enemy off the crest of Mount Meredith, and then shelled the country to the immediate south with, what was afterwards seen, heavy effect.

The 1st Light Horse Brigade fell back at 06:00 from the southern slopes of Wellington Ridge to a ridge in line with and to the west of it, held by some outpost troops of the 52nd Division. The enemy was now fighting desperately for the ridge, and succeeded in gaining it at 07:00. The 1st Light Horse Brigade in falling back came under heavy shrapnel fire, causing some casualties. The brigade then moved just north of the et Maler camp. On the eastern edge of the ridge, the 6th and 7th Light Horse Regiments were also forced to vacate their positions and slowly fell back, moving by alternate squadrons. The last high ground between et

Maler camps and the enemy was left in his hands. The enemy did not, however, move forward at once, apparently not knowing of the retirement, or else reorganising his forces behind the ridge. The enemy (about one brigade, with some mounted troops) were still to be seen pushing between et Maler and Mount Royston, and at 07:45began to outflank the right of the 2nd Light Horse Brigade. The 3rd Light Horse Regiment was then sent to prolong the right of this brigade's front.

Action of the Detachment at Dueidar.

The 5th Light Horse Regiment left Dueidar shortly after midnight on the night 3–4 August. A short halt was made at Bir el Nuss, where the regiment was informed by the post of the Auckland Mounted Rifles that at dusk on the 3rd there had apparently been no change in the situation towards Mageibra, and that the enemy had not advanced during the day. Leaving Bir el Nuss at 02:45, the regiment moved in a south- easterly direction in order to arrive at Nagid from the south. Just before daybreak the advanced guard reported Nagid 'all clear,' but on moving forward to a high ridge 200 yards south of Nagid two battalions of the enemy, strength about 1,500,were seen moving north-west. This force had out small advanced and flank guards of camelmen. These at once took up a position along a high ridge between the 5th Light Horse Regiment and the valley up which they were marching towards Hodel Enna. The enemy opened fire with machine guns and mountain guns at a comparatively close range. Having ascertained the position of the left flank, the regiment moved back to Bir el Nuss. Heavy firing in the Romani direction was heard. The regiment reported the position, and instructions were received from the New Zealand Mounted Rifle Brigade to proceed three miles back on the road towards Dueidar and await instructions. On arrival there, no communication could be got with the brigade, which had, in the meantime, moved towards Romani. At dusk on 4th, still having failed in his efforts to get communication or orders and being absolutely in the dark as to events, the Officer Commanding decided to return with the regiment and the squadron of the Auckland Mounted Rifles to Dueidar, where the 3rd Light Horse Brigade had arrived at 19:30 from Ballybunion.

It was unfortunate that the regiment was not made more use of during the day, but its presence at Nagid had undoubtedly a substantial effect on the Turkish reserves. It later turned out that this force was stationed during the night 3–4 at Bir el Marieh. The two battalions seen by the 5th Light Horse Regiment were part of the Turkish reserves marching to reinforce the attack on et Maler. When the firing opened at Nagid this force was delayed for some two hours before recommencing its march.

Action of the Section Troops.
At 07:00 the New Zealand Mounted Rifle Brigade, which had been at Hill 70, was on the march for Dueidar, but its direction was changed to Canterbury Hill.

By 07:45, one squadron of the 5th Mounted Brigade had moved up from Pelusium and was in touch with the enemy. At 08:30 a column of the enemy, reported at between 2,000 and 3,000, began to appear opposite the infantry work No. 22A. They also began to line the crest of Wellington Ridge, and the camps at et Maler came under a heavy rifle fire. The Ayrshire Battery R.H.A., and one section of the Leicester Battery R.H.A., however, swept the ridge with heavy shrapnel fire, inflicting heavy casualties. The Turks were driven off, and did not again attempt to cross the skyline. At 08:35, a message got through from the 5th Mounted Brigade reporting that they were taking up a position about El Kaseba-Hod Negeiret Ali-Birum Ziad, with one regiment to be kept back at Gilban. The armoured train was ready also at km.37.
Meanwhile, the 42nd Division was being brought up by train to Pelusium, but there was greater delay than anticipated, and, during the morning of 4 August, no infantry was available for an attack on the enemy's flank at Mount Royston. This caused the whole brunt of the fighting in this area to fall upon the 1st and 2nd Light Horse Brigades, whose casualties had not been light, and whose right flank was unprotected. It was not until 15:30 that two battalions of the East Lancashire Regiment, closely followed by a third, were on the march southwards from Pelusium station to take part in the attack against Mount Royston. At 09:45, the

composite regiment of the 5th Mounted Brigade got into touch with the enemy two miles south-west of Mount Royston, where it also got connection with a squadron of the brigade that had been holding off enemy attacks since 07:45. The main result of the Turkish rapid advance was that the section cavalry (New Zealand Mounted Rifle Brigade and the 5th Mounted Brigade), originally destined to operate against the enemy's rear, was diverted to strengthen the line of resistance on the north.

The enemy continued to work his way along Mount Royston, while our right was working forward among the sand hills at the foot of that point. The 5th Mounted Brigade and the right of the Australian and New Zealand Mounted Division got into touch at 10:00. In order to extend our line westwards, two companies 156th Infantry Brigade took over part of the 7thLightHorseRegiment'sline at10:50.At11:00, the New Zealand Mounted Rifle Brigade (less 5th Light Horse Regiment) had got in touch with the 5th Mounted Brigade, and arrangements were made for an attack on Mount Royston by them, from the west. A section Ayrshire Battery R.H.A. opened on the enemy in the hods and valleys east of the hill.

The 42nd Division was asked to support the attack, and the 127th Infantry Brigade, which had been retained at Pelusium, was at once put on the move for this purpose.

Meanwhile, the enemy began to show more activity on our left. They were reported forming for an attack on the infantry line opposite works 22A, 21, 21A, 4 and 5,but this did not materialise.

At 11.30, an enemy mountain battery opened on Bir et Maler, but the dust thrown up by the firing was observed, and the section of the Ayrshire Battery R.H.A. was turned on it, and it ceased fire. Two considerable bodies of enemy were reported entering Abu Hamra at 11:40, and his reinforcements were also observed south of Wellington Ridge. They were also seen making their way into the hods west of that place. All available guns, including two 18-pdr batteries of the 52nd Division, opened on the hods and swept the ground in rear of Wellington Ridge, presumably with effect, as no attack developed.

Interest was now beginning to centre more on Mount Royston, where the 5th Mounted Brigade was hotly engaged. Just before 12:30, heavy rifle fire broke out on our right, caused by the enemy advancing on Bir Abu Diuk, where they were met by the 6th Light Horse Regiment, and a hot fire fight ensued.

The enemy had now reached the farthest point of his advance, and his line ran from Bir Abu Diuk north of Mount Royston (which he held), thence straight to Wellington Ridge, of which he held the southern slopes but not the crest, and thence his line went round to the east and north, encircling the infantry posts.

Attack on Mount Royston.
At 13:10, the attack on Mount Royston began, the New Zealand Mounted Rifle Brigade advancing on the hill from the west, supported by the fire of the Somerset Battery. The 127th Infantry Brigade was on the move from Pelusium, in support, while the 5th Mounted Brigade attacked from the north-west.

The 1st and 2nd Light Horse Brigades were to move forward directly Mount Royston fell. By 14:30, the attack had made some progress into the sand hills, though the Turks on the hill were putting up a hard fight, being specially difficult to dislodge from the deep folds in the ground, which surrounded the hill.

At 16:30, the enemy made his last attempt to move forward in his centre, supported by the fire of his guns from Mount Meredith. Our guns again swept the crest of Wellington Ridge, and drove the enemy back with heavy loss.

By 17:00, the New Zealand Mounted Rifle Brigade and the 5th Mounted Brigade, closely supported by the 127th Brigade, were pushing forward steadily. At the same time, to help the attack, the 156th Brigade was asked to attack Wellington Ridge, but some considerable delay ensued and this attack did not develop.

Just after 18:00, the ridges north of Mount Royston were carried, and parties of prisoners surrendered as each point fell. At 18:30,Mount Royston itself, with 500 prisoners, was taken. A battery of mountain guns to the west of the hill, previously put out of action by the Ayrshire Battery R.H.A., was also captured. The whole line now began to sweep forward, gathering up prisoners as it went. This movement continued until dark. The New Zealand Mounted Rifles and the 5th Mounted Brigades withdrew after dark to Pelusium to water. The 1st and 2nd Light Horse Brigades had been unavoidably mixed during the day. The position of regiments at nightfall was :

```
        S
        |           Wellington    7th      2nd     3rd     6th     1st
E———————W           M.R. Regiment A.L.H.   A.L.H.  A.L.H.  A.L.H.  A.L.H.
        |           ─────────────────────────────  ──────────────────────
        |                  2nd A.L.H. Brigade.         1st A.L.H. Brigade.
        N
```

(1st Australian Light Horse Brigade consisted of the 1st, 2nd and 3rd Australian Light Horse Regiments, and the 2nd Australian Light Horse Brigade of the 5th, 6th and 7th Australian Light Horse Regiments, while the New Zealand Mounted Rifle Brigade was composed of the Canterbury, Wellington and Auckland Mounted Rifle Regiments. The 5th Australian Light Horse Regiment had been temporarily attached to the New Zealand Mounted Brigade and the Wellington Mounted Rifle Regiment had taken its place in the 2nd Australian Light Horse Brigade.)

Firing continued long after dark along the line, the enemy also using his artillery, and the firing did not die down till midnight. The enemy also expended a number of star shells, from time to time, presumably in anticipation of an advance.

Movements of Other Troops.
At 19:30, the 3rd Light Horse Brigade and the Inverness Battery arrived at Dueidar. The mobile column from No. 2 Section, which had left Ferdan Railhead at 12.45, reached Bada, where it

bivouacked that night.

No move during the night of 4–5 was made by our line, and under cover of darkness, the horses were watered.
Our casualties during the day were:

	Killed	Wounded	Missing
1st Light Horse Brigade	71	233	28
2nd Light Horse Brigade			
New Zealand Mounted Rifle Brigade	4	40	-
5th Mounted Brigade	4	40approx	-
Infantry	About 250, but no details		
Other units	About 100, but no details		

Altogether, the battle cost us in killed, wounded and missing about 800.

> The Section Orders for the next day were generally as follows: The enemy had retired to a line of entrenched positions running Hod el Enna-Bir Qatia-Abu Hamra, with covering troops in front. The Section Commander wished to work the enemy southward tithe line Katib Gannit-Hod el Enna, at the same time to envelop his flanks. The Australian and New Zealand Mounted Division was to push forward all along the line with its right on Hodel Enna, its left on the 52nd Division advancing on the line Katib Gannit-Mount Meredith, the 3rdLight Horse Brigade to push forward on Bir el Nuss and attack Hodel Enna from the south, keeping touch with the 5th Mounted Brigade on its left. The 5th Mounted Brigade was under the orders of the 42ndDivision, and was to assist in linking up with the 3rd Light Horse Brigade and the Australian and New Zealand Mounted Division. The 42nd Division was to push forward in full strength on the Canterbury Hill-Mount Royston-Hodel Enna line in close support of the Australian and New Zealand Mounted Division.

Beyond desultory firing by the enemy long range guns, the night passed without incident.

The Pursuit.

At daybreak on the morning of 5 August a brigade of the 52nd Division, with the 7th Light Horse Regiment, took the remainder of Wellington Ridge by assault, capturing about 2,000 prisoners. Elsewhere the mounted troops pressed forward, meeting some opposition, but prisoners continued to come in steadily and it was soon obvious that the enemy's offensive was completely broken. An advance was ordered all along the line and at 09:30 all mounted troops were put under the G.O.C. Australian and New Zealand Mounted Division, with orders to push on as far and as vigorously as the resources at his disposal would admit. The mounted troops pressed steadily forward and found the enemy holding the ridges west of Qatia and supported by artillery. The 3rd Light Horse Brigade, which had moved from Dueidar to Bir el Nuss, came into contact with the enemy near Hamisah and captured 450 prisoners with machine guns and other material. The further advance of these troops was met with heavy fire from field guns and howitzers and no further progress was made.

Cavalry Moving Rapidly Suffer Very Little from Rifle or Shell Fire.

The 5th Light Horse Regiment was ordered to rush that part of Qatia consisting of the strip of timber separated from the main oasis by the salt pan and about a half mile to the south of the road. Enemy guns were reported to be in the timber. The regiment with fixed bayonets was formed in two lines, squadrons in line of troop columns. After galloping half a mile, the squadrons formed line, and covered a front of about 500 yards. In this formation, they galloped another half a mile and charged into the oasis. No guns were there, but a few prisoners were taken. In the gallop, only one man was hit and several horses slightly wounded. As the regiment was reforming, artillery and machine guns were turned on them. Men were dismounted and went into action while the led horses were galloped back out of range. A strong attempt was made to eject the enemy by dismounted action, but the attack failed to make progress and darkness found our troops and the enemy's facing each roughly on parallel lines.

On the morning of the 6th, the enemy retired from Qatia and, while the cavalry pressed on in pursuit, the infantry moved forward and occupied the line Bir el Mamluk-Qatia-Er Raba. The day was intensely hot and it is doubtful if the infantry could have made another forced march over the heavy sand. Those Australian Light Horse Regiments(1st and 2nd Light Horse Brigades) which had borne the brunt of observing and harassing the enemy's advance since 19 July were given a day's rest in camp while the remainder of the cavalry (3rd Light Horse Brigade, New Zealand Mounted Rifle Brigade and 5th Mounted Brigade) continued the pursuit. The enemy's rearguard was found to be occupying his previously prepared position extending across the road and telegraph line between Hod el Reshafat and Hod el Dhaba. Our attempts to turn his flanks by Hod en Negiliat and Hod el Sagia on the south were frustrated by heavy shell fire.

On the same morning the Camel Corps detachment of Smith's Mobile Column occupied Bir el Mageibra without opposition.

On the 7 August, the cavalry maintained their pressure on the enemy's rearguard, which had fallen back to the line of his first entrenched position running from Oghratina to Hod el Masia, with flanks thrown well out to the north and south. There was continuous fighting throughout the day, but the enemy was too strongly supported by artillery for the cavalry to drive him from his position. Meanwhile the mobile column, operating from Bir el Aweidia, had fought a very successful action with an enemy force consisting of a thousand rifles, three machine guns and two twelve-pounders, in the neighbourhood of Hod el Muhammam. The camel detachment and a regiment of cavalry, the whole under the command of Lt-Colonel Grant, drove the enemy out of several successive positions, capturing 53 prisoners. This threat to his flanks was probably an important factor in determining the enemy to continue his retreat.

On the 8 August the enemy was found to have abandoned Oghratina and by the evening to have taken up a position covering Bir el Abd, his advanced base. It was here the enemy made his final stand, to cover the evacuation of his camp and stores. Touch was now gained between the cavalry and Smith's Mobile Column and was maintained from this time onwards.

The Action at Bir El Abd, 9 August.
On 9 August, the cavalry made a desperate effort to encircle both flanks of the enemy at Bir el Abd and cut off his further retreat. It was, perhaps, the hardest fought action in this campaign. The cavalry, five weak brigades, attacked an enemy in position and whose numbers and artillery were greatly superior.

Royston's Column (the 1st and 2nd Light Horse Brigades) struck the enemy in position on a line with his right on the Sabkhet Bardawil, thence a mile west of Hod el Hisha and thence towards Abd. The Ayrshire Battery came into action and dispersed a small body of the enemy, but the advance was checked about 04:30. The New Zealand Mounted Rifle Brigade, moving direct on Abel, encountered and drove in the enemy's advanced patrols and, pushing on, occupied the high ground overlooking Bir el Abd by 06:15. The 3rd Light Horse Brigade was, in the meantime, moving forward to the south in the direction of Hod el Bada. The 5th Mounted Brigade was in reserve at Oghratina. A counterattack was made by the enemy, some 10–12,000 strong. in two columns each 5–6,000 strong. These were dispersed by the fire of the Somerset Battery and rifle fire and some prisoners taken. By 06:30,theNewZealand Mounted Rifle Brigade was engaged all along the line with the enemy, holding a position about two and a half miles west of Bir el Abel. Royston's Column was in position two miles south of Hod Hamada, the 1st Light Horse Brigade on the left facing south-east with the right on the 2nd Light Horse Regiment in the sand dunes, and connected with the 2nd Light Horse Brigade on their right, whose right in turn was extended towards the left of the New Zealand Mounted Rifle Brigade but separated by a gap of 800 yards. Both brigades had a regiment in reserve. The Ayrshire Battery was in action, firing south-east. To the south, the 3rd Light Horse Brigade was meeting opposition and was in touch on its right with patrols of the mobile column near Hod el Muhammam.

At 07:30, the enemy was reported to be working round the right of the New Zealand Mounted Rifle Brigade, their objective apparently being the long ridge running north and south across the telegraph line. A general move of camels out of Bir el Abd continued and the Somerset Battery made good practice on them. At 08:30, the 3rd Light Horse Brigade was ordered to get close touch with the New Zealand Mounted Rifle Brigade and to make Bir el Abd their objective instead of Salmana. At 08:50, it seemed probable that the New Zealand Mounted Rifle Brigade would get into Bir el Abd, as they were able to advance a little. They were, however, shortly afterwards held up. Meantime, the 3rd Light Horse Brigade had reached a point just west of Likmirdeh, where they were strongly opposed. The 8th and 9th Light Horse Regiments were attacking. By 10:30, the enemy's guns were showing great activity, and at 11:30, the Warwick Yeomanry was put in to reinforce the New Zealand Mounted Rifle Brigade. By 11.40, our advance was completely checked. Our line was in a semicircle facing south-east, east and north-east and from three to three and a-half miles distant from Bir el Abd. The enemy had brought a large number of guns into action. Parties could be seen removing material and stores. From midday onwards, the enemy made several counterattacks against the Canterbury Mounted Rifles, which was in advance on the left of the New Zealand Mounted Rifle Brigade. The Ayrshire Battery was at the same time heavily shelled and four men and 37 horses killed and seven men and seven horses wounded before it could be got to another position. At 12:35, very heavy shell fire was opened on Royston's Column and the enemy began to advance against the centre of the line. At 12:58, the enemy made another determined counterattack on the centre of the New Zealand Mounted Rifle Brigade. Heavy firing was going on all along the line. All guns were turned on the enemy columns and the counterattack broke, the enemy retreating hurriedly. His heavy guns were firing on our line the whole time. Half an hour later, the enemy delivered an attack on the left of the

New Zealand Mounted Rifle Brigade with three battalions. The gap, which had existed, had been filled by the Warwick Yeomanry, which met the attack; the Leicester Battery was turned on to it also and the pressure was relieved. At 14:00, the 3rd Light Horse Brigade reported that all troops, except the reserves, were in the firing line. The enemy was strong along the whole line and the continual pressure by the enemy had forced the right back a little. At the same hour, a determined attack was made on Royston's Column, supported by heavy artillery fire.

The Ayrshire Battery was ordered back, but owing to casualties among the horses could not move. All reserves were called up and put into the fight, so that the guns could be withdrawn. By 14:30 the left flank of Royston's Column began a gradual withdrawal and at the same time the enemy pressure forced back the 3rd Light Horse Brigade for nearly a mile and the enemy concentrated about Um Diek, making apparently for the ridge which runs from the 'H' of Hod Umm Zaghiya to Hod ed Debabis. The attacks on Royston's Column continued and at 14:48, he reported that he was just holding on but he would have to retire probably. All men were now in the firing line. By 16:30, his left was forced back, the enemy to the number of 3,000 pressing on the centre and about 1,000 against his left. The shell fire along the line was heavy and our line was going back gradually. The column succeeded in getting away all the wounded. At 17:00, a counterattack was made on the 3rd Light Horse Brigade but was repulsed by the 8th Light Horse Regiment. By the forcing back of both flanks, the New Zealand Mounted Rifle Brigade became very exposed. Preparations were now made to withdraw, the regiments in front slowly falling back. At 18:30, as the withdrawal was taking place, the enemy delivered an attack on a front of about two and a half miles. The rifle and the machinegun fire was intense and continued until dark. The enemy was, however, held off and the withdrawal completed. During the day, the Leicester and Somerset Batteries fired over a thousand rounds each and the Inverness about 500. In view of the large numbers of fresh enemy troops that appeared, the Division, less

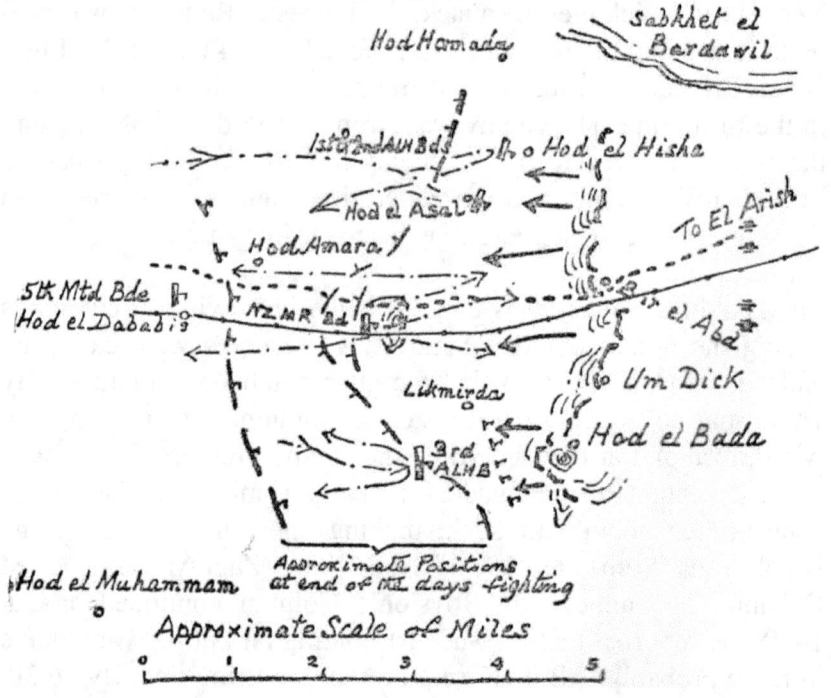

SKETCH MAP OF THE BATTLE OF BIR EL ABD

the 3rd Light Horse Brigade, fell back to Oghratina. The 3rd Light Horse Brigade bivouacked at Hod Abu Dhaba. Officers' patrols kept a watch on the enemy during the night.

Our casualties in this action were heavy, but those of the Turk greater, as was evidenced by the large number of killed still unburied when we occupied Bir el Abd on the 12th.

(This action is a fine example of the ability of the cavalry to break off an action and withdraw in the face of greatly superior numbers.)

During the next two days, our cavalry was unable to do more than maintain continuous pressure, but the mobile column that occupied Bayud on the 9th continued to menace the enemy wide on his right flank. On the 10th, a strong reconnaissance was made against the enemy, who was in strength at Hod el Mushalfat south-east of Bir el Abd. On the 11th, an enemy force with two mountain guns approached Bayud. A sharp action, which commenced at 05:30, was fought, and in the course of it all the enemy's baggage camels and ammunition mules were destroyed. Towards the afternoon, the enemy evacuated this position and retired on the main body of his rearguard. On the following day, patrols from the neighbourhood of Bayud found the country to the east and north all clear.

Early on the morning of the 12th it was found that the enemy had retired from Bir el Abd and, though there was a small encounter with his rear troops about Salmana, the general pursuit stopped at this point, the enemy retiring through Bir el Mazar to el Arish. The cavalry were ordered to hold the line Bir el Abd-Homossia with two brigades and keep touch with the mobile column that remained at Mageibra. The infantry at Qatia (the farthest point of their advance) returned to the Mahemdia-Romani line.

The result of the operations in the Qatia district was the complete defeat of an enemy force amounting in all to some 18,000, of which 15,000 were rifles. Nearly 5,000, including 50 officers, were captured, and from the number of enemy dead actually buried it is estimated that the total number of enemy casualties amounted to 9,000. In addition, there were captured one Krupp 75mm. mountain battery of four guns, complete with all accessories, and 400 rounds of ammunition, nine machine guns and mountings, especially constructed pack saddles for camel transport, 2,300 rifles, one million rounds small arm ammunition, 100 horses and mules, 500 camels and a large amount of miscellaneous stores and equipment. Two field hospitals complete fell into our hands, and large quantities of stores were burnt by the enemy at Bir el Abd to prevent their capture.

Notes on the Romani Operations.
1. The construction of infantry posts on Wellington Ridge would have relieved the cavalry of close outpost work at night on the right flank. The position overlooked the Romani line, and would have also relieved the cavalry for its legitimate purpose – pursuit.

2. It is difficult to understand why the 42nd Division and three brigades of cavalry were kept back until 4 August. An additional cavalry brigade forward would have relieved matters. The strain on two cavalry brigades for 16 days harassing and checking the enemy was great, and when the opportunity came, the cavalry brigades at Romani were too exhausted to take up the pursuit with anything like real vigour. It can only be said that there were difficult problems of feeding then and they must have been too great to allow of a concentration forward earlier.

3. The question of the use of the reserve cavalry in the hands of No. 3 Section on 4 August is interesting. The deflection of the march of the New Zealand Mounted Rifle Brigade from Dueidar may have been influenced by the reports received by No. 3 Section.Boththe52nd and the ANZAC Mounted Divisions believed early that morning that the main attack was on their front. Even if the 52nd was taking the main attack, it looked as if greater opportunities would come through Dueidar. There seems to be no great reason why the 3rd Light Horse Brigade was not brought upon the 3rd instead of the 4th. The two cavalry brigades at Romani held the Turkish attack and could have done so until the arrival of the 42nd Division

Sketches are shown: (1)the actual direction of the attack, and (2) as if the main attack was coming in opposite the 52nd Division. It looks as if the great chance lay through Dueidar. There was practically all day on 4 August when this might have been put into execution. If done earlier in the day, so much the better. The force available would have been the New Zealand Mounted Rifle and the 3rd Light Horse Brigades complete. There would have been some time to add to this force certain units of the 5th Mounted Brigade, which were not already engaged and possibly some from that body, which were acting independently to the south. It is suggested that they should have been put under one commander and given the role of acting against the enemy's left flank and rear. Even taking the situation as in sketch 2, it still

MOUNTED TROOPS OF E.E.F.

1. The MAIN ATTACK as it actually occurred, being met by the ANZAC Mounted Division (2 Bdes)

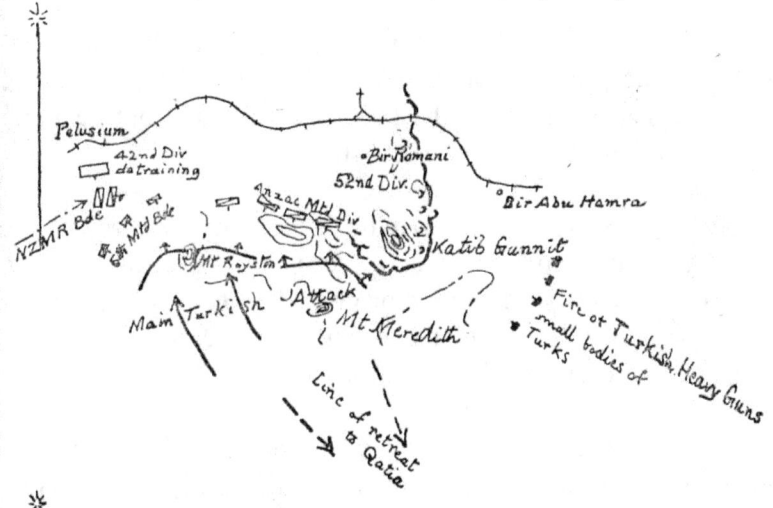

2. HYPOTHETICAL MAIN ATTACK as it might have been, opposite the 52nd Division and through Abu Hamra

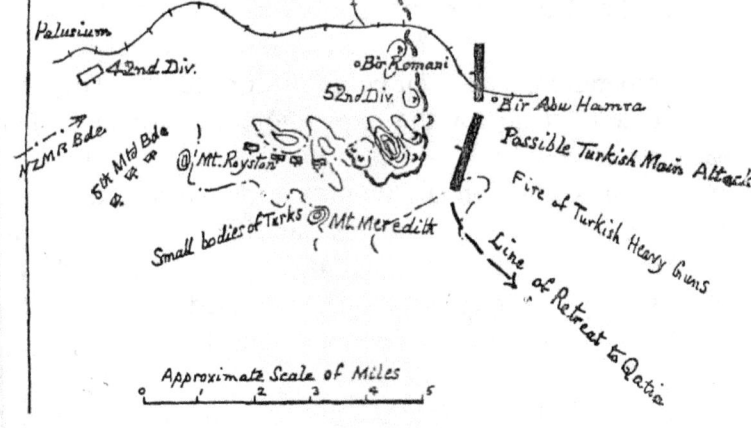

looks as if greater results would have been obtained by an attack from the direction of Dueidar.

4. Section Headquarters were at Kantara, 24 miles away. Early on the morning of 4 August, all the lines back were cut (presumably by enemy agents) and our only means of communication for some two hours was by wireless.

5. The impossibility of infantry moving any great distance over the desert and fighting. On the 7th, the 42nd Division made strenuous efforts to get up to the fight beyond Qatia but heat and thirst stopped them from sheer exhaustion.

6. Touch was lost several times with the enemy, due mainly to lack of water and supplies, which necessitated a withdrawal at night and advance again next morning. The enemy was never really on the run. He conducted a skilful retirement, using the positions he had prepared during his advance.

7. The available camel transport was not enough for a long distance pursuit. It did not allow of the mounted division and one infantry division operating more than two days' march from railhead. In the final pursuit, all camel convoys had practically to be concentrated on keeping up the supply for the mounted troops.

8. Turkish preparations had been going on for months. They had special equipment made for the expedition in Germany. Their camel-pack equipment and saddles were quite the best thing of their kind. The machine gun and mountain gun packs taught us a great deal. Their camel equipment was especially good. A manual printed in Arabic on the care and treatment of camels, which was given to the supply and transport trains, contained nothing but the soundest advice, and it has since been found useful in our service.

8. It was not thought that the Turk could bring heavy guns across the desert. They adopted an ingenious plan for securing a sufficiently stable track. Practically all the way from El Arish to Qatia they constructed an artillery road by cutting two trenches, each a foot deep and about 18 inches wide, which they filled with brushwood and tough scrub found all over the desert, and covered

the whole with a layer of sand. When the sand was exceptionally soft, wide planks were used instead of brushwood, and a battalion of labourers were employed in carrying the timber from the rear of the batteries to the front of them until the soil became firmer and the scrub tracks could be resumed.

9. Later we constructed a wire netting road along which infantry and light cars could move.

10. The main lessons to cavalry that were brought out were:
    (1) Picketing an enemy and close observation of his movements while avoiding being brought into an engagement, 19 July to 3 August.
    (2) Cavalry seizing the chance of a local success by an enemy's mistake. (Action at um Ugba.)
    (3) Delaying action against a greatly superior enemy. (1st Light Horse Brigade, night of 3–4 August.)
    (4) Ability of cavalry to break off an action and withdraw in face of greatly superior numbers. (Abd, 9 August.)
    (5) Cavalry moving rapidly suffer very little from rifle or shell fire.
    (6) Where it is impossible to bring off a mounted attack, cavalry can make use of suitable ground to gallop into action and then begin a dismounted attack.

9. RAID ON BIR EL MAZAR, EXTENSION OF THE RAILWAY EASTWARDS AND FINAL PREPARATIONS FOR THE CLEARANCE OF THE SINAI PENINSULA.

There is little to record beyond reconnaissances and patrols for the next month. On 17 September a successful reconnaissance in force was made against the enemy's camp at Bir el Mazar. The troops engaged were the 2nd Light Horse Brigade, 3rd Light Horse Brigade and one company of camels, while the 1st Light Horse Brigade came as far as a point 12 miles west of Bir el Mazar to act as covering force and protect the water supply for the returning troops. Sufficient water was brought forward by a camel convoy to allow one complete watering for horses as well as drinking water for the men. The nearest adequate Supply was Bir el Abd, 26 miles away.

The force was concentrated near Salmana on the night 15–16, and remained hidden on the 16th in the palm groves. Aeroplanes provided continuous contact patrols. The force moved forward on the night 16–17, and at dawn on the 17th the camp was attacked from the west and from the south and south-east. On the west the troops occupied a ridge about 800 yards from the enemy's second line trenches and several small posts were rushed and taken. Our batteries came into action in a favourable position, partially enfilading some enemy trenches, which were seen to be occupied in strength, and inflicting considerable loss. The enemy replied actively with artillery and heavy rifle fire. On the south and south-east the troops drew fire on a front of two miles and in many instances occupied the enemy's original first line trenches. The instructions were that a general action against the enemy in entrenched positions was to be avoided. The action was broken off about midday and the column, having successfully carried out its mission, withdrew without any attempt on the part of the enemy to molest it. The aeroplanes cooperated effectively throughout the operation and the action of the seaplanes off el Arish diverted the attention of the enemy's aircraft from our troops at Bir el Mazar. Our casualties were slight, and the captures included 1 officer and 13 men of the enemy's Camel Corps, besides a number of camels.

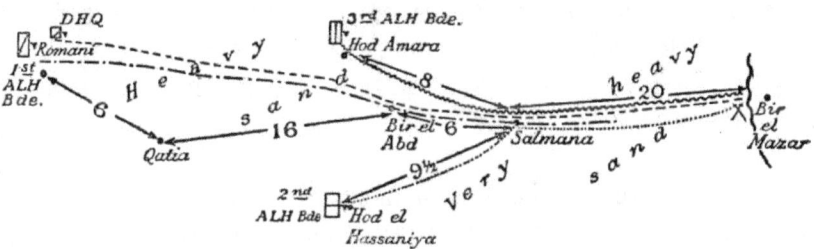

Plan showing Distances in Miles from Camps to Bir el Mazar.

The distances covered were:
1st Light Horse Brigade – 72 miles between 08:00 on the 15th and 13:30 on the 18th
2nd Light Horse Brigade – 59 miles between 02:00 on the 16th and 07:30 on the 18th
3rd Light Horse Brigade – 56 miles between 02:00onthe 16th and 07:30 on the 18th
D.H.Q. and certain divisional units – 96 miles between 08:00 on the 15th and13:30 on the 18th
(Times shown include the start from and return to camp, as well as five and a half hours while in concealment at Salmana.)

The success of the operation, apart from the casualties inflicted, which were heavy, lay in the fact that it gave the enemy a new and unexpected proof of our extended radius of action, and induced him in the course of the next few days to evacuate his camp at Bir el Mazar and withdraw the troops to camps near el Arish. The enemy's force at Mazar consisted of the Turkish 31st Regiment, about 2,000 strong. Remnants of the 39th Regiment, about 300, with four mountain guns, were also attached to this force. The whole operation was carried out in intensely hot weather and the marches were over very heavy sand.

Gradual Extension Eastwards.
From now on, until November, the railway was gradually pushed on towards el Arish, covered by the cavalry. The infantry were advanced as food and water supplies became available. During the month the railway reached Mazar. Reconnaissances by the cavalry were pushed forward to within eight miles of el Arish by 17 November, and on 28 November a patrol got through to Bir el Masmi, a little more than three miles south-west of el Arish. From now on our patrols were constantly in touch with the enemy's position at el Arish-Masaaid.

A successful reconnaissance against the enemy's position at Maghara, 65 miles east of Ismailia, was carried out between 13 and 17 October by a small force of Australian Light Horse, Yeomanry and Camel Corps. This operation not only needed careful preparations but entailed two night marches over exceedingly difficult country, the difficulties being increased on the second night by the presence of a thick fog. On the morning of 15 October the enemy was located holding a strong position on the precipitous hills of Maghara. The force, attacking in two columns, dislodged the enemy from his advanced position, capturing a few prisoners. At the same time the enemy's camp was repeatedly bombed by our aeroplanes. The force then withdrew unmolested and reached Bayud without any loss.

Throughout the month the enemy's aircraft showed considerable activity, attacking the railhead and the bivouacs of our advanced troops with bombs. Little damage was done. Our own aircraft visited Magdhaba, Sheikh Zowaid and Khan Yunus for reconnaissance purposes, and on 11 November made very successful bomb attacks on Bir Saba and Magdhaba. At Bir Saba special attention was paid to the aerodrome and the railway station, both of which were damaged.

By 1 December the railway was east of Mazar. In the meantime the enemy maintained his position at El Arish and Masaaid, and in order to afford him no inducement to withdraw until such time as the force was ready to strike, the patrols were ordered to be as unostentatious as possible.

Since January the force had gradually pushed across the desert, fighting when necessary, organising and constructing in the heavy sand and hot sun. The main factor of our success was work, intense and unremitting. To regain the peninsula, the true frontier of Egypt, hundreds of miles of road and railway had been built, hundreds of miles of water piping had been laid, reservoirs and filters capable of supplying 1,500,000 gallons of water a day had been installed, and tons of stone transported from distant quarries. Kantara had been transformed from a small canal village into an important railway and water terminus, with wharves and cranes and a railway ferry; and the desert, till then almost destitute of human habitation, showed the successive marks of our advance in the shape of strong positions firmly entrenched and protected by hundreds of miles of barbed wire, of standing camps where troops could shelter, of tanks and reservoirs, of railway stations and sidings, of aerodromes and signal stations and wireless installations. Thus was the desert subdued and made habitable and an adequate line of communication established between the advancing troops and their ever receding base. While British troops had laboured incessantly through the summer and autumn, the body of organised native labour had grown. The necessity of combining the protection and maintenance, including the important work of sanitation, of this large force of workers, British and native, with that steady progress on the railway, roads and pipes which was vital to the success of the operations, put the severest strain upon all energies and resources. But the problem of feeding the workers without starving the work was solved by the good will and energy of all concerned.

Organisation had kept pace with construction. The equipment of the fighting units with camel transport, which had reached its first stage of completion at the time of the Romani battle, had been perfected by the middle of December, the allotment of camels to units having been worked out with minute precision. A large number of additional camels were provided for convoying supplies and water from the railhead to the front. The striking force was now completely mobile, and the troops had grown skilful in solving the special problems of desert campaigning.

But no organisation could entirely overcome the chief difficulty, which had to be faced all through the year, the adequate provision of water for the troops. In fact, during this final period, this difficulty was accentuated by the rapid advance of troops and railway, with which the water supply could not keep pace. Moreover, the troops had passed out of the water bearing Qatia basin and had reached a tract in which local water was almost nonexistent. From Romani to Bir el Abd the local water, though generally somewhat brackish, had always been employed for the horses, mules and camels, and it had been found that, if the necessary precautions were taken, it had no ill effect upon our troops, at all events for a limited period. East of Bir el Abd the situation was altogether different. Water is found in comparatively few and widely separated localities. Such as exists is generally too brackish for human consumption, and the wells east of the water line are so widely separated and are of so small capacity that it is a matter of great difficulty, sometimes a complete impossibility, to water any large number of animals. This latter fact greatly restricted the employment of mounted troops during the first half of November, also the pipeline was not yet delivering water at Romani, and the water for the advanced troops had therefore to be brought up by rail in tank trucks and stored in improvised tank sat railway sidings made for the purpose. Since the railway had reached km. 109 (about 60 miles east of Kantara) considerable strain was thrown on its resources for this period owing to the necessity of maintaining the rate of construction, for forwarding material for the construction of the pipeline, for supplying the troops, and for undertaking the long haulage of great quantities of water in addition. By 17 November, however, the water situation was somewhat relieved by the delivery of water through the pipeline at Romani. Thereafter the water difficulty again increased as the railway advanced until the pipeline delivered water at Bir el Abd, thereby again reducing the distance over which rail-borne water had to be carried. But, as the month advanced, the water question presented itself more insistently than ever. Every tactical preparation for the offensive had been made, naval cooperation planned, and the arrangements made for the landing of stores and construction of piers as soon as el Arish was in our possession. But the difficulty of water supply, even with the advanced railhead, was immense. (The enemy was so disposed as to cover all the available water in the neighbourhood of El Arish and Masaaid.) Between his position and ours, and south of his position, no water could be found; nor had search in the Wadi el Arish south of the town, by parties sent in by night, proved more successful. If, therefore, he should be able to force us to spend two days in the operation of driving him from his position it would be necessary to carry forward very large quantities of water on camels for the men and animals of the formations engaged. This entailed the establishment of a very large reserve of water at railhead, and the preparation of elaborate arrangements for the forwarding and distribution of water.

The Turkish garrison at el Arish consisted of 1,600 infantry in a strongly entrenched position. Between 9 and 14 December increased activity was shown by the Turkish and our aircraft. Mounted patrols reported the construction of new works. Enemy camps at Magdhaba and Abu Aweigila increased in size. On these indications of a probable reinforcement of the enemy the final preparations were pushed on with strenuous determination. Had rain only fallen an earlier move could have been made, but as it was the water supply for the striking force was not adequately secured until 20 December.

The swiftness of the final preparations was rewarded, but not immediately, by a successful engagement. We had been too quick for the enemy, but he had recognised it and, knowing that reinforcements would arrive too late, had hurriedly withdrawn his troops from Masaaid and el Arish. This retirement was reported by the Flying Corps on 20 December late in the evening. As some doubt still existed as to whether the whole or only part of the Turkish forces had gone, the cavalry were ordered to move that night on el Arish.

The Dash For el Arish.
It was a long night march by the Australian and New Zealand Mounted Division and the Imperial Corps in order to effect a surprise at dawn. It was quite successful and the troops arrived in their positions under cover of night, but the Turk had already evacuated the place. It was a dark, moonless night and the march lay over the usual heavy sand. Scottish troops were to move in support of the mounted troops and arrived at el Arish on the 22nd.

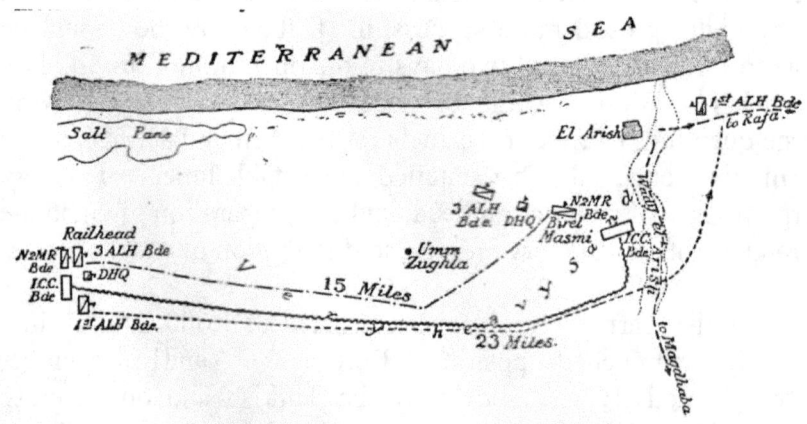

SKETCH TO SHOW MOVES OF TROOPS NIGHT 20TH-21ST DECEMBER, 1916.

By dawn the place was surrounded and reoccupied by us after an interval of over two years

The 1st Light Horse Brigade left the starting point at 22:15 on 20 December and, after a 23 miles march, was at its objective at 05:15 on the 21st.

Divisional headquarters, 3rd Light Horse Brigade and the New Zealand Mounted Rifle Brigade left the starting point at 22:25 on 20 December and arrived at the objective at 03:45 on 21 December, which is 15 miles in five and a half hours. Divisional headquarters and divisional units had to do eight miles before reaching the starting point.

Turkish Retirement.
During the day our aircraft reported about 1,600 of the enemy on the march in two columns in the neighbourhood of Magdhaba and Abu Aweigila. Sheik Zowaid and Rafa appeared to be clear of the enemy. Maghara had been evacuated and the enemy was apparently in the process of withdrawing from the neighbouring posts. By the night of 21 December, therefore, the reoccupation of el Arish had been effected and the enemy was evacuating or had evacuated his positions west of a north and south line through that place, except those at Nekhl and Hassan. The aircraft, moreover, reported that the garrison of the latter place seemed also to be reduced.

On 22 December the Scottish troops were about el Arish and Bittia. Minesweeping operations were at once commenced in the roadstead, while the preparation of piers was taken in hand. In 48 hours the Navy had cleared the roadstead of mines and the supply ships from Port Said began unloading stores and supplies on the 24th.

The enemy having temporarily succeeded in eluding us, it was of the utmost importance to strike any of his forces that remained within reach. It had always been anticipated that, should the enemy choose to abandon el Arish, his lines of retreat would be through Magdhaba and Abu Aweigila towards el Auja. These anticipations were confirmed by the report of the Flying Corps that an enemy force of about two regiments was at Magdhaba. It appeared likely that this force consisted of the 1,600 infantry which had composed the garrison of el Arish, and that it was preparing to hold Magdhaba as a rearguard. Orders were given for the mounted force to push forward with all haste against the enemy, and a Flying Column of the available mounted troops and the Camel Brigade was quickly organised and left el Arish the same night.

10. ACTION AT MAGDHABA.

Starting at 01:00 on 23 December, the Flying Column (consisting of the 1st and 3rd Light Horse, New Zealand Mounted Rifles and the Camel Brigades, the whole under Major-General H. G. Chauvel, C.B., C.M.G.) reached a point in open plain about four miles from Magdhaba at 05:00, whence the enemy bivouac fires could plainly be seen. General Chauvel, with his staff and subordinate commanders, immediately undertook a personal reconnaissance of the enemy's position, and soon after 08:00, by which time the first aeroplane reports had been received, the attack was set in motion.

The enemy had taken up a position on both banks of the Wadi el Arish, and was very strongly posted in a rough circle of from 3,000 to 3,500 yards in diameter. Five large closed works, exceedingly well sited, formed the principal defences, and between these works was a system of well constructed and concealed trenches and rifle pits. General Chauvel's plan of attack was as follows:

> The New Zealand Mounted Rifle and the 3rdLight Horse Brigades. both under the command of Brigadier-General E. W.C. Chaytor, C.B., were to move to the east of Magdhaba and to swing round to attack the enemy's right and rear. The Imperial Camel Brigade were to move direct against Magdhaba to attack the enemy in front – that is, from the north-west. The 1st Light Horse Brigade was at the outset in reserve.

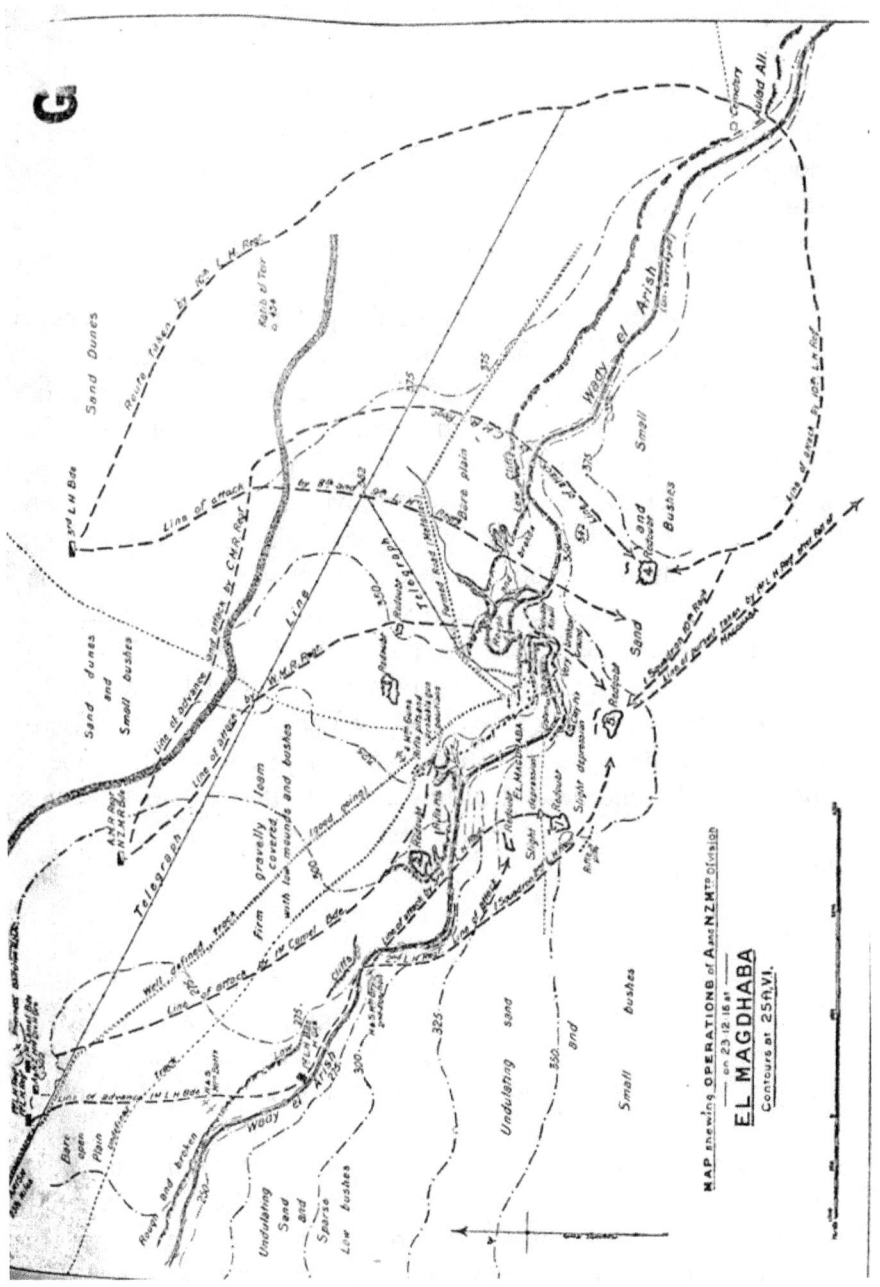

Between 08:45 and 09:30 the attack developed and, at the latter hour, General Chaytor moved the 10th Light Horse Regiment and part of a machine gun squadron on a wide turning movement round the rear of the enemy's position, with orders to come in from the south. A little later two regiments of the New Zealand Brigade were despatched in more or less the same direction, though making a less wide detour, with orders to move on Magdhaba from the east. In the meantime the Imperial Camel Corps was making progress, though somewhat slowly.

At 10:00 aircraft reports indicated the possibility that the enemy might try to escape. The mounted troops in reserve, less one regiment, were ordered to push in from the north-west. The troops moved forward at a trot and, coming under shrapnel fire, increased the pace to a gallop. The enemy then opened a very heavy shrapnel and machine gun fire, whereupon the force swung to its right and gained cover in the wadi, dismounted and began an attack against the left of the enemy position. Between noon and 13:30 the enemy's position was practically surrounded, but for some little time it had been found increasingly difficult to make progress. The Horse Artillery batteries had been greatly hindered by the mirage and the difficulty of getting forward observation, the ground round the enemy's position being absolutely flat and devoid of cover but scattered over with very small bushes and excrescences in the ground which completely hid the trenches and pits.

In the meantime reports were received from the field squadron that no water could be found. Unless Magdhaba could be taken during the day it was probable that our troops would have to withdraw, as none of the horses had been watered since the evening of the 22nd and the nearest water, except that in the enemy's position, was at el Arish. The situation was reported to the Desert Column and orders received to maintain the attack. But before this communication arrived the situation had begun to improve. The 1st Light Horse Brigade, pressing in against the enemy's left captured a work on the west of the wadi, taking about 100 prisoners. At 14:00 two regiments of the 3rd Light

Horse Brigade, coming in from the north-west, were within 200 yards of the position, in close touch with the Camel Corps advancing from the north-west. A quarter of an hour later the attack of the third regiment of this force was pressing heavily on the enemy from the south. By 15:00 the New Zealand Mounted Rifles were within 600 yards of the enemy's trenches on the east. From this time forward the pressure on the enemy increased from all sides. Before 15:30 the 1st Light Horse Brigade and the Camel Corps attacked the enemy's second line trenches. At 16:00 the former carried one of the main redoubts, taking 130 prisoners, including the Turkish commander. Immediately after this, part of a Light Horse Regiment charged in from the south and by 16:30 all organised resistance was over and the enemy were surrendering everywhere.

The total number of prisoners taken was 1,282, including some 50 wounded. A large number of the enemy were buried by our troops on the position. Four mountain guns, one machine gun and 1,052 rifles were captured and 200 more rifles were destroyed.

Our casualties were 12 officers and 134 other ranks killed and wounded. It was possible to give every attention to the wounded before moving them back to el Arish, owing to the fact that the enemy had a permanent and well equipped hospital at Magdhaba, to which the wounded were taken as soon as the action was over. The troops marched back to el Arish during the night 23–24 December, our third night march in four days.

11. ACTION AT RAFA, 9 JANUARY 1917

On 27 December the Air Force reported that an entrenched position was being prepared by the enemy at Magruntein, near Rafa. Work on this position was continued during the following day, and it was occupied by a garrison equivalent to about two battalions with mountain guns. Lieutenant-General Sir Philip Chetwode, who commanded the Desert Column, set out from el Arish on the evening of 8–9 January with a force consisting of the Australian and New Zealand Mounted Division (less the 2nd Light Horse Brigade), 5th Mounted Brigade and the Imperial Camel Corps with a battery of artillery attached.

It was a long distance raid of some 29 miles, with a view of completely surprising the enemy. So efficiently was the approach march carried out that the enemy by dawn on 9 January found himself almost entirely surrounded before he became aware of the presence of any large forces in his vicinity. The position was a formidable one. It consisted of three strong series of works connected by trenches, one series facing west, one south-west and one south-east. The whole was dominated by a central keep or redoubt, some 2,000 yards south-west of Rafa. Moreover, the ground in front of these works was entirely open and devoid of cover and in their immediate neighbourhood was almost a glacis.

The guns with aeroplanes observing began to register at 07:20. The main attack was carried out by Major-General Sir H. G. Chauvel with the Australian and New Zealand Mounted Division and was timed for 10:00. The New Zealand Brigade on the right attacked from the east, while the 1st and 3rd Light Horse Brigades attacked from the east and south-east, and the Camel

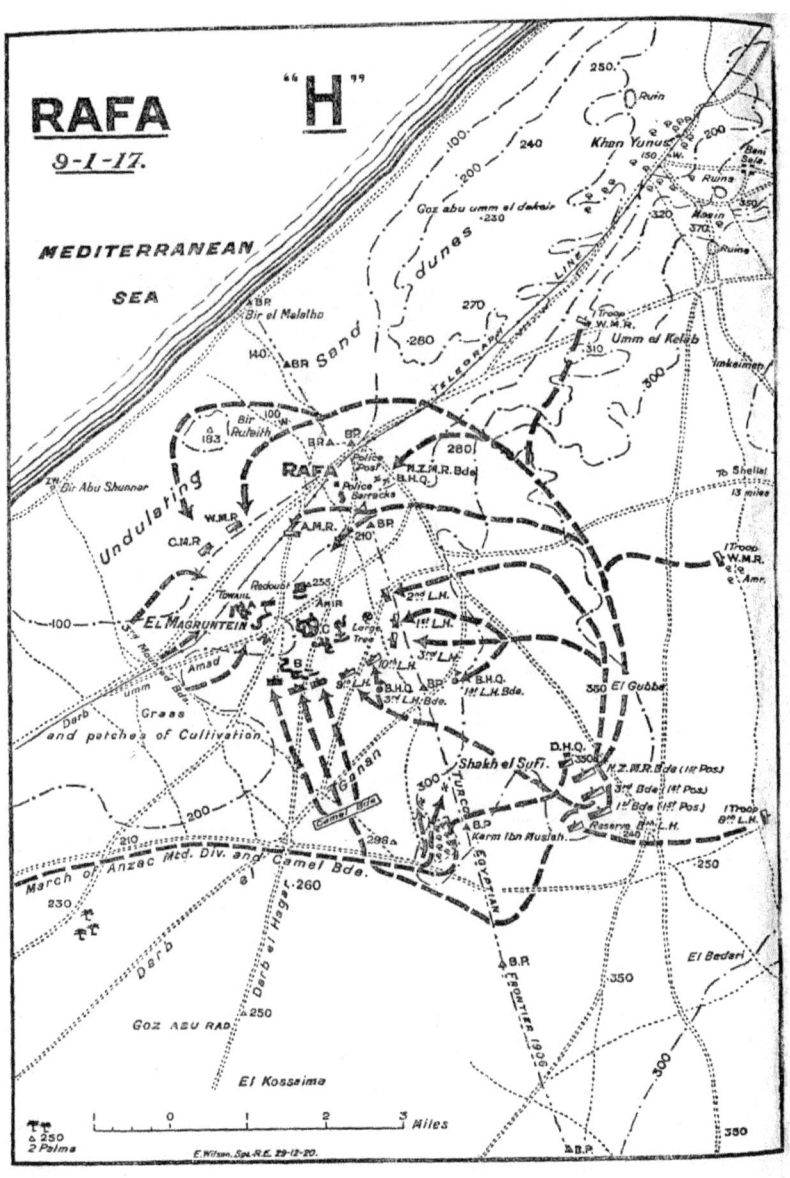

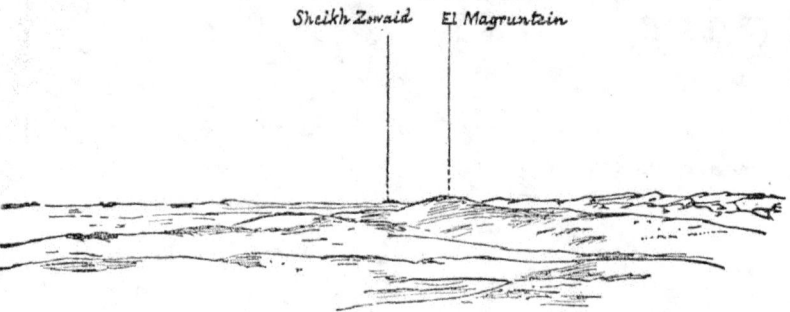

VIEW OF THE BATTLEFIELD OF RAFA FROM THE NEW ZEALAND MOUNTED RIFLE BRIGADE HEADQUARTERS.

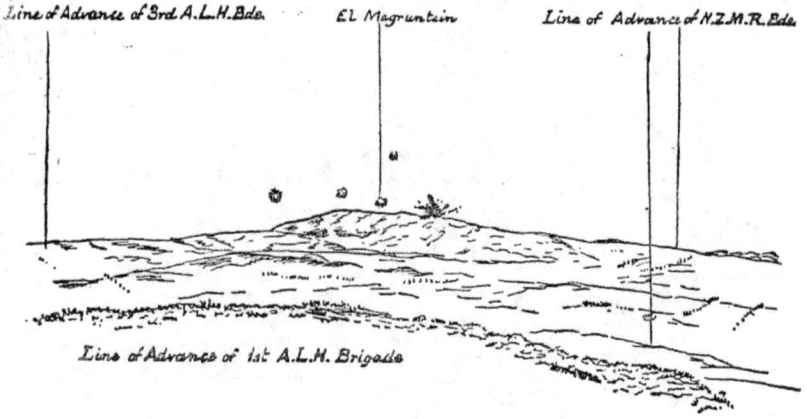

ATTACK ON EL MAGRUNTEIN AT THE ACTION OF RAFA, DRAWN FROM THE "LARGE TREE."

Corps attacked the works on their front from the south-east also. One regiment of the 3rd Light Horse Brigade was in reserve with the 5th Mounted Brigade in column reserve.

Shortly after 10:00 parties of Turks who were attempting to leave Rafa by the Khan Yunus road were met and captured by the New Zealand Brigade, who galloped the police barracks and machinegun post, capturing six Germans (including one officer), two Turkish officers and 163 other ranks.

Before 11:00 Rafa was occupied. The Australian Light Horse and the Camel Corps were ordered to press their attack on the works facing south-west, and about the same time the New Zealand Brigade, with a body of Light Horse, galloped an open space south of the police post and established themselves 300 yards east of the nearest enemy work. The Yeomanry were also ordered to deploy against the western works, and to attack in conjunction with the Camel Corps. The encircling movement was now practically complete, save for a gap in the north-west between the New Zealand Brigade and the Yeomanry.

At 12:20 one of the Horse Artillery batteries moved forward 1,500 yards to support the attack of the Yeomanry. By 13:00 our troops were within 600 yards of the southern and western trenches, which were being shelled by our artillery. By 14:00 the right of the New Zealand Brigade had linked up with the left of the Yeomanry and was pressing its attack on the rear of one of the enemy's works. The column commander now issued orders for a concentrated attack on the 'redoubt' or central keep by the New Zealand Brigade, and all other available troops of the Mounted Division to commence at 15:30. The Yeomanry was ordered to cooperate against the rear of the work. By 15:15 two of the enemy's works had been captured and further prisoners taken.

While the attack on the central redoubt was developing, information was received both from patrols and from the Air Force that an enemy relieving force was marching from Shellac on Rafa. This force was attacked frequently with bombs and machinegun fire by our aeroplanes with success. At 16:45 the New Zealand Brigade captured the redoubt with brilliant dash, covering the last 800 yards in two rushes, supported by machinegun fire. By this achievement they were able to take the lower lying works in reverse and these soon fell to the Camel Corps, the Yeomanry and the Australian Light Horse. By 17:30 all organised resistance was over, and the position with all its garrison was captured. A detachment of the Australian Light Horse, which had come in contact with the force marching from Shellal, drove the enemy off without difficulty. Our troops now withdrew, taking with them all prisoners, animals and material captured. One regiment (8th Light Horse) and a light car patrol were left to clear the battlefield and withdrew unmolested on the following day. In this action, which lasted for 10 hours, the entire enemy force was accountedfor.Morethan1,600 unwounded prisoners were taken. The Turkish killed were about 252. In addition, six machine guns, four mountain guns and a number of camels and mules were captured. Our casualties were comparatively light, amounting to 487 in all, of whom 71 were killed, 415 wounded and one missing.

The result of these successful operations was that the province of Sinai, which for two years had been partially occupied by the Turks, was freed of all formed bodies of Turkish troops. The destruction of his rearguard at Magdhaba compelled the enemy to withdraw by 31 December, and the victory at Magruntein had driven him over the frontier at Rafa, which he did not attempt to reoccupy.

Notes on Rafa and Magdhaba Actions.
A criticism was made that the attacks of the mounted division at both of the above fights were made on too wide a front and that, as a result, there ensued want of control, hence it became practically impossible to bring off an assault at a given time. In addition, that such an unduly dispersed line has no depth, makes slow progress, and if held remains stuck until it overpowers the enemy by rifle fire.

At Rafa and Magdhaba we sallied out to round up an enemy in an entrenched position. This meant blocking all exits and hence getting right round. The ground by which the enemy could retreat had to be observed at any rate. The effect was to draw our encircling lines out, and as numbers were, to say the least of it, rather limited for the task in hand, the force became spread over a great area.

PLAN OF ATTACK AS ACTUALLY CARRIED OUT AT RAFA.

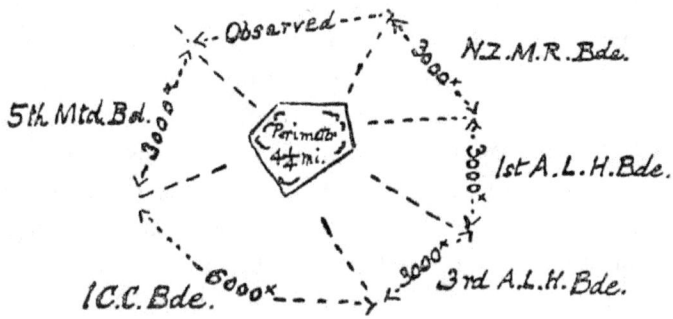

This method of course leads to an extraordinary extension and, as a matter-of-fact, troops in some cases were extended right across the front of attack.

In working this out at 5,400 rifles to 18,000 yards, it means about three and a half yards per rifle, provided all units adopted the same extensions. Once we got round the enemy it was not possible for anybody to escape, and it is suggested that brigades might have driven home their attack on a narrower front and more depth and at the same time keeping under observation the ground between units by means of patrols.

AN ALTERNATIVE PLAN OF ATTACK.

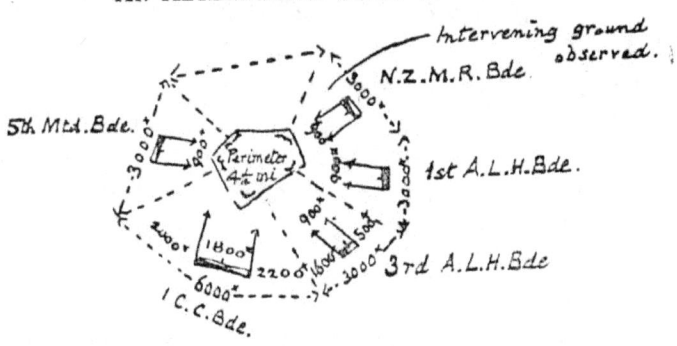

Frontage of attack thus
Remainder of ground under observation

The problem at Rafa was a difficult one. It was whether a force of

5,000 men could first cut off the retreat of a force of about 2,000 and then carry an entrenched position held by the enemy with six machine guns, four mountain guns and well placed modern entrenchments, backed up by a force of unknown strength within 12 miles. The attacking force also had only field guns to support the attack, and were operating 29 miles from a base and carrying out a long day's fight after a night march. The place had to be taken against time and, if it did not fall, there was some doubt if part of the attacking force would ever get away.

Ammunition.
The expenditure of ammunition was heavy. Something like 410,000 rounds was expended. The Turkish killed were 250 and 162 wounded. Taking it at 2,700 rifles at the most, 108 Lewis guns and 36 machine guns, it looks excessive. In addition, the three batteries expended 1,637rounds.

It must be remembered that :
(a) The attack was over a glacis slope on all sides. The field guns were not effective in keeping down the Turkish fire, which, having an ideal field of fire, prevented an advance. It therefore finally came to the point that only by a sustained rifle and machine gun fire on the Turkish trenches could any advance be made.
(b) The attack, particularly during the last three hours, when the enemy reinforcements were approaching was against time. The attack had to be helped forward at all costs.
(c) The morale effect must also be considered. Once an attack has reached a certain point, and been obliged to drop back again, it would be difficult to get forward again. Since the artillery was ineffective, the only other means of helping the attack forward was by rifle fire.
(d) No doubt there were certain faults in this great expenditure. Some Lewis guns were used as if they were machine guns, with the inevitable result, they were soon out of action.

Timing of an Assault.
Even though there may have been undue extensions, there was

not sufficient time given in the Rafa action to bring off a concerted assault. To bring it off at a given time plenty of notice must be given. The assault should be carried out by those nearest the enemy, and to be successful it must be delivered at once. There is no possibility of that unless all those about to take part in it know about when it is to come and can rise at the same time and go on.

Notes on the Sinai Campaign Generally.
In addition to the lessons brought out in the various actions, the following were found to be of general application:

(1) Framing of orders and reports. The value of orders is dependent on something more than a matter of regulations ; they require practice, clearness of thought and military knowledge. A mounted division operates over a large field, and consequently brigade commanders are required to adopt an independent role and act on their own initiative in a manner, which is exceptional with infantry. Orders will therefore be frequently more general in tenor than would be permissible with the other arms. From this arises the enhanced necessity for uniformity of thought in a mounted division. Orders are not a thing apart; they are intimately connected with training as they are with operations. A true interpretation of cavalry orders can only be ensured by means of a clear and unmistakable doctrine inculcated during the period of training. It is not a new lesson, but one that is emphasised by the result of these operations.

As regards reports, a framework is doubtless helpful to the framer, but too often leads to a generalisation which is the reverse of helpful to the recipient. When are port is called for, it is generally with reference to some particular information which is especially required. This information should form the principal subject of the report, and should find its place in the first paragraph, whatever the form of a report may be. The information a commander or staff requires should be explained clearly to whoever is detailed to obtain it. If, in the course of acquiring this information, other information of a useful nature is gained, well and good, but this should only be treated as incidental to the main object, which should never be obscured by a quantity of irrelevant matter.

(2) The country did not lend itself to shock tactics, as the going was all against it, nor were the troops employed armed with the sword or lance. Nevertheless, whenever the opportunity offered and the ground was hard enough to go right home at the gallop, the troops availed themselves of the chance. Time and time again instances showed that mounted troops are today, as in the past, capable of crossing a fire-swept zone.

(3) Fire Control. The tendency to open fire at excessive ranges was noticeable. The disadvantages of long range fire, except in special cases, such as rearguard actions, are
(i) Waste of ammunition, for it does no damage.
(ii) Disclosure of one's position prematurely.
(iii) Morale effect and discipline because:
   (a) The morale and discipline of men, who retain their fire till the enemy is close, is good, and per contra, fire at long ranges leads to, if it does not originate from a deficiency in these two essential qualities, and
   (b) The effect on the enemy is multiplied a hundredfold if we advance against the enemy, of whose presence we are aware, but show no signs of his existence till it is to our advantage to do so.

(4) Camel Brigade. As this brigade was with us during the greater part of our operations in the desert, the following notes may be useful:
   (a) If a camel brigade is working with mounted troops it should be considered the infantry of the column, and kept on the inner flank, because even in heavy sand horses move a great deal faster. In the Mazar operation the camel company with us was given the wide turning movement through Birel Kasseiba. Although they were given two hours start they did not appear until the end of the action, some four hours after we had been engaged.
   (b) They should be used by themselves for a specific duty in waterless country where they will be away two days or more, as

the camels do without water for that period and the men are self-contained for five days.

(c) They should be kept back on a night march, especially if a halt is intended. Camels when barracking or getting up again always roar and grunt and give away their position.

(d) As they carry 500 rounds of ammunition per man and five days' rations, they can in extremity supply rations and ammunition (to a limited extent) to troops working with them. (Remarks as to pace refer principally to the Sudan camel, which was always slow in the heavy sand.)

(5) Communications. Visual was possible over large areas of country, but had the disadvantage that there was usually a considerable haze; if a *khamseen*[4] sprang up, it was impossible. Although the high sand hills gave a great view, any slight wind caused a continuous cloud of sand on the top, which greatly handicapped visual.

Cable was much used. Either we repaired and made use of the old air line that ran through Sinai or laid down our own cables. In connection with this, however, we got gradually to rely on cable and, as a result, we missed it later, when moves became longer and more rapid in Palestine. The danger of using a telegraph line, which also runs through an enemy country, was exemplified by the Turks when they were at Oghratina after the retreat from Romani. They were using the line back to Abd but had forgotten to cut out forward of their station, and for some three hours on 7 August we were listening to their conversations and obtained some really useful information as to the state of their morale.

Wireless was used in Sinai but was not so important a feature as it became later. With the greater practice in later operations, we found that the pack wireless station could be setup and pulled down again very quickly.

In the desert, owing to the heavy sand, any system of despatch

---

[4] A sandstorm, more particularly a hot south-west wind, often blowing for about 50 days from about the middle of March.

riders and relay posts was not of much use. In hard sand desert, such as existed on the western desert of Egypt, they may have been of use. Later in Palestine motor despatch riders were invaluable.

12. PERIOD PRIOR TO THE OPERATIONS FOR THE FIRST ATTACK ON GAZA.

While the mounted troops were at el Arish the Imperial Mounted Division was formed and cameintobeingon16 March 1917.The 3rd Australian Light Horse Brigade left the ANZAC Mounted Division and the 22nd Mounted Brigade came to it. The Desert Column commanded by Lieutenant-General Sir P. W. Chetwode therefore became as follows :

ANZAC Mounted Division.
1st A.L.H. Brigade.
2nd A.L.H. Brigade.
N.Z. M.R Brigade.
22nd Mounted Brigade.
With Ayrshire, Inverness, Leicester and Somerset Batteries R.H.A.

Imperial Mounted Division.
3rd A.L.H. Brigade.
4th A.L.H. Brigade.
5th Mounted Brigade.
6th Mounted Brigade.
With Berks, Notts, A and B Batteries H.A.C., R.H.A.

IMPERIAL CAMEL BRIGADE.

The Turks had meantime been strengthening their position at Weli Sheikh Nuran, South of the Wadi Gaza, and were also reported to be holding Khan Yunus. Reconnaissances were carried out daily by the mounted troops; but the Turks did not come far from their trenches. The pushing forward of the railway and pipeline continued, covered immediately by the infantry, while a brigade of cavalry was pushed forward sufficiently far ahead to ensure full notice of any hostile enterprise.

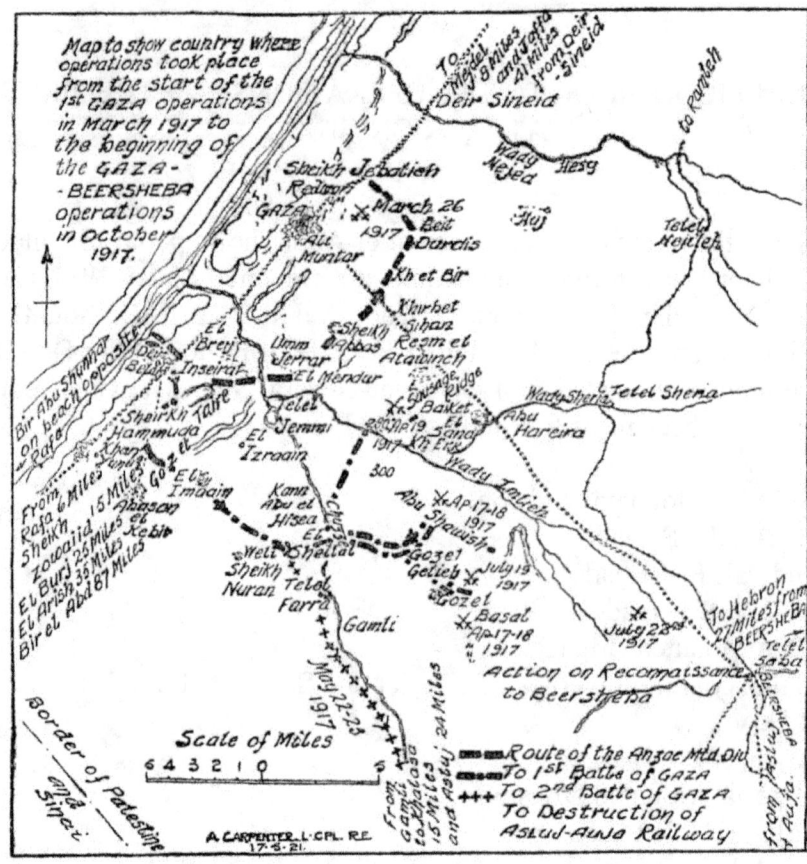

As soon as the railway was well beyond El Burj, the whole of the ANZAC Mounted Division (less one brigade) went forward on 19 February to Sheikh Zowaiid, and General Chaytor, commanding the New Zealand Mounted Rifle Brigade, went forward with his own brigade and the 2nd Australian Light Horse Brigade and reconnoitred Khan Yunus, which was found strongly held. On (or about) 27 February, however, the Turks left Khan Yunus, and on 5 March they retreated from the whole of their prepared position at Well Sheikh Nuran, leaving a few posts on the Wadi Ghuzze. These were chased away by the cavalry, who now patrolled beyond the wadi.

The Gaza Operations.
On 23 March the position of the Desert Column was as follows:
Headquarters at Rafa.
ANZAC Mounted Division (less one brigade) along the beach about Bir Abu Shunnar, close to the Sinai-Palestine border.
Imperial Mounted Division on the track south of the ANZAC Mounted Division.
Imperial Camel Brigade, Abasan el Kebir.
Armoured cars, Abasan el Kebir.
Railhead was a little beyond Rafa.

The Turks were entrenching round Gaza, and were reported to have 4,000 in the place. Strong detachments were also known to be at Nejed, Huj, Abu Hareira, Tel el Nejileh and Beersheba.

General instructions for the coming operations were issued. These were for the Desert Column to move round the east side of Gaza by night and cut the town off from the north, while the infantry attacked from the south and south-east. Prior to this the troops had to be assembled within striking distance, and the ground beyond the wadi, as near as possible to Gaza, had to be reconnoitred.

The mounted troops especially had to reconnoitre the route to be followed by night over the Gol el Taire, a rough ridge broken up by wadis and the crossings over the Wadi Ghuzze. Orders for the assembly and the reconnaissance were issued on 24 March.

At 02:30 on 25 March, the ANZAC Mounted Division left their bivouacs on the beach, crossed the two miles of heavy sand hills, and went through Rafa, moving a little north of east, so as to get on the right flank of the infantry, who were to march north-east from Rafa.

The result was that they struck the marching infantry columns in

Rafa, and some delay and crossing of columns occurred.

The mounted troops then marched east of Khan Yunus, skirting Abasan el Kebir, and pushed across the Wadi Ghuzze, only encountering opposition when about two miles from the town. The route to be followed that night was then carefully reconnoitred as far as the Wadi Ghuzze, a selected officer from each brigade was taken over it, sign boards put up where required, and a trench cut across the track at one point where the column had to leave it and go across country forabout150 yards to another one.

After dark this route was again reconnoitred for a considerable distance by the Divisional Staff.

The reconnaissance completed, the mounted troops withdrew to Deir el Belah, the ANZAC Mounted Division bivouacking just north-east and the Imperial Mounted Division just west of the village.

Orders were issued at 17:00 by the Desert Mounted Corps and got to brigades by 19.15.

The Night March to Encircle Gaza.
At 02:30 on 26 March, the ANZAC Mounted Division left Deir el Belah. The Imperial Mounted Division followed them. In spite of all the arrangements a check occurred at once.

Between the time of the last reconnaissance of the road to be followed by the mounted troops and the hour of starting, a body of infantry had marched in and camped across the track. A deviation had to be made to avoid the infantry bivouacs, and, in the darkness, some difficulty was experienced in picking up the track again. Moreover, while this was going on, the column parted owing to an accident, and some anxious minutes were spent before it was joined again.

As the head of the column reached the foot of the Goz el Taire a thick fog came on and was absolutely dense when the column was at the top of the hills.

The leading brigadier was obliged to halt his brigade until he got a message back from his advanced guard that they had made good the crossing over the Wadi Ghuzze.

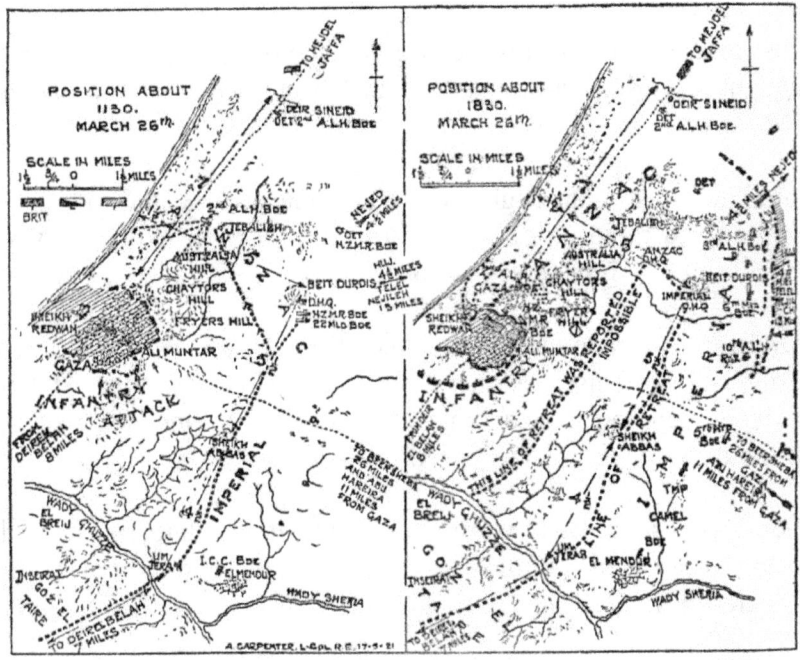

In the map showing the 1st Battle of Gaza at 18.30, the 22nd Mounted Brigade is indicated one mile east of Gaza and of the New Zealand Mounted Rifle Brigade below Fryer's Hill.

At 04:50 the leading brigade of the division crossed the wadi; but for some time, owing to the fog, advanced and flank detachments had to keep close in to the column.

At 07:55 the fog began to lift, just as the head of the column passed Sheikh Abbas, and it cleared about 20 minutes later.

In front, along the top of a slight rise, ran the main road from Gaza to Beersheba, with the telegraph line alongside it. Here the first shots were fired; the Turkish camelmen occupying some rough ground near the road. They were driven off at once, and the march went on.

At 08:15, 08:35 and 08:55 the hostile aeroplanes attacked the column, coming low over it and using machine guns. Parties had to dismount and fire back at them to drive them off; and some slight delay was caused.

Just after 09:00 the advanced guard, coming over a rise, nearly caught a Turkish aeroplane on the ground; but it rose and got away.

The 2nd Australian Light Horse Brigade now swung to the left, and moved rapidly north-west, towards Jebalieh, with the object of cutting off Gaza from the north.

Divisional Headquarters reached Beit Durdis at 09:30, and established themselves there, the New Zealand Mounted Rifle Brigade sending a detachment to the high ground north of that place to watch the country northwards.

Some pools of water were found, due to the late rains, in the wadis near Beit Durdis, and here many of the horses were watered.

Communication was established with Desert Column by 10.10A cable was laid from Desert Mounted Corps as the troops advanced.

At 10:30 the 2nd Australian Light Horse Brigade Headquarters was established at Jebalieh.

As the leading regiment of this brigade galloped down on to the road running into Gaza from the north, they caught the Turkish Commander of the 53rd Division and Staff, just driving into Gaza in a carriage, on his way from his division to take command of the troops in Gaza. The division itself was coming down the road, and the brigadier of the 2nd Australian Light Horse Brigade sent a detachment from his brigade up the road towards Deir Sineid to watch its movements. This detachment reported later that the Turks were bivouacking north of Deir Sineid.

In addition to the Turkish Commander the brigade also captured a convoy of 30 wagons, driven by Germans and Turks.

The first Turkish guns opened fire from Gaza at this time, dropping shells near the troops approaching Beit Durdis. At 11:30 the 2nd Australian Light Horse Brigade reported that their right was on the sea, so that Gaza was now completely cut off from the north. A body of Turks trying to march north-east from the town had been caught in column on a road between cactus hedges and driven back with loss.

13. THE FIRST BATTLE OF GAZA

The attack on Gaza by the infantry had begun and shells were bursting about Ali Muntar and neighbouring points. Only that part of the attack that was directed on Ali Muntar could be seen from Beit Durdis.

At 13:33 orders came to General Chauvel, from Desert Column, to tell him to reconnoitre towards Gaza to assist the infantry attack, and, acting on these orders, the 2nd Australian Light Horse Brigade began pushing southwards, through the olive trees and gardens which lie to the north of the town, while their extreme right pushed forward through the sand towards Sheikh Redwan. The Turks up north of Deir Sineid were still quiet, but reports from the Imperial Mounted Division and from the detachment from the New Zealand Mounted Rifle Brigade north of Beit Durdis showed that there was some movement going on, both from Nejed and Huj.

A heavy Turkish gun was shelling from Abu Hareira towards Sheikh Abbas.

At 14:00 the following order came from Desert Column: General Chauvel was put in command of General Hodgson's Division as well as his own. He was to attack Gaza from the north, using his own division and such troops of the Imperial Mounted Division as were not required for other purposes. He was to use the Imperial Mounted Division to keep off the enemy advancing from the direction of Huj and Nejed.

Orders were got out at once for brigadiers of the 2nd New Zealand Mounted Rifle and 22nd Mounted Brigades to meet General Chauvel at a point two miles nearer Gaza, whither

Divisional Headquarters were to move at once. General Hodgson was asked to send one brigade to General Chauvel, to be in reserve, as he intended to put in the whole of the ANZAC Mounted Division (less certain detachments) to attack Gaza. Hodgson was ordered to move his headquarters to Beit Durdis.

By 14.35 ANZAC Divisional Headquarters was at its new position, north-east of Gaza. General Chauvel explained the plan of attack to the brigadiers, and at 15.40 it began.

The 2nd Australian Light Horse Brigade attacked from the north, keeping their right on the sea.

The New Zealand Mounted Rifle Brigade, in touch with the left of the 2nd Australian Light Horse Brigade, attacked along the continuation of the Ali Muntar Hill, one point being now called Chaytor's Hill.

The 22nd Mounted Brigade attacked on the left of the New Zealand Mounted Rifle Brigade.

At this time the infantry could be seen moving rapidly up to Ali Muntar, and apparently making good progress. By 17:00 they had taken the hill.

The position now was as follows:
Around Gaza everything was going well. On the right the 2nd Australian Light Horse Brigade were pushing their way south on foot, through cactus hedges and sand. Their right-hand regiment was into Sheikh Redwan.
The New Zealand Mounted Rifle Brigade had got the ridge east of Gaza, and were into the outskirts of the town.
The Somerset Battery had silenced two Turkish guns, which the New Zealanders then captured and turned on to buildings still held by the Turks, compelling their hurried evacuation.
A detachment of the Canterbury Mounted Rifles was with the infantry on Ali Muntar Hill.
The 22nd Mounted Brigade was concentrated close to a hill now

called Fryer's Hill.

Prisoners were coming in, and the report of the brigadiers pointed to complete collapse of resistance in their front.

Towards the north and east, however, matters had taken a turn that gave cause for anxiety. The Turks north of Deir Sineid appeared to have woken up, and small bodies had pushed south and were engaged with our detachment at Deir Sineid.

The Turks from Nejed and Huj were now in considerable strength, and General Hodgson was hotly engaged. He was obliged to send to General Chauvel to ask him to send back the 3rd Australian Light Horse Brigade, which Chauvel did, keeping one regiment of that brigade; while the brigade went off at a gallop to Beit Durdis, arriving just in time to save an awkward situation.

The advanced troops of the 5th Mounted Brigade, facing Abu Hareira, were also engaged with bodies of Turks pushing forward from that place.

The Imperial Camel Brigade were in the gap between General Hodgson's right and the left of the 5th Mounted Brigade; but the gap was too wide and the enemy appeared likely to work round Hodgson's right, so that he was obliged later to ask for the remaining regiment of the 3rd Australian Light Horse Brigade, the 10th Light Horse, to be returned to him to fill the gap. The fighting in this area increased as darkness came on.

It was at 17:00 that orders came from Desert Column that all slow moving stuff should be sent back. The camels with wireless and some of the wheels therefore left.

At 18:10 a conversation took place on the telephone between Desert Column and General Chauvel. It lasted sometime, as the information the General gave as to his true position had to be considered at Headquarters East Force, which was alongside

Desert Column. At any rate the outcome of the conversation was that the mounted troops were to concentrate at once and withdraw during the night to Hill 310, close to Insert.

The Withdrawal from Gaza.
The difficult operation of a night march was rendered far more so by several circumstances. It was dark when the order arrived. The troops, thinking naturally of the success they had won, were still pressing on among the cactus hedges and houses of Gaza, taking prisoners and material. The two captured guns and a large party of prisoners, including many wounded, had already been sent in to Divisional Headquarters. Owing to the enclosed nature of the ground the horses of the attacking troops, and particularly those of the right-hand regiment of the 2nd Australian Light Horse Brigade, had been left far behind; and just before dark these horses had been sent to water in a large pond north of Gaza. The 2nd Australian Light Horse Brigade and New Zealand Mounted Rifle Brigade were on a front of over three miles.

There was also the detachment to the north to be withdrawn.

And it was not until the ANZAC Mounted Division had passed Beit Durdis on its way back that the Imperial Mounted Division could even begin to withdraw its detachments.

Under ordinary circumstances it would be light enough by 06:00, and all the mounted troops should be back at least as far as Sheikh Abbas by that time, so that allowing everything to go well the Imperial Mounted Division should at least start its arrangements to withdraw not later than 03:00.

It was not until 23.55 that the ANZAC Divisional Headquarters were able to close down and march. They went via Beit Durdis and Sheikh Abbas, passing Beit Durdis at 00.45. The New Zealand Mounted Rifle Brigade made a march across country to Beit Durdis.

The division reached a point nearElMendurat05:15, and crossed the Wadi Ghuzze at 06:00, south of Ummjerar, and bivouacked about Inseirat, being held in readiness for the rest of the day.

On 28 March, when it was definitely decided that the first attempt to take Gaza should be abandoned, the division withdrew to a bivouac north-west of Deir el Belah.

The results of this battle for the ANZAC Mounted Division were as follows:

Captured Material – 2 Krupp 75mm. guns.
Prisoners – 462.

	Horses	Casualties Personnel Officers	Other Ranks
Killed	-	6	23
Wounded	6	40	30
Missing	-	2	3
	6	48	56

Shells Expended – 304 rounds.
S.A.A. Expended – 150,000 rounds.

Points With Regard to the First Battle of Gaza.
The first Battle of Gaza was a success for the mounted troops as far as they were allowed to go. The situation at dark was dangerous; but all those round Gaza considered they had won. Hence the order to break off the action and withdraw was very hard to carry out. The description of the infantry part of the battle does not belong to this account.

The following questions naturally arise:
(a) Did the fog cause much delay, and hence influence the course of the battle?

The distance that ANZAC Divisional Headquarters had to cover from the bivouac at Deir el Belah to Beit Durdis was about 17 miles, of which the first seven included the rough and difficult

Goz el Taire and the crossing of the Wadi Ghuzze, had been carefully reconnoitred and marked. The remainder was unknown ground.

It was just light at this period at 06:00. The column left their bivouac at 02:30. Normally, therefore, they would have marched for three and a half hours under night conditions, whereas they had to go for nearly five and a half hours under those conditions, as the fog began to dissipate at 07:55.

This does not mean that the pace of movement is so much affected as that the advanced guard and flanking detachments have to keep close in to the column, and that the movement to successive positions is very restricted. At the ordinary rate of marching, taking the two periods, in the dark and after daylight, the division should have reached Beit Durdis by 08.50. They did reach it at 09:30, 40 minutes later.

There were two other causes for delay, however:
1. The check and detour, which had to be made immediately after starting, to avoid the infantry bivouacs; say 10 minutes.
2. The action with the camelmen, and three aeroplane attacks, which between them may have caused another 10 minutes delay.
The delay by the fog to the mounted troops is hardly half an hour. On the other hand, it certainly must have seriously delayed the infantry arrangements for attack by delaying reconnaissances, which could have started immediately after daylight. This would put the whole sequence of events back two hours, and one has only to consider the great difference had Ali Muntar fallen at 15:00 instead of 17:00 as it did!

One must also admit the fog had its effect on the enemy. Their forces from Huj and Nejed would have marched sooner had our attack come sooner.

(b) It has been stated that the cavalry were short of water. This may have been the case with the Imperial Mounted Division,
though there were pools in the wadis near Beit Durdis due to recent rains, where ANZAC Divisional Headquarters and some other troops had already watered.

As regards the ANZAC Mounted Division, however, apart from these pools already mentioned, the large pond on the northern outskirts of Gaza was in their hands, and horses of both the 2nd Australian Light Horse Brigade and the New Zealand Mounted Rifle Brigade were already watering there.

(c) Could the attack by the ANZAC Mounted Division have been pushed in sooner?

It must have been apparent that the longer the delay before Gaza fell the more would the Turkish forces from the north and north-east begin to make themselves felt. The order came at 14:00. However, the whole timing of the infantry attack was probably affected by two hours, as has been suggested before. Otherwise the order might have come at midday. The division was in a position to attack by 11:30, so that they were really doing nothing for two hours; but through no fault of their own.

(d) Could the mounted troops have held on where they were and continued the fight next morning? (All the facts of this battle not being in my possession, I can only state what was known at Divisional Headquarters.)

The situation, as far as we know, is shown in Map II. The enemy seemed in greatest strength opposite Beit Durdis, and had been only just checked at dusk. They were holding on opposite the Imperial Mounted Division. To hold off the Turks coming from this direction, and including Abu Hareira, next morning the Imperial Mounted Division and the Imperial Camel Brigade would have had to fight on a front of 10 miles at least, to include Beit Durdis in the north and the Wadi Ghuzze in the south.
The rifles available would be about as follows :
   Imperial Mounted Division about 3,600 rifles.
   Imperial Camel Brigade   ,, 2,000 ,,
         or   5,600 in all.

 And as regards guns : 4 R.H.A. Batteries.
          1 Mountain Battery.

This was not a great force to hold off a probably very superior enemy force, which might, moreover, put in strong attacks at three different points, that is, north or south of Beit Durdis or from Abu Hareira.

And in addition to this there was the force coming down from the north, and already engaged about Deir Sineid. General Chauvel could hardly have continued his attack on Gaza with his whole division. He must have taken steps during the night to pull back certainly one, and probably two, brigades. The 22nd Mounted Brigade were easy to get hold of; but to disengage either the New Zealand Mounted Rifle Brigade or 2nd Australian Light Horse Brigade would have been difficult, and even then it is not certain that the force available would have been enough. If Gaza fell early next day all would be well. But if it did not, one can see that the mounted troops would have to stand determined attacks from three or four directions. Except for the attack from Deir Sineid, if any of these were successful, the retreat of at any rate part of the mounted troops would have been cut off.

A further consideration was that, if any hard fighting occurred before Gaza fell, these troops would be in a very difficult situation as regards ammunition supply. Another possibility is, that even if the Imperial Mounted Division and Imperial Camel Brigade could not hold back the Turkish attack, could they delay it for such time as to enable the ANZAC Mounted Division, with the help of the infantry, to mop up what was in Gaza, and withdraw through it? After this the Imperial Mounted Division and Camel Brigade to effect their own withdrawal. This all again depends on the unknown quantity of the Turkish resistance in Gaza. The following point is, however, of interest and is, I believe, not generally known.

The Gaza garrison sent wireless messages out to say 'all was lost,' and this was picked up in Cairo ; but did not reach East Force in time. One final point about the route taken by the ANZAC Division in its withdrawal. Late in the day an officer was sent by General Chauvel to reconnoitre a possible route back direct from ANZAC Divisional Headquarters, passing west of Sheikh Abbas, and thus avoiding the long and possibly dangerous way east of Sheikh Abbas. The officer got back and reported the route impracticable. Sometime later, when the ground was examined, it was found that it would have been quite easy to retire that way. The difference in the situation for the General Officers Commanding ANZAC and Imperial Mounted Divisions is obvious.

It may be asked why a possible alternative route for retirement was not reconnoitred before. There was no idea of any retirement as regards the ANZAC Mounted Division until the order came at 17.00 for all slow moving stuff to go back.

14. THE SECOND BATTLE OF GAZA.
PREPARATIONS FOR THE BATTLE.

At the beginning of April preparations for the second attempt on Gaza were begun. During the period following the first battle the Turks had concentrated their main force in and about Gaza, and thus gave the opportunity for a very similar operation to the last one. But they changed their dispositions, putting a strong force to hold Gaza, detachments at Khirbet Elbir, Rijm Atawineh and

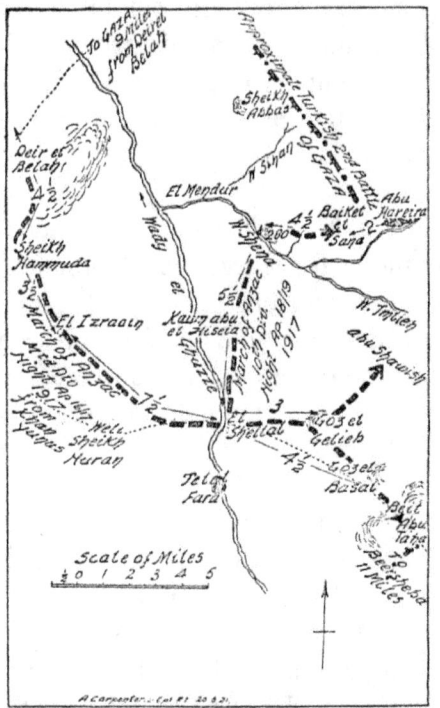

The map shows the approximate Turkish *line* facing S.W.
For " March of Anzac 10th Div." *read* " Mounted Div."

Khirbet Erk; a strong force at Abu Hareira and a reserve in rear about Beit Durdis. Beersheba was strongly held.

They began to extend their trenches at Gaza, along the high ground towards Abu Hareira, and constructed redoubts. This work progressed rapidly. This disposition of the Turkish forces precluded all chance of a turning move by the mounted troops round the flank, which was now Abu Hareira; and therefore the battle took the form of forcing a gap in the enemy's line through which the mounted troops could pass.

From the cessation of the first Gaza operations the mounted troops kept out a day line of observation beyond the Wadi Ghuzze. The night outpost line was along the Goz el Taire, up to and including Sheikh Hammuda.

The Turks made no move forward; but any attempt of our patrols to push forward beyond the Wadi Ghuzze met with opposition.
Under cover of this outpost line a reserve of water was put into the cisterns at Tel el Jemmi and Umm Jerar, being brought from Deir el Belah on camels.

Preliminary instructions for the next operations were given out, and as the first move for the ANZAC Mounted Division was a night march from Deir el Belah, through Sheikh Hammuda and El Imaain, through ruins west of Weli Sheikh Nuran to El Shellal on the Wadi Ghuzze, the route was carefully reconnoitred, and as far as the ruins west of Well Sheikh Nuran was marked by heaps of earth dug every 50 yards.

On 15 April, at 15:00, there was a conference at Desert Column Headquarters, in which instructions for the next operations were given. These were, shortly, the infantry to secure the Sheikh Abbas ridge, while the ANZAC Mounted Division, after completing the night march, helped this operation by strong demonstrations towards Abu Hareira and Beersheba.

On 16 April, at 07:00, a final conference was held by Sir A. Murray at Khan Yunus. This was attended by all Divisional

Commanders.

In the afternoon officers from the Divisional and Brigade Staffs of the ANZAC Mounted Division rode over the first five miles to be followed that night.

The route wound through the infantry bivouacs before striking the western slopes of the Goz el Taire, where it turned south-east. As an additional precaution a signaller with a lamp was put at this point, with orders to flash A.V.A. from 19:00 onwards, this being the hour of starting.

The 1st Australian Light Horse Brigade also had marched into Khan Yunus from Bir el Abd, and the point where they joined the column had to be arranged.

The Operations, 17 and 18 April
At 19:00 the head of the division passed the starting point.

Two points made the march difficult at the start. The country was now very dry, and the marching of columns of troops had cut it up. Hence, a thick dust cloud added to the difficulty of the darkness. The lamp, however, in front helped the direction. Beyond that the route was marked with the heaps of earth ; but with no moon these were invisible at 50 yards and progress was slow.

17April. At 04:25 the advanced guard crossed the Wadi Ghuzze at El Shellal. A cable was run into El Shellal by Desert Column, but it was cut several times by enemy agents, and communication was not at first obtained.

The division crossed to begin the demonstrations as ordered, and as the 2nd Australian Light Horse Brigade were crossing they were attacked by enemy aeroplanes, which inflicted some damage on men and horses with bombs. The two light armoured motor-cars joined the division after daylight.

The 22nd Mounted Brigade moved towards Abu Hareira with the armoured cars, and the New Zealand Mounted Rifle Brigade went along the road towards Beersheba. Scattered bodies of enemy were met and their guns, about Abu Hareira, came into action. A good deal of firing went on, and after dark, the division withdrew to the southern side of the Wadi Gaza. The infantry took Sheikh Abbas during the day.

On 18 April the division again pushed forward towards the Wadi Imlieh. Enemy aeroplanes attacked the column from time to time; but practically the only damage was an unlucky shot that struck one of the Leicester Battery ammunition wagons. In the afternoon General Chauval interviewed Sir P. Chetwode at Tel el Jemmi, and orders for the next day's battle were given.

In this battle the ANZAC Mounted Division were in reserve; but most of its units were engaged throughout the day.

The Battle.
At 01:00 on 19 April, the division was assembled on the northern side of the Wadi Gaza and marched.

1st Australian Light Horse Brigade led with orders to cross the Wadi Imlieh at Point 280, and thence turn east and occupy Bimetal Sana, and hold up any enemy who might push forward from Abu Hareira.

The 22nd Mounted Brigade remained on the Wadi Ghuzze with orders to watch the country towards Beersheba and the south, and prevent any hostile advance from that direction.

At 03:50 the head of the 1st Australian Light Horse Brigade reached the Wadi Imlieh where a delay occurred, as the tail of the Imperial Mounted Division was still crossing on their way north. The 1st Australian Light Horse Brigade finally crossed at 04.15, and went off to Baiket el Sana, the Leicester Battery R.H.A. going with them.

Divisional Headquarters was established on a small hill just north of Point 280.

The 2nd Australian Light Horse Brigade and New Zealand Mounted Rifle Brigade were held in reserve south of Wadi Imlieh, opposite Point 280. At 05:40 an officer attached to Divisional Headquarters was sent out to select a position for a line of posts to connect Point 280 with El Shellal, where the 22nd Mounted Brigade were. As the ground was practically dead flat there was not much choice of position.

By now, the battle had begun, and at 06:00, the C.R.A. went forward to select gun positions to support the attack of the Imperial Mounted Division.

Two batteries went forward shortly afterwards, and at 07:45 the Inverness Battery opened fire on the Sausage Ridge, and the Ayrshire Battery on the Atawineh Redoubt.

At the same time, orders came to General Chauvel to send up a squadron to temporarily fill a gap in the front line. It was promised back as soon as another regiment from the Imperial Mounted Division was available ; but it did not return.

At 08:50, General Chauvel, by orders of Desert Column, sent up the Wellington Mounted Rifles. They were brought up on the right of the 5th Mounted Brigade, and put in the attack on the Sausage Ridge.

At 09:15, Khor Sihan was taken by the 4th Australian Light Horse Brigade. The 5th Mounted Brigade were close to Atawineh, and the Wellington Mounted Rifles were working up the Sausage Ridge, closely supported by the Inverness and Ayrshire Batteries.

At 10:28, matters seemed to be going well, and orders came for the ANZAC Mounted Division to be ready to go through the gap.

Two cars of the Light Armoured Motor Battery were put in to help the advance of the Wellington Mounted Rifles up the Sausage Ridge, which was still pushing on. Patrols of the 7th Australian Light Horse Regiment, who were pushed out in observation in the direction of Beersheba, reported patrols of the enemy could be seen coming from that direction. The 5th Australian Light Horse Regiment was already engaged in digging on the line already selected between Point 280 and El Shellal.

At 11:28, to help the advance of the Wellington Mounted Rifles, the guns of the Leicester Battery were turned on the Sausage Ridge from Baiket el Sana. So far the 1st Australian Light Horse Brigade were not seriously engaged but their advanced troops to the east and north-east were engaged with scattered parties of the enemy.

At 12:20, the two Light Armoured Motor Battery Cars returned much damaged. The advance of the Wellington Mounted Rifles was held up by 13:22, though the Commander of the Ayrshire Battery pushed his guns forward and engaged the enemy in their trenches at 700 yards.

At 14:15, the enemy counterattacks began, and most of the ground gained was lost. Orders came to General Chauvel to send up a brigade to report to the Imperial Mounted Division, and the New Zealand Mounted Rifle Brigade (less the Wellington Mounted Rifles and a squadron Auckland Mounted Rifles, who were already up) went up at once.

This left the 6th Australian Light Horse Regiment with the 2nd Australian Light Horse Brigade, forming General Chauvel's only reserve, and as it was intended that this regiment should go up with the New Zealand Mounted Rifle Brigade to make that brigade complete. Orders were sent to tell General Fryer, General Officer Commanding 22nd Mounted Brigade, to send two of his regiments up at once to report to Divisional Headquarters.

About the same time a message came in from General Fryer to say that he was engaged with the enemy's cavalry coming from Beersheba, and shortly afterwards the 2nd Australian Light Horse Brigade reported that the 7th Australian Light Horse Regiment was engaged about Hill 350.

At 14:30, the Turks counter-attacked north-east of Sausage Ridge, and a quarter of an hour later the 1st Australian Light Horse Brigade reported Turks advancing on Baiket el Sana.

Both these attacks were stopped; but the Leicester Battery had to change position under heavy shell fire.

At 16:00, Turkish cavalry moved against the right of the 1st Australian Light Horse Brigade; but were driven off by the Hotchkiss rifles and mounted attack of the 3rd Australian Light Horse Regiment.

At 17.35, came a big attack of Turkish cavalry and camelmen from the direction of Beersheba, coming off the high ground in the direction of that place and over Goz el Basal and Goz el Gelieb, towards Tel el Jemmi. They brought several batteries of light guns down and these shelled the crossings of the Wadi Ghuzze, getting right into the field squadron working at El Shellal and causing some casualties.

It seemed likely at one time that the Turks would press right on; but, except for small bodies, they did not come beyond Goz el Gelieb, from which place they kept up fire until dark.

No further progress was made in the main battle, and night found both sides as they had started the day.

At 19:45, the ANZAC Mounted Division got orders to withdraw to Izraain. This was done after dark ; but, owing to the dispersion of the division, it took some time to collect them.

The division reached Izraain at 22:00.

No material or prisoners were taken by the ANZAC Mounted Division in this battle, and it had the following casualties:

	Personnel		Horses
	Officers	Other Ranks	
Killed	2	17	119
Wounded	2	170	102
Missing			10
Injured			2
Sick			60
	9	187	293

Points About This Battle.
As regards the ANZAC Mounted Division, since it was mainly in reserve as a division, there are few points to bring out. The

following, however, should be noted:

1. The great dispersion of the troops of the division.
The intention was to use the ANZAC Mounted Division as soon as the gap was forced in the line. Yet from 08:50 up to 13:00,the period during which this was probable, the only troops on whom General Chauvel could lay his hands for immediate action were the 2nd Australian Light Horse Brigade (less two regiments), the New Zealand Mounted Rifle Brigade (less one regiment and one squadron) and the Somerset Battery, as the following list shows:
Divisional Headquarters on Point 280.
1st Australian Light Horse Brigade, Baiket el Sana.
2nd Australian Light Horse Brigade (less two regiments), just south of Point 280.
5th Australian Light Horse Regiment, digging on the Point 280-El Shellal line of defence.
7th Australian Light Horse Regiment, watching country towards Beersheba.
New Zealand Mounted Rifle Brigade (less one regiment and one squadron), just south of Point 280.
Wellington Mounted Rifles, attacking Sausage Ridge.
1st Auckland Mounted Rifles, in front line with the Imperial Mounted Division.
22nd Mounted Brigade, on the Wadi Ghuzze watching country south and south-east.
Ayrshire Battery, in action supporting attack on Sausage Ridge
Inverness Battery and Atawineh.
Leicester Battery, Baiket el Sana.
Somerset Battery, just south of Point 280.Available for going through the gap.

After the time for attack had passed and we were on the defensive, the New Zealand Mounted Rifle Brigade, Somerset Battery and later the 6th Australian Light Horse Regiment (the remaining regiment of the 2nd Australian Light Horse Brigade), were sent to help in the defence, and two regiments of the 22nd Mounted Brigade coming up to Point 280.
2. Could any mounted troops have been sent to deal with the

Turkish cavalry when it advanced late in the day?

This was probably what the Turks intended, and, except for small bodies, they did not come beyond Goz el Gelieb, so that any troops sent after them would have had to go a long way. The only troops who could have been used at that hour would have been the 7th Australian Light Horse Regiment, possibly the 5th Australian Light Horse Regiment, and the two regiments of Yeomanry. But as the main battle was still going on it would not have been justifiable to send these troops off on a chase, when they might at any moment be urgently needed elsewhere.

Subsequent Operations.

In the early morning of 20 April the division was collected, and two brigades sent off to take up a defensive line along the old Turkish position at Weli Sheikh Nuran, facing south, as it was expected that an attack might come that way. When there they were attacked by enemy aeroplanes, and had 30 killed and wounded and about one hundred horses hit.

For the next few days, 21 April and onwards, the division was employed in patrolling north of the Wadi Ghuzze in the direction of Abu Hareira and Beersheba. The Turkish cavalry were met daily at first; and there occurred the case of a troop of light horse charging a troop of Turkish lancers, though they themselves were only armed with rifles and bayonets. A hand-to-hand fight occurred, in which the Australians accounted for the whole Turkish troop, in either killed, wounded or prisoners.

All the mounted troops were also engaged in digging a defensive line, which, after several changes, was chosen to run along the northern side of the Wadi Ghuzze. A chain of redoubts were dug and wired. These were taken over by the infantry about the second week in May.

From the end of the Gaza operations until the operations against the Gaza-Beersheba line in October, 1917, was a period of trench warfare for the infantry and of minor enterprises for the mounted troops.

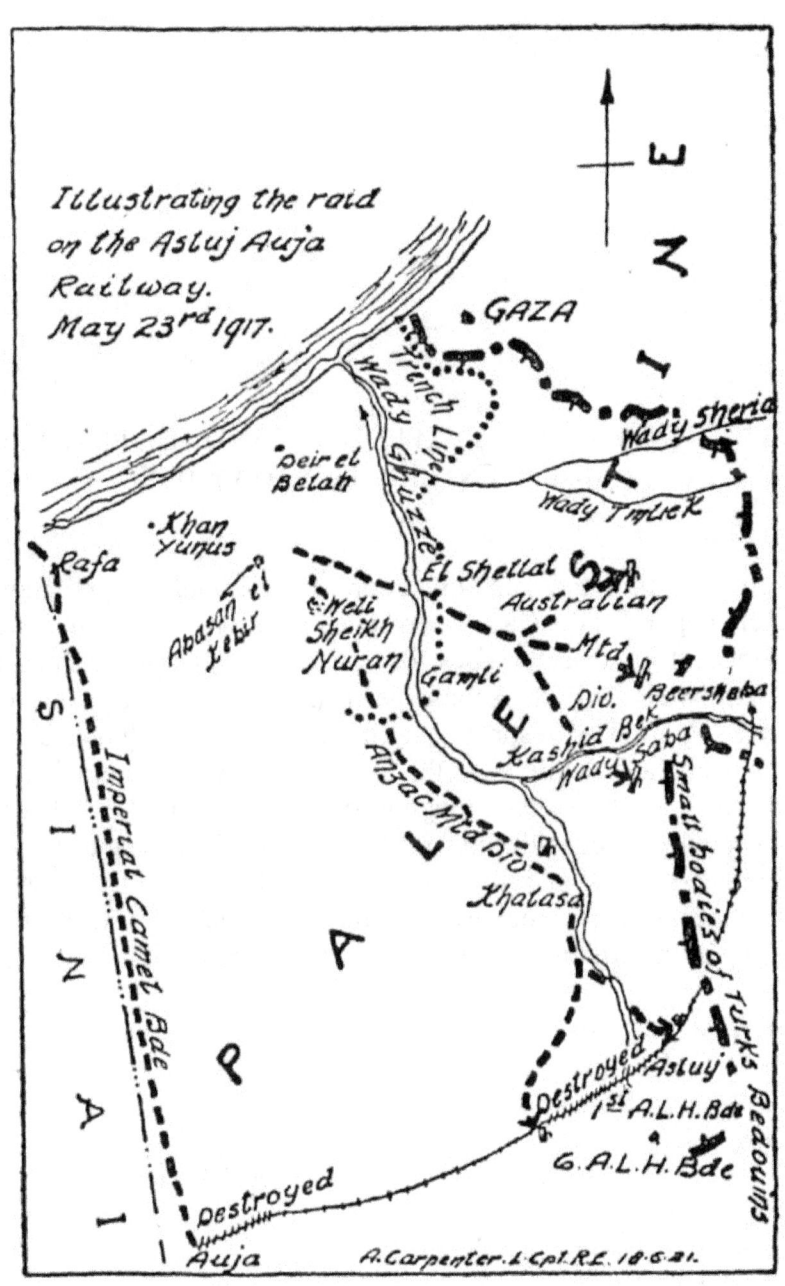

15. THE ASLUJ-AUJA EXPEDITION AND THE PERIOD OF MINOR ENTERPRISES, MAY 1917.

From the time the Gaza operations ceased until the preparations were begun for the Gaza-Beersheba operations, In October, was a period of minor enterprises for the cavalry. It was arranged that each division in turn should be in the forward line, while each took a period of resting. At first only the two divisions were available, and the division that was resting was kept at Abasan el Kebir, so as to be near enough to support if required. But later the Yeomanry Mounted Division was formed, and the Imperial Mounted Division renamed the Australian Mounted Division. Each division became also one of three brigades, instead of four as up to the present, and were organised as below:

ANZAC Mounted Division.
1st A.L.H. Brigade.
2nd A.L.H. Brigade.
N.Z.M.R. Brigade.
With the Ayrshire, Inverness and Somerset Batteries.

Australian Mounted Division.
3rd A.L.H. Brigade.
4th A.L.H. Brigade.
5th Mounted Brigade. With three batteries.

Yeomanry Mounted Division.
6th Mounted Brigade.
8th Mounted Brigade.
22nd Mounted Brigade. With three batteries.

One mounted brigade, the 7th Mounted Brigade, became corps troops. The whole of the above formed the Desert Mounted Corps. Once this organisation was completed divisions could take a period in the front line, a period in support at Abasan el Kebir, and a period resting on the beach.

As regards the minor enterprises, each division was left a free hand in their inception, only reporting to Desert Mounted Corps what they intended to do.

The object of the enterprises was :
(a) To obtain moral superiority over the enemy.
(b) By making it dangerous for his patrols and posts to push forward, to stop him gaining information.

And as would possibly follow from his inability to gain information by small bodies to induce him to send larger ones, and so give a chance of inflicting loss on him.

There is no record available of the minor enterprises carried out by the ANZAC Mounted Division between April and May,1917.

On 23 May was undertaken the expedition to the Asluj-Auja railway, by which it was still possible for the Turks to rail troops as far as Auja, and thus be a threat, if not a danger, to our communications. The ANZAC Mounted Division and Imperial Camel Brigade carried out this raid. Before undertaking it parties of men from the division were put through a regular drill of placing, securing and firing a charge to cut a rail. In the end it was possible to cut every rail for a mile in 20 minutes. To cover the operation, the Australian Mounted Division marched across the Wadi Ghuzze, and at dawn on 23 May, they pushed out strong parties towards Abu Hareira, the Wadi Imlieh and Beersheba.

Some opposition was encountered from Turkish cavalry, and armed Bedouin; but the Turks kept well within their defences.

The ANZAC Mounted Division left their bivouac near El Shellal on the evening of 22 May and took up a position some four miles north of Khalasa. The 1st Australian Light Horse Brigade, with 6th Australian Light Horse Regiment and raiding parties, pushed on in advance, reaching the railway about Asluj at 06:55 on 23 May, destroyed four miles of railway, all points, switches, et cetera, in Asluj station, and one 8-arch bridge, one 5-arch and one 3-arch, and two smaller bridges by 10.20 and returned. The covering troops had some fighting with some hostile Arabs.

The Imperial Camel Brigade destroyed the railway about Auja; but I have no details.

The force were back at El Shellal by 22:30 on 23 May.

The demolition and covering parties of the ANZAC Mounted Division did 58 and 64 miles respectively between 15:00 on 22 May and 22:30 on 23 May.

From 4 July to 8 August the ANZAC Mounted Division were again in the front line. Sixty-two minor enterprises were carried out, which took the forms of:
(a) Drives by day or night; or surprises of certain localities by forces up to one brigade.
(b) Small parties lying up to catch patrols.
(c) Raids on to the Beersheba-Gaza railway.

The enemy were very cautious, and gave no chances; but now and then some loss was inflicted.

On 19 July the Turks attempted a reconnaissance in force, which led to a long day's desultory action, in which a great deal of shell fire occurred; but practically the only casualties to the division were caused by an aeroplane bomb.

On 22 July a report came that the Turks were evacuating Beersheba, and the whole division went out, and were able, by 09:00 that day, to report that the defences were strongly held.

At the end of the third week in October preparations for the attack on the Gaza-Beersheba line were begun.

16. PHASE III[5]

In July, 1917, when General Allenby arrived in Palestine, the Turkish Army in Southern Palestine held a strong position extending from the sea at Gaza, roughly along the main Gaza-Beersheba road to Beersheba (see Plate VI).

Gaza had been made into a strong modem fortress, heavily entrenched and wired, offering every facility for protracted defence. The remainder of the enemy's line consisted of a series of strong localities, viz.: the Sihan group of works, the Atawineh group, the Baha group, the Abu Hareira-Kauwukah trench system and, finally, the works covering Beersheba. These groups of works were generally from 1,500 to 2,000 yards apart, except that the distance from the Kauwukah group to Beersheba was about 4½ miles.

During the period from July to October, the enemy's force on the front had been increased. It was evident, from the arrival of these reinforcements and the construction of railway extensions from Et Tine, on the Ramleh-Beersheba railway to Deir Sineid and Beit Hanun, north of Gaza, and from Deir Sineid to Huj, and from the reports of the transport of large supplies of ammunition and other stores to the Palestine front, that the enemy was determined to make every effort to maintain his position on the Gaza-Beersheba

---

[5] This narrative is mainly based upon the official reports compiled by the G.O.C. Desert Mounted Corps. The writer is greatly indebted to Lieutenant-Colonel G. Browne, C.M.G., D.S.O., 14th Hussars, for complete information as to the operations of the Australian and New Zealand Mounted Division; also to Lieutenant-Colonel the Hon. R. M. P. Preston, D.S.O., for Map A, taken from his most valuable and readable *The Desert Mounted Corps.*

line (see Plate VI). He had considerably strengthened his defences on this line, and the series of strong localities mentioned above had, by the end of October, been joined up to form a practically continuous line from the sea to Kauwukah south of Sharia, except for a gap just east of Gaza. The defensive works round Beersheba remained a detached system, but had been improved and extended.

The Turkish communications were efficient. The Jerusalem-Beersheba and Jerusalem-Gaza roads were metalled and capable of carrying heavy mechanical transport.[6] The Gaza-Beersheba road, connecting up all his defended localities, was hard, and the open country north of it generally was passable for horsed transport. His front was served by the Junction Station-Beersheba railway (3ft 6in gauge), with its branch line, Et Tine-Deir Sineid.

The Turkish forces consisted of XX and XXII Corps and the 3rd Cavalry Division, in all nine divisions; about 50,000 rifles, 1,500 sabres and 300 guns.

XXII Corps had its Headquarters about Gaza and held the western groups of works.

XX Corps had its Headquarters at Sharia and held the centre groups of works, with the 27th Division and 3rd Cavalry Division about Beersheba (see Plate VI).

Army Headquarters and the main reserve centre was near Huj.

BRITISH FORCES.
The E.E.F. in October, 1917, consisted approximately as follows (the fighting strengths given for each Corps total 100,000, and only include infantry and mounted regiments):

XX Corps (Lieutenant-General Sir Philip Chetwode, Bt);

---

[6] Map A fails to show the metalled road from Junction Station north-east to Latron.

(fighting strength, 45,500), consisting of:
10th Division
53rd Division
60th Division
74th Division
23 Batteries R.G.A. (Mountain, Heavy and Siege)

XXI Corps (Lieutenant-General Sir Edward Bulfin); (fighting strength, 36,000), consisting of:
52nd Division
54th Division
75th Division
18 Batteries R.G.A. (Mountain, Heavy and Siege)

Royal Flying Corps:
3 Squadrons and 1 Balloon Wing

Army Cavalry:
Imperial Service Cavalry Brigade (Jodhpur, Mysore and Hyderabad Lancers)

Desert Mounted Corps (Lieutenant-General Sir Harry Chauvel, A.I.F.)
(fighting strength, 18,700), consisting of:

(a) Australian and New Zealand Mounted Division (Major-General Sir E. W. C. Chaytor, N.Z.I.F.):
1st Australian Light Horse Brigade
2nd Australian Light Horse Brigade
New Zealand Mounted Rifles Brigade
18th Brigade R.H.A. (Inverness, Ayr and Somerset Battalions)

(b) Australian Mounted Division (Major-General Sir H. W. Hodgson):
3rd Australian Light Horse Brigade
4th Australian Light Horse Brigade
5th Mounted Brigade (Yeomanry)
19th Brigade R.H.A. (A and B Batteries H.A.C., 1/1st Notts.

Battery)

(c) Yeomanry Mounted Division (Major-General Sir G. de S. Barrow):
6th Mounted Brigade (Yeomanry)
8th Mounted Brigade (Yeomanry)
22nd Mounted Brigade (Yeomanry)
20th Brigade R.H.A. (Berks., Hants and Leicester Batts)

(d) 7th Mounted Brigade
(Yeomanry, and including Essex Battalion R.H.A.)

(e) Imperial Camel Corps Brigade
(three battalions and one Mountain Battalion R.G.A.)

Note.
(1) Of the above nine brigades, only the five mounted brigades (Yeomanry) were armed with the sword, as well as the rifle and bayonet, and were trained in accordance with the manual, *Cavalry Training*.[7] The four A.L.H. Brigades and the N.Z.M.R. Brigade relied solely upon the rifle and bayonet, and had been trained in accordance with the manual, *Yeomanry and Mounted Rifle Training*.
(2) With the above exception the mounted divisions were almost identical in every way with the cavalry divisions in France in 1917–1918. They each had, however, a divisional train; and the M.T. was retained under control of Desert Mounted Corps.

In October, 1917, the British situation was approximately as follows :

XXI Corps was strongly entrenched in front of Gaza, from the sea to a distance of about six miles inland. In this sector months had been spent in perfecting the defensive arrangements, and the

---

[7] *Cavalry Training*, (London: HMSO 1912, reissued with amendments, 1915).

conditions were practically those of fortress warfare.

The right flank was open, and in this area Desert Mounted Corps operated. One mounted division, with its camps on the Wadi Ghuzze at Fara, sent out one Mounted Brigade daily to the high ground El Buggar-Pt. 720-Pt. 630[8] – Bir in Bir el Girheir (Map A) to overlook the wadis about Bir Imleih and Bir el Girheir and keep the hostile cavalry patrols at a distance. Each night this outpost Mounted Brigade withdrew and took up a night outpost line behind the barbed wire which protected the Wadi Ghuzze to as far south as Gamli. The remainder of Desert Mounted Corps and XX Corps were echeloned back to the coast, resting.

Topography.
The line Gaza-Beersheba is practically the southern edge of the Plain of Philistia. From this line, for 80 miles northwards, the topographical conditions are remarkably constant. Along the sea coast there is a belt of sand dunes, varying from two to four miles in width. The Plain of Philistia running as far north as Jaffa, and the plain of Sharon which continues to Mt Carmel, lie between the sand dunes and the foothills of the Jude An Mountains. The average breadth of the plain is 20 miles, reaching its maximum breadth of 30 miles on the line Gaza-Beersheba, at which latter place a deep re-entrant runs into the mountains. The Plain of Philistia is for the most part rolling downland. It is wonderful barley country, under crops from April to June. It is sparsely populated, partly by tent-living Arabs with their flocks and partly by the Fellahin, who live in the mud villages. The inhabitants find ample water for their needs in the deep village wells, and there is a regular rainfall from November to March.

The winter rains descending from the Jude An Mountains have cut deep wadis across the plain. These wadis are the only serious obstacle to movement in the plain. In general it might be said that the Plain of Philistia is perfect 'cavalry country'; while there is

---

[8] These are obviously map references but the authors do not make it clear which map they were referring to.

freedom of movement everywhere, the country is not flat; on the contrary, for mile upon mile gentle hills and valleys give promise of covered approach to large cavalry forces. Even the wadis are comparatively easily crossed by cavalry, and give refuge from artillery fire or attack by hostile aircraft. The Jude An Mountains run from Beersheba northwards. The watershed is marked approximately by the metalled road Beersheba-Hebron-Jerusalem-Nablus. From Hebron northwards the mountains rise to a height of 3,000ft.

The western slopes are much more gradual than the eastern, and the western foothills extend westwards to within about two miles of the Beersheba-Sharia-Junction Station-Ramleh railway. The eastern slopes of the Jude An Mountains are very steep and in places precipitous.

Between Beersheba at the south end of the mountains, and the Plain of Esdraelon, 100 miles to the north, several valleys descend westwards from the summit to the plain, up which modern troops without wheels might reach the summit. The spurs run from east to west, descending comparatively gently to the west, and it is up these spurs, rather than up the valleys, that infantry could most easily force their way. Any advance into the mountains, however, from the west, in the face of opposition, would be a most difficult operation.

An advance from Beersheba northwards along the backbone of the mountains would be met by position after position of great natural strength; later experience showed that an advance of five miles in one day, in face of determined opposition, was the most that could be expected.

It is clear, therefore, that a commander seeking a decision will always avoid the mountains, if he can.

Lord Allenby has described his plan in his despatch dated 16 December 1917.
    I had decided to strike the main blow against the left flank

of the Turkish position, Hareira and Sharia. The capture of Beersheba was a necessary preliminary to this operation, in order to secure the water supplies at that place, and to give room for the deployment of the attacking force on the high ground to the north and north-west of Beersheba, from which direction I intended to attack the Hareira-Sharia line.

This front of attack was chosen for the following reasons. The enemy's works in this sector were less formidable than elsewhere, and they were easier of approach than other parts of the enemy's defences.

When Beersheba was in our hands we should have an open flank against which to operate, and I could make full use of our superiority in mounted troops; and a success here offered prospects of pursuing our advantage and forcing the enemy to abandon the rest of his fortified positions, which no other line of attack would afford.

It was important, in order to keep the enemy in doubt up to the last moment as to the real point of attack, that an attack should also be made on the enemy's right at Gaza, in conjunction with the main operations.

Lord Allenby discloses the fact that he had his mounted troops in mind. He intended them to exert a decisive influence. He selected for his main attack that area in which the mounted troops would find the conditions most favourable; the hostile positions in the east were less formidable than to the west; the hostile reserves were mainly behind Gaza; the enemy's main L. of C. ran from Gaza northwards to Junction Station; the ground about Sharia and to the north of it was suitable for the rapid movement of large mounted forces. Exploitation by cavalry, in its initial phases at least, requires ground giving freedom of movement and a minimum of hostile opposition. Lord Allenby's plan, therefore, was designed to give his cavalry every chance.

It is certain that Lord Allenby looked far ahead. Success in the main attack at Hareira-Sharia might lead to the rolling up of the whole line, to pursuit to Junction Station, and even to the capture of Jerusalem.

Battle of Beersheba.
The strategic plan depended upon an initial tactical success, the capture of Beersheba, for which the C-in-C formed the following plan. XX Corps (60th, 74th, 53rd and 10th Divisions and Imperial Camel Corps Brigade) was to move out from Esani and Fara and capture the enemy's main works, south-west of Beersheba, between the Beersheba-Khalasa road and the Wadi Saba (see Map A).

The Desert Mounted Corps, less detachments, was to concentrate far to the south, at Bir Asluj and Khalasa, and moving through the rough country to the east, to attack the enemy's defences on the east and north-east of Beersheba and the town of Beersheba itself.

Narrative
Preparatory Measures.
The situation of Descorps prior to the operations was as follows (Map A):

Corps Headquarters	South of El Fukhari
	Tel el Fara, with one Mounted Brigade on outpost on the ridge El Buggar – Pt. 720-Pt. 630
ANZAC Div.	Abasan el Kebir
Yeodiv	On the beach near Khan Yunus
7th Mounted Brigade (Corps Troops)	El Fukhari
I.C.C. Brigade (Corps Troops)	South of El Fukhari

The preparatory measures of Descorps aimed at placing ANZAC Div. at Bir Asluj, Ausdiv at Khalasa and 7th Mounted Brigade at Esani. Yeodiv and I.C.C. Brigade were to be detached from Descorps before the operations began, as there was no hope of finding water to the south and east of Beersheba for more than two mounted divisions and one mounted brigade.

Descorps was also required to protect the advance of XX Corps to their preliminary positions on the line Ma El Mallaka-El Buggar.

31 October was the date fixed for the capture of Beersheba, but it was necessary to start the moves some days earlier, in order to re-establish the wells at Asluj and Khalasa, which had been destroyed by the enemy, and to store at each place sufficient water, about 100,000 gallons, for a Mounted Div. for one day.

At Esani also, water had to be collected into reservoirs to supply one Mounted Div. in its march to Khalasa.

Preliminary Moves
The preliminary moves, therefore, consisted of:
(a) An advance of the line of cavalry observation eastwards as far as the line from a point two miles east of Esani-El Buggar –
Pt.720-Pt.630 – Bir in Bir el Girheir-nearly to junction of the big Wadis Ghuzze and Sharia.
(b) A gradual extension of our line southwards as far as Bir Asluj.

Advance of Line of Observation.
The line of observation, which was under the command at the G.O.C. Ausdiv, was established on 24 October, on the general line Esani-El Buggar – Pt. 720-Pt. 630[10] – Bir in Bir el Girheir thence W.N.W.

---

[10] These are obviously map references but the authors do not make it clear which map they were referring to.

This line was 15 miles long, and one mounted brigade was

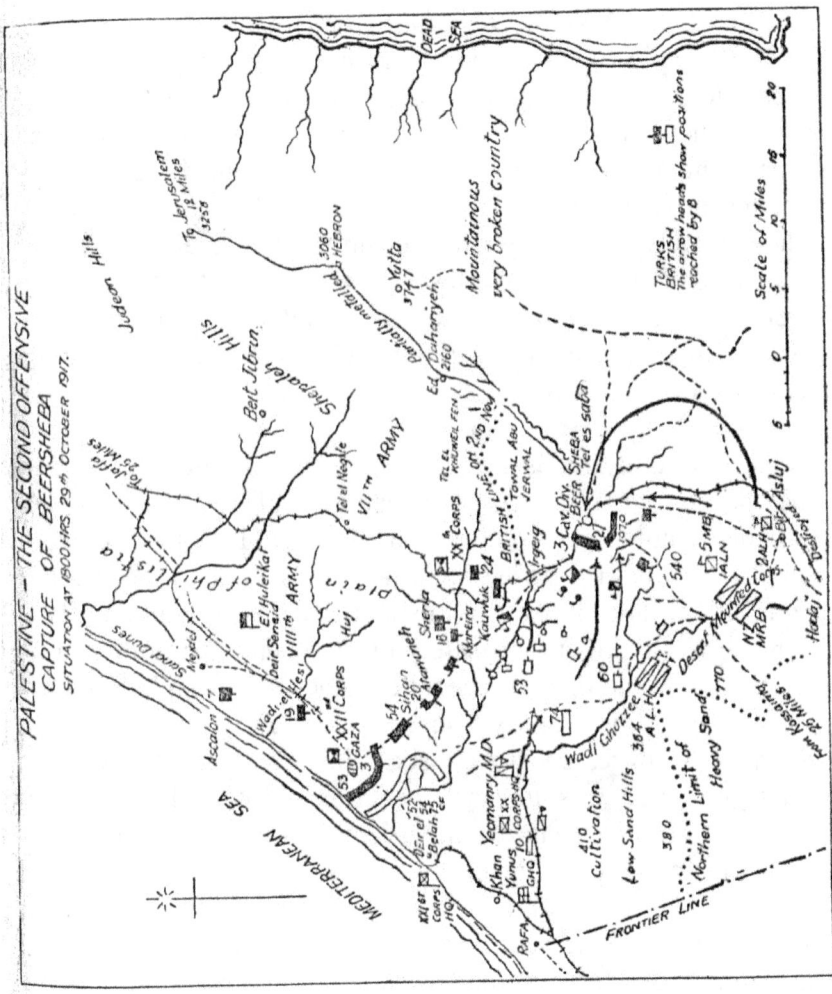

PLATE VI.

detailed daily as outpost brigade for a tour of duty of 24 hours.

The main object was to deny to the enemy, from 17:00 hours on 24 October onwards, positions from which he could bring observed artillery fire on to the railway construction parties, who were extending the railway from Shellal to Karn.

Previous to 24 October the mounted brigade on outpost duty was withdrawn each night behind the wire on the Wadi Ghuzze, reoccupying the position each morning. The position El Buggar – Pt.720-Pt. 630 – Bir in Bir el Girheir is a ridge from which observation can be obtained to El Gamli and Shellal. It was decided, therefore, that this ridge must, from 24 October onwards, be permanently occupied both by day and night by the outpost mounted brigade. This decision meant that the mounted brigade, besides merely 'observing' from Esani to El Buggar and from Bir in Bir el Girheir for four miles W.N.W. of it, a total distance of seven miles, must entrench itself in an outpost line of resistance from El Buggar, through Pts 720 and 630, to Bir in Bir el Girheir, a distance of eight miles.

It was thoroughly realised that only about one regiment and the machine gun squadron and two batteries of artillery, would be available to hold the entrenched position, that little more could be done than to hold fortified localities at Pt. 720, Pt.630 nadir in Birel Girheir, and that the troops actually dug in could easily be overpowered and that their safety must depend upon other troops coming quickly to their rescue when attacked. From before dawn on 26 October one infantry brigade of 53rd Div. was to be east of the Wadi Ghuzze, encamped six miles west of Pt.630. This infantry brigade was to stand to arms daily at dawn, and be prepared to move at short notice, if necessary, to the support of the outpost mounted brigade.

The mounted brigade next for duty of Ausdiv, encamped at Tel el Fara, nine miles from Pt. 630, was also to be ready to march at three-quarters of an hour's notice to the support of the outpost mounted brigade.

These two brigades were so far away that quick support could not be expected; there was no water east of the Wadi Ghuzze, so they could not be maintained further forward.

Further, the enemy's entrenched positions south of Kauwukah

and Hareira were only four miles from Pt. 630, and were occupied by large Turkish forces.

The orders received could only be interpreted in one way. The ridge, in particular the most important localities, Pts. 720 and 630, must be denied to the Turks. The garrisons of these localities must resist to the last, giving time for supports and reserves to intervene; these localities were therefore entrenched, but there was no time to erect wire.

This line, partly of observation and partly of resistance, was occupied successively by 3rd and 4th A.L.H. Brigades and 5th Mounted Brigade of Ausdiv, during the period 23 to 26 October.

At 17:00 hours on 26 October, 8th Mounted Brigade, temporarily detached from Yeodiv, was put into the outpost line by Ausdiv, but came under command of G.O.C. 53rd Div., at midnight, 26–27 October.

The distribution of the outpost mounted brigade to carry out its task on the 15 mile front had been worked out by the Div. Staff of Ausdiv, with the mounted brigade commanders.

8th Mounted Brigade occupied the line as follows:
(a) Middlesex Yeomanry (two sub-sections 21st machine gun squadron attached), El Buggar to Pt. 630 (inclusive).
(b) 3rd County of London Yeomanry (one sub-section 21st machine gun squadron attached), Pt. 630 (exclusive), to eight miles W.N.W. of it.
(c) City of London Yeomanry and 21st machine gun squadron (less three sub-sections), were in mounted brigade reserve about Karm.

Hants Battalion R.H.A. was in action near Karm, one section covering Pt. 720 and one section covering Pt. 630.

The dispositions of the Middlesex Yeomanry are given, as they show how weakly the line of resistance was held.

B Squadron (Major Lafone).
(a) 1 Troop as standing patrol at El Buggar
(b) Sqn Headquarters and 2 Troops and 1 sub-section 21st machine gun squadron, dug in on the crest of Pt. 720
(c) 1 Troop a mile in rear of Pt.720 in reserve

C Squadron (Capt. A. McDougall).
(a) 1 Troop dug in half mile south of Pt. 630
(b) Remainder of Sqn and 1 sub-section machine guns dug in at Pt. 63; all the led horses were sent 1½ miles to the rear of Pt. 630.

Regimental Headquarters and A Squadron, near Karm.

As it was realised that the enemy could develop greatly superior artillery and machine gun fire against these isolated posts, it was decided to dig cruciform posts, about 70 yards behind the crest, so that the enemy could not see and direct artillery fire onto them; further, the distance of 70 yards was chosen so as to be out of bombing range from the crest.

The troops were to hold the crest until driven off, when they were to retire down into the cruciform posts.

These posts would, without doubt, be surrounded, but as effective artillery fire or bombing could not well be developed against them they could only be taken by assault.

The Brigade Commander ordered the posts to be held at all costs.

The decision to dig troops in behind a crest, whence they could only see 70 yards ahead of them was a desperate decision. But the localities had to be held; only three squadrons were available for fixed defence from Pt. 720, through Pt. 630 to Bir in Bir el Girheir, a distance of five miles; the enemy could attack with almost unlimited numbers, and it was impossible to maintain effective reserves close at hand. The commanders who drew up the plan realised that they were making tremendous demands on the troops ; the problem as set from above was an extraordinarily difficult one, and it will well repay thinking out.

Early on 27 October, Pts. 720 and 630 were attacked by a force of about six battalions, 2 regiments of cavalry and 2 batts. No praise can be too high for the magnificent defence put up by the Middlesex Yeomanry and 21st machine gun squadron.

The following accounts of events at Pt. 720 and Pt. 630 are taken from the official reports of officers who took part.

B Squadron, Middlesex Yeomanry, at Pt. 720.

We relieved the Australians about 17:00 hours, October 26th. Major Lafone, with Lieutenants. Van den Bergh and Edmondson, 2 troops of B Sqn. and 2 M.G.s, took up his position in some trenches near the crest of Hill 720. His right flank was protected by a troop under Lieutenant Jehu (Note. Presumably the standing patrol at El Buggar). The horses were sent a mile or so back. Sometime before dawn we saw green lights go up on our left, presumably from Pt. 630, and heard rifle fire, which rapidly increased in volume. Shortly after this we were surprised to hear the neighing of horses and a deal of uncouth jabbering to our right, and to see about six horsemen appear over the crest about 300 yards away. It was not sufficiently light to see plainly who they were, but their speech betrayed them, and a few rounds dispersed them. There must have been a gully in front of the hill, for we could heat the Turks talking not more than 30 yards away. The force opposed to us has been variously estimated, but perhaps it is best described as 'a little army.' At dawn the enemy opened accurate fire on us with shrapnel and machine guns. They kept this up for about two hours, by which time a half of our small force were casualties, and we were nearly surrounded. The enemy then made a strong attack on our left flank, which was held by a Hotchkiss and a few men. All the Hotchkiss team were killed or wounded, but when the enemy got to within 50 yards the few surviving rifles, reinforced by Major Lafone, who took up a rifle and shot down the Turks one by one, counting them as he did so, beat off the attack. This was immediately followed by a cavalry attack on our right flank. We had scarcely changed flanks to meet it when the enemy swept across our front, but he was routed by our machine gun, which took heavy toll. In the meantime a small body of enemy cavalry had managed to creep round our flank and attack our led horses, which had come up earlier in the day. The horse-holders had suffered casualties in the shelling and the survivors had about 10 horses each, but a Hotchkiss was quickly got into action and the enemy fled. All this time Major Lafone was directing the fire, and encouraging the men regardless of personal danger. The shelling became more intense. Major Lafone and Lieutenant Van den Bergh were killed, Lieutenant Edmondson was wounded, and the remaining force did not exceed half a dozen men, but when the Turks made another dismounted attack they were beaten by one machine gun, worked by a single man, and two rifles. About 10:00 hours, the Turks were seen to be preparing another cavalry charge, so realising the impossibility of holding out any longer, the four unwounded men and a few of the slightly wounded withdrew as the enemy swarmed over the position. Several were hit as they ran back, and it was impossible to remove those who were too badly wounded to help themselves.

B Sqn. obeyed its orders to the letter and fought to the bitter end.[11] It is certain that the siting of the cruciform posts did not prevent the enemy from directing artillery and M.G. fire, as had been hoped.

The trenches, however, were originally attacked at 05:15 hours, and were not taken until the final assault, which took place at 11:15 hours; two troops and two machine guns therefore maintained their position for six hours, and this part of the plan

---

[11] The gallant squadron leader, Major Lafone, was posthumously awarded the Victoria Cross.

can hardly, therefore, be called a failure. The failure lay in the fact that in six hours no effective reinforcements arrived to save the situation.

C Sqn. Middlesex Yeomanry at Pt. 630.Report by Capt. McDougall., D.S.O.

It was at Shellal on October 26th, 1917, about 08:00hours, that we first heard that the regiment was for the outpost line that night. Our orders were:

The regiment will take over from the Light Horse at dusk today, on the line, 720–630, both inclusive. B Squadron will hold the right, from 720; C Squadron the left, from 630; Headquarters and support (A Squadron),near Karm; two guns of the 21st Machine Gun Squadron will accompany each squadron; one section of Hants R.H.A. will support 720, and one, 630; signalling will be by visual ; alarm signals signifying the need of artillery support and reinforcements, red flares from 720, green and white flares from 630. During the morning the officers moved out across the Wadi Ghuzzi to reconnoitre the ground, and the regiment followed later in the day. Two of us visited the Australians on 630 in the afternoon. It was already an unhealthy locality, for the Turk had two guns beautifully trained on the crest, and we soon found by experience that he let drive at the slightest sign of movement. Between720 and 630 is a gap of three and half miles, and with our weak squadrons it was not possible for either B or C to hold any intervening points, so it was left to A Squadron in reserve to watch this ground by means of patrols. C Squadron and two guns of the 21st M.G.S., under Lieutenant Gardham, relieved a similar force of A.L.H. at dusk. The position consisted of three partially dug cruciform trenches on the reverse slope 30 yards apart and about 70 yards from the crest. There were also two machine gun emplacements close by. Just beyond the right and left shoulders of the hill, on the forward slope, were two small trenches, each large enough for four men. Eight hundred yards to the south-east was a smaller hill, overlooking the Wadi Hannafish, up which an enemy patrol or attack was to be expected. On this hill there was one partially finished cruciform trench on the reverse slope, and a smaller trench on the forward slope. It was held by No. 4 Troop, under Lieutenant Abraham, MC. This troop was given an extra Hotchkiss rifle for the defence of the right flank. Sixty yards south of Lieutenant Abraham's position was a small trench, from which the right flank could be protected. Here it was that Corpl Stott, M.M., and his gallant Hotchkiss section fought all day and saved the flank. Three times the enemy attacked them. Twice the Hotchkiss drove them back, and the third time they did it with two rifles and two revolvers, their Hotchkiss having jammed. The remainder of the dismounted men was divided between the two trenches on 630, under the command of Capt. A. McDougall, D.S.O. and Lieutenant (now Capt.) G. H. Matthews, M.C., respectively. The led horses were sent back one and a half miles, under Capt. Carus-Wilson, M.C. Each of the small forward trenches was at once occupied by a corporal and three men. Their orders were (1) to fire on any small parties of enemy; (2) not to fire if the enemy came on in force, but to get back to the main trenches on the other side of the crest and warn us so that we should all be ready the moment the enemy topped the crest. For the remainder, the order was: 'Dig until the moon goes down.' We were all to realise soon that this irksome labour had really been a blessing in disguise. An artillery wire was found on 630, about 200 yards south of the trenches. This was used throughout the night of 26th, and up to half an hour after the attack had commenced, when the line was cut by the enemy's fire. Pte Finlay, M.M., brought a message up to the trenches and went back with the reply. This he did under very heavy fire, and later carried a message back to Headquarters, thereby winning the Military Medal. Even if this wire had not been cut, it would not have been possible to have used it throughout the day, owing to the two hundred yards of fire-swept ground between the telephone and the trenches. At 04:00, in the darkest hour, just before dawn, the right-hand forward post on 630 opened rapid rifle fire. This soon stopped and the corporal in charge came back to report that he had driven back a party of cavalry. So far so good, and all was quiet again. At about 04:15 the whole section came back, this time without firing, and the corporal reported: 'There's an army coming, Sir.' Well, then we waited and watched that crest, and waited and watched. There was nothing to be heard or seen. The left-hand forward section was still out and had reported nothing, so after about five minutes the corporal and his section were again sent to occupy their trench. But the Turk was there first, and they came back under a hail of bullets. Our left-hand forward post also now came in at the double, and reported large numbers of the enemy advancing up the other side of the hill. We fired our green lights, and white lights were going up from Lieutenant Abraham's hill. Unfortunately, the lights failed to bring the much desired reply shells from our two guns. Our friends behind mistook our flares for those of the enemy, which had been going off at intervals ever since the moon went down. It is a pity, as there must have been a wonderful target just behind that hill. (An aeroplane later in the day reported two thousand Turks there.) It was now quarter light, and at last the enemy appeared on the crest. We let him have it full blast from two Hotchkiss rifles, 25 rifles and the two Vickers guns. It stopped him, and through- out the whole day he never appeared on the top again. When it was light, from the right-hand trench on 630 a Hotchkiss did good execution with flanking fire against the Turks advancing up the forward slope of Lieutenant Abraham's hill. Twice they fell back, and then that particular Hotchkiss jammed and had to be taken to pieces. As a result, the enemy established a machine gun there, and was quickly dropping bullets into us. By now the enemy had established several machine guns on either shoulder of 630, and between them they quickly put out of action our own two Vickers guns, but not before the latter had taken a goodly toll of Turks, and their officers and the whole of both crews had become casualties. When the fight was hottest, Capt. Carus-Wilson appeared suddenly in our trench, carrying several bandoliers of spare ammunition, having on his way delivered a similar quantity at Lieutenant Matthew's trench. To do this he had had to cross 200 yards of open, under very heavy machine gun and rifle fire. There being no telephone, he at once volunteered to go back and report on the situation to the colonel. This he did. Later on he again appeared carrying two boxes of Hotchkiss ammunition. One of these he safely delivered to Lieutenant Matthew's trench, and finally fell into our trench, shot through the thigh at point-blank range. For the most gallant efforts made by our own A Squadron, and by two squadrons of the City of London Yeomanry to come to our aid, those on 630 who could see it all quite clearly have only one word – magnificent! We had seen the Turks registering their machine guns on the ridges to which our fellows were advancing, and it was awful to watch them approaching the fatal ridge. With our supports driven back and the Turks practically all round us, things looked black. A volunteer was called for to run back to Headquarters with a message. It was then that Sergt Randall won his D.C.M. He ran the same gauntlet that Capt. Carus-Wilson had done three times previously, and got back safely. As a result, our guns opened on the crest and did some beautiful shooting. Lieutenant Abraham, from his position on the right, could see the shells mowing down the enemy. Thanks to these guns, which kept on firing at intervals during the afternoon, the enemy's machine guns and snipers were very much less active. To the writer, the extraordinary thing was that the enemy had neither shelled us nor tried to rush us with bomb and bayonet. It seemed certain that he was only waiting for the cover of darkness to do the latter. About 17:00, what at the time seemed like a miracle happened, so unexpected was it. We were relieved. The enemy's fire suddenly ceased. After a little while we made good our crest, and there below us across the wadi went the enemy in a long cloud of dust, legging it back as quickly as he could. Then on our left we saw from the crest what we could not see from our trenches, the reason why. The 53rd Division was advancing on the hill in attack formation and the sight of it was enough for the Turk. Soon our horses were sent up for us, and then it was that our intense joy at being relieved was so greatly damped by the news of the sad fate which had befallen so many of our friends in gallant B Squadron. It was a red letter day for the Middlesex Yeomanry when, on October 30th, on the eve of the attack on Beersheba, the Commander- in-Chief himself found time to motor over to Shellal to congratulate the regiment in person.

The plan for holding Pt. 630 was therefore made a complete success by the great gallantry of C Squadron Middlesex Yeomanry. The Turks, in hugely superior numbers, failed in 13 hours to establish themselves on the hill; 53rd Div., according to programme, took over the ridge about17:00 hours, and the Turks retired to their defensive positions. The railway construction and other arrangements for the coming offensive continued practically undisturbed.

There are many lessons to be learnt from this operation.

Extension Southwards (Plate VI)
The extension southwards began on 22 October, with ANZAC Div. leading, 2nd A.L.H. Brigade moved to Esani and I.C.C. Brigade to near Ma el Mallaka. Thenceforward the work of water development was carried on at high pressure by night and day. Tracks were improved and marked. The bulk of the work, which was very heavy, fell on the two brigades mentioned above, and upon the 1st and 2nd Field Squadrons, Australian Engineers.

ANZAC Div. and Ausdiv reached Asluj and Khalasa respectively by night marches. During the movement, the left flank was picketed by day and night to afford protection from the direction of Beersheba, but the enemy took no steps to interfere. A hostile detachment was reported 18 miles south-east of Asluj on

23 October, but a regiment of 2nd A.L.H. Brigade, sent after them, learnt that they had retired.

The leading of a night march in such country is most difficult. The country was sandy and broken up by small watercourses made by the last year's rains. Colonel Preston gives two photographs of the country traversed, in his book, *The Desert Mounted Corps*, facing page20. The maps gave no indication whatever of the ground; at night no tracks could be seen, and the marches were conducted by compass and the stars.

Preparatory Dispositions.
By the evening of 30 October, all arrangements were complete and Descorps was disposed as follows :

Asluj	ANZAC Div. and Descorps Headquarters.
Khalasa	Ausdiv
Esani	7th Mounted Brigade
Shellal	Yeodiv (in G.H.Q. reserve)
North of Shellal	I.C.C. Brigade (under G.O.C. XX Corps)

The operations of Descorps were to be of a decisive nature, and the C-in-C would doubtless have employed all his available mounted troops in the attack from the east had it been possible; but on the edge of the desert it was impossible to water the whole corps; under these circumstances it was wise to remove Yeodiv and the I.C.C. Brigade completely from Descorps, as it permitted the Corps Commander and his staff to devote their entire energies to their main task.

Capture of Beersheba
Task of the Corps.
The task of Descorps was to attack the town of Beersheba from the north-east and east, while XX Corps attacked the main trenches protecting it on the south-west and west.

The objects of Descorps attack were :
(a) To assist XX Corps by threatening the enemy's rear, pinning down his reserves and, generally, by throwing him off his

balance.
(b) To prevent the enemy retreating deliberately and destroying the water supply.

Comments on G.H.Q. Plan.
The attack of Descorps was intended to embarrass the enemy before the infantry attack, which was expected to take place about 09:00 hours on 31 October.

The main feature of the C-in-C's plan was the cooperation of the Cavalry Corps with the attacking corps. To each was assigned the role most suited to its characteristics. The cavalry objective was well chosen, as the east and north-east of Beersheba was the enemy's weakest point; his main entrenched system did not extend farther east than Ras Ghannam; the few fortified localities to the east of Beersheba were known to be isolated from each other, and it was thought that they were not wired; the eastern flank was open and it was practically certain that little opposition would be met in the turning movement.

The approach march consisted in a night march by ANZAC Div. and Ausdiv from Asluj and Khalasa respectively, commencing at dusk,17:00 hours, 30 October. The track was most difficult to find and it had been considered unwise to reconnoitre it thoroughly. Only one track was available along the Wadi el Shreikiye and Ausdiv followed on the tail of ANZAC Div. The column was 20 miles long and the hills on each flank of the march were so rough that it was impossible to employ a moving flank guard.

The distance to be traversed, under these difficult conditions, by about 06:00 hours, 31 October (i.e., in a space of 13 hours of darkness and moonlight), worked out at 24 miles for ANZAC Div., 30 miles for Ausdiv

As no effective flank guard could be detailed, and the march led across the front of the enemy, the transport could not be divisionalised, but had to march with brigades for safety, each brigade being made entirely responsible for its own flank protection. The presence of so much transport sandwiched between the columns of mounted troops delayed the latter very considerably.

Under the peculiarly difficult circumstances, the demand made on these two cavalry divisions by the C-in-C was a stupendous one; it is considered that such a march had never previously been attempted; the fact that it was carried out successfully proved how thoroughly the C-in-C understood the capacity of the arm.

On 30 October, the corps moved off from the preliminary position as follows:

(a) ANZAC Div. From Aslujat 17:00 hours, via Wadi el Shreikiye-Thaffa-Iswaiwin, with 2nd A.L.H. Brigade, moving via Arara.

Objectives :
(i) Bir el Hamam-Bir Salim Abu Irgeig.
(ii) Bir el Sakati-Tel el Saba.
(iii) A position astride and across the Hebron road, facing north-west, with left flank on north side of Beersheba.

(b) Ausdiv from Khalasa, at 17:00 hours, following ANZAC Div. as far as Iswaiwin, where the division was to halt and be prepared to act, either northwards in support of ANZAC Div., or westwards towards Beersheba.

(c) 7th Mounted Brigade from Esani, at 21:30 hours, to move by a circular route to the south, and reach the neighbourhood of Bir ibn Turka. Its task, to observe the enemy's defences at Ras Ghannam, and be ready to follow up the enemy if he retired, or to cooperate with the left of Descorps or right of XX Corps.

Narrative of ANZAC Div.
The head of ANZAC Div. reached Thaffa at midnight, where the 2nd A.L.H. Brigade continued straight on Arara, with objective

Tel el Sakati. The remainder of ANZAC Div., with N.Z.M.R. Brigade leading, turned north from Thaffa on Khasm Zanna. Turkish flares sent up from Beersheba assisted the maintenance of direction; but it was a very fine performance on the part of the General Staff and leading troops of ANZAC Div. that no error of direction was made.

At 06:45 hours, 31 October, the New Zealanders had the first encounter with Turks about Iswaiwin. These were driven off, and the brigade concentrated about Khasm Zanna and sent reconnaissances forward. Advanced troops of 2nd A.L.H. Brigade could be seen well on, moving towards Tel el Sakaty.

The view from Khasm Zanna towards Beersheba was perfect. South of the Wadi Saba, which ran through Bir el Hamman and past Tel el Saba to Beersheba, a flat open plain stretched from Beersheba for six miles to the south-east, towards Khasm Zanna. The plain was six miles long, from north-west to south-east, and about four miles broad, from north to south. This plain was surrounded on all sides by hills of various sizes (see Plate VII).

Only small groups of the enemy could be seen; but, soon after the attack by XX Corps was seen to have begun, transport and men could be seen leaving the town by the north side.

Orders were issued to N.Z.M.R. Brigade to occupy Tel el Saba, which was now known to be strongly held, and to 2nd A.L.H. Brigade to take Tel el Sakaty as soon as possible.

One regiment of Ausdiv had meanwhile been despatched from Iswaiwin, to take up a position of observation about one mile west of Khasm Zanna, looking towards Beersheba.

At 10:00 hours, the N.Z.M.R. Brigade attacked Tel el Saba, supported by Somerset Battalion R.H.A. They moved against the position, partly along the Wadi Saba and partly north of it. There was no cover except in the wadi, and the place was defended by well-concealed machine guns, both on the Tel el Saba and to the north of it. The Turkish artillery nearer Beersheba fired on the attacking troops and on the Corps and Div. Headquarters and reserve brigades at Khasm Zanna. Turkish aeroplanes also attacked Khasm Zanna, with bombs and machine gun fire.

The New Zealanders were reinforced on their left by one, and later by another, regiment of 1st A.L.H. Brigade; finally, 3rd A.L.H. Brigade and two H.A. Batteries from Ausdiv were sent to assist in the capture of Tel el Saba.

PLATE VII.

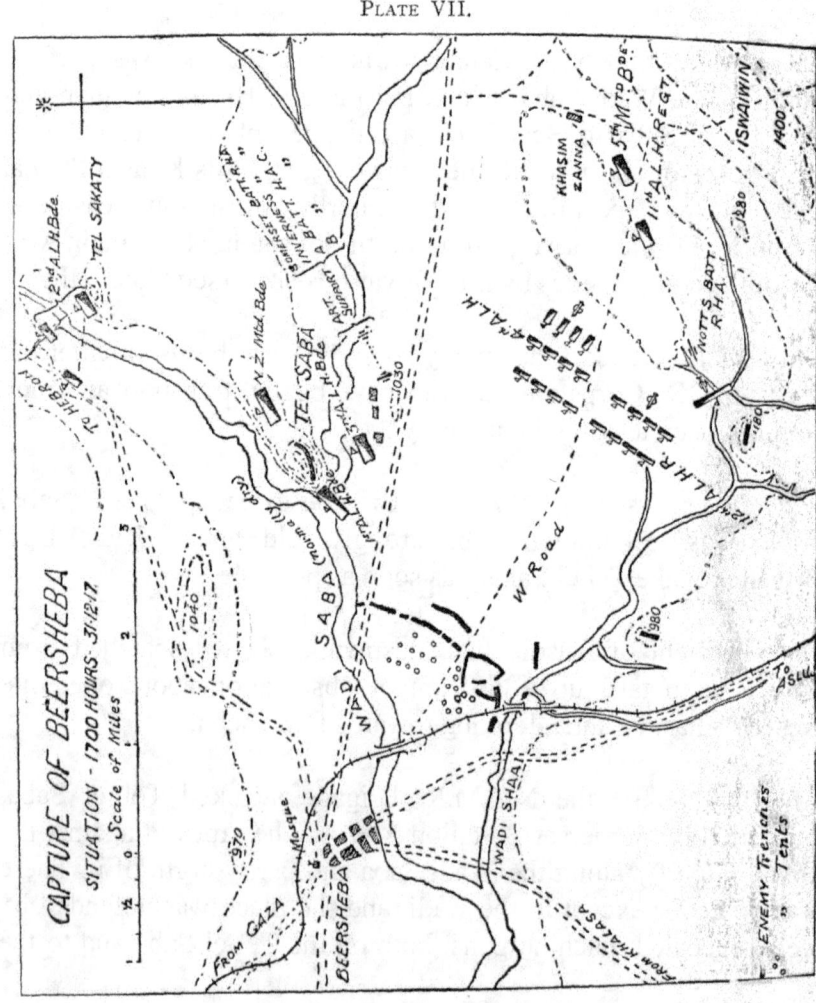

In the meantime, 2nd A.L.H. Brigade had taken Tel el Sakaty at 12:30 hours, and had cut the Hebron road. They met fairly heavy shell fire in their advance and took 50 prisoners and some transport. They had moved rapidly over the open ground in column of sections, at wide and irregular intervals, and suffered very little.

The attack on Tel el Saba was making way slowly, the machine guns north of the hill giving most trouble. Finally, a section of Somerset Battalion was pushed to within 800 yards of the hill, and opened on these machine guns at 1,900 yards range; the Inverness Battalion was also brought forward to 2,300 yards from the hill, and at 13.05 hours the New Zealanders rushed the hill.

After the capture of Tel el Sakaty and Tel el Saba, all attempts to push on, on the part of the 2nd A.L.H. Brigade and N.Z.M.R. Brigade, were frustrated by machine gun fire.

Narrative of Ausdiv
Ausdiv reached Iswaiwin about 10:00 hours, on 31 October, and moved forward into reserve at Khasm Zanna, with observation posts out towards Beersheba and in touch with 7th Mounted Brigade in the vicinity of Ras Gbannam.

At 13:30 hours, news was received that XX Corps had taken nearly all their objectives and orders were issued by Descorps Headquarters, for 3rd A.L.H. Brigade and two battalions R.H.A. to be placed by Ausdiv at the disposal of G.O.C. ANZAC Div., who was ordered to press home the attack on Tel el Saba after thorough artillery preparation. 5th Mounted Brigade was in Corps Reserve, and the G.O.C. Ausdiv had only the 4th A.L.H. Brigade remaining at his disposal.

By 16:00 hours, Descorps had been fighting for nine hours, and while its operations had undoubtedly weakened the enemy's hold on the main defences, west and south-west of Beersheba, and had thereby assisted XX Corps, yet the main objective of Descorps, Beersheba, had not been taken, and ANZAC Div. was unable to get on north of the Wadi Saba.

Only one hour remained before dusk, and. whatever could be done must be done quickly. Descorps therefore gave Ausdiv an order to take Beersheba by dusk. The G.O.C. Ausdiv had no option but to pass the order on to General Grant, Commanding 4th A.L.H. Brigade; at the same time 7th Mounted Brigade was ordered to turn the defences of Ras Ghannam and cooperate with the attack of the 4th A.L.H. Brigade

Attack of 4th A.L.H. Brigade.
It will be remembered that ANZAC Div. consisted of three brigades of mounted rifles. They had no swords. Ausdiv consisted of the 3rd and 4th A.L.H. Brigades. and 5th Mounted Brigade This latter brigade had swords, but the two A.L.H. Brigades had not. The ANZAC Div. was content to remain a mounted rifle division, as it had proved itself of magnificent quality at mounted rifle work, and the Divisional Commander was by no means certain that it would gain anything by adopting the sword.

General Hodgson, commanding Ausdiv, did not agree. He considered that the 3rd and 4th A.L.H. Brigades of his division were seriously handicapped for want of a sword or lance; further, he considered that the great physical strength and dash and other wonderful military qualities of the men of the A.L.H. singled them out amongst all mounted troops as swordsmen par excellence.

Prior to the Beersheba operation, he had applied to be allowed to arm his two A.L.H. Brigades with a sword. The Australian military authorities, quite naturally, having no experience of the weapon, were doubtful as to the wisdom of this step, and it was not sanctioned.

The two Australian Brigadiers in Ausdiv were, however, quite open- minded on the subject, and on 26 October, five days prior to the Beersheba battle, the G.O.C. Ausdiv issued the following instructions :

> (i) It is to be noticed that the country is built for mounted action, whereas any dismounted attack is handicapped for want of cover. The Divisional Commander hopes that all brigades will endeavour to profit by their knowledge of these facts.
>
> (ii) To manoeuvre an attack mounted an *arme-blanche* weapon is necessary. The Divisional Commander suggests that the bayonet is equally as good as the sword, if used as a sword for pointing only; it has the same moral effect as a sword, as it glitters in the sun and the difference could not be detected by the enemy.
>
> (iii) If used in this manner, the point only should be sharpened, to ensure that the men point instead of striking.
>
> (iv) The Divisional Commander suggests that the bayonet, used thus, will be more effective as an *arme-blanche* weapon than the rifle with bayonet fixed, as he fears that the latter method would render the control of the horse difficult in manoeuvre, and would leave the right arm too tired to give the final thrust.
>
> (v) The G.O.C. directs that steps be taken at once to have the points of all bayonets sharpened by the armourers.

The value of the bayonet is perhaps overstated, but the arms and bodies of the A.L.H. are very long indeed, and give them a tremendous reach.

At 16:00 hours, when General Grant, commanding 4th A.L.H. Brigade, received the order, his brigade was six miles east-south-east of Beersheba, and it would be dusk in one hour. The open plain stretched before him, magnificent galloping ground; the enemy had been attacked from front and rear and was weakening;

success must come now and quickly, or never. All the conditions suitable for a mounted attack were present, and no other kind of attack could promise equal results.

The action taken by General Grant is described below in his official report (Ref. Plate VII):

> At 16:00 hours on October 31st, 1917, ANZAC Div. was operating to the east and north-east of Beersheba, and was pushing back the enemy down the Wadi El Saba. This division was operating dismounted, but, owing to the stiff opposition, the progress was slow and it appeared as if the town would not be taken from that direction before dark. It was essential that the place be taken quickly, as the horses had not been watered since the previous day and had made a night march of over 30 miles.
>
> At 16:15 hours orders were received from the G.O.C. Australian Mounted Division, and also direct instructions from the Corps Commander, for the 4th A.L.H. Brigade to attack direct on Beersheba, moving on the left of the ANZAC Mounted Division, and to take the place before dark.
>
> The brigade was then in reserve in a valley about six miles east of Beersheba, and the horses were being fed. It was realised by the Brigadier that he would have to act quickly, as only a little over an hour of daylight remained in which to carry out the operation.
>
> The brigade was assembled in a valley near Hill 1280, with the exception of the 11th L.H. Regiment [*sic*], which was on detached duty about two miles south-west of that position.
>
> Orders were sent to the 11th A.L.H. Regiment to concentrate and follow the brigade, and the brigade was ordered to saddle up and move when ready, under the

Seconds in Command of Regiments, the senior to command. The Brigadier and Brigade Major, accompanied by the C.O.s 4th and 12th Regiments, galloped forward to reconnoitre a covered way of approach for the brigade to the point of deployment, and for the direction of the attack. This was necessary, as the 3rd A.L.H. Brigade had just previously been heavily shelled in attempting to cross exposed ground.

The brigade started about 16:30 hours and moved at the trot. Shortly afterwards two enemy planes passed over and dropped bombs and, on return, one flew low and machine-gunned Brigade Headquarters personnel and Signal Troop, which was moving in rear of the brigade. No material damage was done beyond one horse wounded, but it somewhat delayed the establishment of communications.

The route taken was along the wadi about quarter of a mile south of W. road, and the brigade deployed where the road crossed the 1100 contour.

The 4th L.H. Regiment was ordered to advance on the sector from the left of A., and N.Z. Mounted Division to W. road. The 12th A.L.H. Regiment was ordered to advance on the left of the 4th L.H. Regiment; these two regiments were ordered to attack mounted, each in three successive lines, of a squadron each line. The files were at about four yards interval and 300 yards distance between squadrons. They were ordered to charge with drawn bayonets held in the hand, as no swords were issued to these troops.

The 11th A.L.H. Regiment was ordered to follow on in rear and act as a reserve.

One sub-section of 4th A.M.G. Squadron was sent with each of 4th and 12th A.L.H. Regiments, and the Machine Gun Squadron, less one section, was ordered to move down the wadi and cooperate with the reserve squadron of the

12th A.L.H. Regiment, in protecting the left rear of the line from attack by the enemy, who were seen in trenches on Hill 1180.

Both the 4th and 12th L.H. Regiments went forward at a gallop and took successive lines of trenches until reaching the wadi at Beersheba. The left flank of the 12th Regiment came under heavy machine gun fire from trenches on Hill 1180. The Machine Gun Squadron immediately opened fire on this redoubt and the Brigadier ordered Major Harrison, O.C. Notts. Battery R.H.A., which had then come up to the point of deployment, to open fire on these trenches. It was then practically dark and impossible to take distances with the range finder, but Major Harrison opened fire and found the range with his second shot, and quickly drove the Turks off the ridge.

On it being reported that the trenches in front of the town had been taken, the 4th and 12th L.H. Regiments were ordered to push right through the town and capture as many prisoners as possible.

This movement was carried out in a very able manner and resulted in the capture of 9 field guns, 7 ammunition limbers, 4 machine guns and about 700 prisoners.

The 11th A.L.H. Regiment, which had arrived at the point of deployment after the battery had come into action, was moved forward together with the Notts. Battery and A Battery H.A.C. to Beersheba. On reaching that place the C.O.s 4th and 12th Regiments reported that they had captured the place. The 11th Regiment was accordingly ordered to push through the town and hold it against any counterattack from the north-west and south-west. This was carried out and the 11th Regiment captured about 400 prisoners who were retreating from the south-west.

The 4th and 12th Regiments were ordered to withdraw from

their line and reorganise. When this was done, the 4th L.H. Regiment took up an outpost line from the Wadi El Saba to the Mosque, and the 11th Regiment from the Mosque to the Khalasa road, the 12th Regiment being held in reserve near the railway viaduct.

The two batteries were placed in position on the bank of the wadi, south of the town, so as to cooperate in driving back any counterattack by the Turks.

The brigade remained disposed as above until relieved by the 5th Mounted Brigade and the infantry the following morning.

The rapidity of the mounted attack seemed to demoralise the enemy, as they mostly fired high, and it was afterwards found that the sights of their rifles were never lowered below 800 metres. The enemy artillery was also unable to estimate the pace, and the shells all went over the heads of the advancing troops.

From the location of the enemy's trenches as shown on the accompanying sketch (i.e., Plate VII) it would appear that they were prepared for any advance down the Wadi Shaai, which would have offered a certain amount of cover while in the wadi bed, but they did not anticipate a mounted attack across the plain.

If a dismounted attack had been made from the Wadi Shaai, it is certain that we would have suffered heavy casualties, as the trenches were very strong, and in the bends machine guns were placed to enfilade the wadi bed.

On 19 April 1917, at the second Battle of Gaza, this brigade made a long advance on foot, with two regiments (11th and 12th) and the Machine Gun Squadron, and had 187 casualties without any satisfactory result being obtained. Here the casualties were 32 killed and 32 wounded, total 64, which is about one-third of the number sustained in the second Gaza battle, and resulted in the capture of 59 officers and 1,090 other ranks, besides 10 field guns, 5 machine guns, and a large number of vehicles, stores and animals. In addition, the enemy did not have time to destroy the water supply, which was the most important factor in the situation.

The high percentage of killed to wounded was due to the hand-to-hand fighting against superior numbers at the trenches. The majority of the wounded fell before the trenches were reached.

The dash of this exploit was magnificent; it thoroughly confirmed the G.O.C. Ausdiv in his opinion that his two A.L.H. Brigades were seriously handicapped for want of a sword, and he determined to continue to press this question the moment operations came to a halt. He knew that his opinion was fully shared by the C-in-C himself.

The writer feels sure that he is correct in saying that, from that day, the G.O.C. and all ranks of 4th A.L.H. Brigade wished to be armed with a sword. It is not known what, at this date, was the view of the G.O.C. and regimental commanders of 3rd A.L.H. Brigade

Anyhow, by this brilliant exploit with a comparatively inferior *arme blanche* weapon in hand, the 4th A.L.H. Brigade set an example of cavalry dash, which raised the morale of Descorps very high, and set many brigades thinking how they could eclipse it.

Narrative of 7th Mounted Brigade
7th Mounted Brigade reached its appointed position north of Bir ibn Turka, and throughout the morning maintained contact with the enemy in his works at Ras Ghannam. At 15:30 hours the brigade was ordered to turn the defences of Ras Ghannam and cooperate with 4th A.L.H. Brigade in the attack on Beersheba. Its

move was somewhat delayed by flanking fire from Ras Ghannam, but it arrived at Beersheba at 18:30 hours.

General.
Until Beersheba was captured there appeared little prospect of watering more than two brigades in the area. Close to the town, however, there were found pools of surface water, caused by two thunderstorms a few days previously; these enabled the whole of the horses to be watered during the night, after being without for 36 hours. In Beersheba the Turks had partially destroyed five out of seven wells ; the engineers worked night and day at restoring them, but the water problem gradually became more and more serious.

17. OPERATIONS NORTH-EAST OF BEERSHEBA
(Map A and Plate VI).

The capture of Beersheba laid open the left flank of the main Turkish position, the Kauwukah and Sharia works, for a decisive blow. During the next few days the role of Descorps was to protect the right flank of XX Corps, while the latter corps was assembling for the main attack on Sharia and Kauwukah; water and transport difficulties were found to be greater than anticipated, and the preparations of XX Corps were delayed.

During this period Gaza was heavily bombarded; several heavy infantry attacks, with limited objectives, were made by XXI Corps, and Turkish reserves were drawn westwards. The protective role of Descorps involved it in hard fighting in the hills north-east of Beersheba, as the enemy brought up his general reserve against the line Ras El Nukb-Tel Khuweilfeh.

Water became a great difficulty. Surface water dried up; the wells in Beersheba were not equal to the demands made upon them by both Descorps and XX Corps, and the Turks prevented us from obtaining possession of the water supply at Khuweilfeh. For this reason it became necessary to relieve mounted brigades every 24 hours. The country is mountainous and so stony as to be in many places impassable for horses.

1 November. On 1 November, Ausdiv was withdrawn into reserve, and ANZAC Div. was ordered to occupy the line Bir El Makrune-Toweil Abu Jerwal. This line was reached after considerable opposition, 179 prisoners and four machine guns being captured. The I.C.C. Brigade and 53rd Div. came up to the line Toweil Abu Jerwal-Kh El Muweileh.

2 November. On 2 November, 2nd A.L.H. Brigade and 7th Mounted Brigade were ordered to occupy El Dhahariyeh and the area Tel Khuweilfeh-Ain Kohleh respectively. They were unable to do so, but by nightfall had reached the line Bir El Nettar-Deir El Hawa-Ras El Nukb–thence a straight line south-west to within one mile of Toweil Abu Jerwal, where the I.C.C. Brigade, now under Descorps, joined with 53rd Division; the salient at Ras El Nukb was taken by 7th Mounted Brigade.

Succeeding Days. During the succeeding four days, 3–6 November, little or no change occurred in the line held by the mounted troops. The Bir Makrune area was occupied continuously by 2nd A.L.H. Brigade, who were unable to find sufficient water in pools in the wadis south of Dhahariyeh. The enemy were found to be firmly entrenched in front of Dhahariyeh. Patrols were able to work round his left flank, but attempts to force him to withdraw were not successful. One patrol reached a point near the Hebron road two miles north-east of Dhahariyeh, whence three lorry loads of enemy troops were seen moving into the village.

The Ras El Nukb line was held successively by 7thMounted, 1stA.L.H., 5th Mounted, New Zealand, and I.C.C. Brigades, all operating under G.O.C. ANZAC Div. The enemy launched counterattacks against 5th Mounted, New Zealand, and I.C.C. Brigades, which were repulsed with considerable loss. The severe fighting and great difficulties in getting water, were having a serious effect upon the mounted troops, especially in view of the coming operations. ANZAC Div. suffered 250 casualties in personnel and 345 in horses, but captured 330 prisoners and five machine guns.

53rd Division came under orders of G.O.C. Descorps and succeeded after hard fighting in taking Tel Khuweilfeh on 6 November. The enemy delivered several determined counterattacks with strong forces against this division, which behaved with great gallantry and caused the enemy very heavy losses.

On 4 November Ausdiv was sent back to Karm on account of water difficulties and relieved Yeodiv in the role of protecting the Karm-Shellal railway by filling the gap between the left of XX Corps at Bir el Girheir and the right of XXI Corps, which was thrown back to near the junction of the Wadis Ghuzze and Sharia (due south of Gaza).

On 6 November, Yeodiv arrived in the forward area and took over from the right of 74th Division, the right-hand division of XX Corps, two miles south-west of Ain Kohleh, in order to free the latter to move into its position of deployment facing west. The horses of Yeodiv were sent back to Beersheba to water.

On the evening of 6 November, as a result of the successful attack by XX Corps on the Kauwukah works, Descorps was required to take up the pursuit and to occupy Bir Jemameh and Huj. A detachment for the defence of the right flank of the Army was therefore formed under Major-General Barrow, G.O.C. Yeodiv, consisting of I.C.C. Brigade, 53rd Div., Yeodiv, N.Z.M.R. Brigade and two squadrons and eight machine guns of 2nd A.L.H. Brigade.

By the night of 7–8 November, in spite of several counterattacks, Yeodiv had forced its way to one and a half miles north-east of Khirbet Mujeidilat, and remained in occupation there, waiting for 53rd Div. to drive the enemy north of Tel Khuweilfeh, but owing to Yeodiv being required to rejoin Descorps in the main pursuit up the Philistine Plain, the operation was broken off and Yeodiv marched to Tel El Sharia.

**The Main Attack of XX Corps
on The Shari-Kauwukah-Hareira Works.**
On 6 November, 74th, 60th and 10th Divs., from the south-east, attacked the system of trenches and redoubts covering Sharia and Kh. Kauwukah. Stubborn resistance was encountered, but our artillery bombardment was overwhelming and the wire was well cut. 74th Div. stormed all positions east of the railway by 15:15

hours, and moved to the high ground near Tel El Sharia (near the railway bridge over the big Wadi Sharia).

60th Div. attacked the Kauwukah system and broke through after two hours' sharp fighting and, about 15:15 hours, occupied Sharia station where the railway crosses the Wadi Sharia; but Tel El Sharia still held out.

The main stroke of the C-in-C's operations had been a complete success. The moment for cavalry exploitation had arrived; if the entire Descorps had been assembled behind 74th and 60th Divs. at 16:00 hours on 6 November, it is considered that the enemy could not have prevented them pushing north along the railway from Tel El Shariato Tel El Nejila on the Wadi Hesi.

But the cavalry were not there. Descorps commander and the staff were at Beersheba, preparing to hand over command of the operations in the hills about Tel Khuweilfeh; Yeodiv was in action, dismounted, about Ain Kohleh and operating, during 7 and 8 November, in the mountains north of Tel Khuweilfeh, and did not become available for pursuit in the Philistine Plain until 8 November, and by then had a long way to catch up. ANZAC Div. was endeavouring to disengage its brigades from the fighting in the mountains, and at 13:00 hours on 6 November received orders to march, relieve Yeodiv on the right of XX Corps, and be prepared to pursue next day. ANZAC Div. did not complete the relief until 03:15 hours on 7 November.

Ausdiv was stretched from Bir el Girheir to nine miles W.N.W. of it, covering the Karm-Shellal railway.

During the afternoon, as soon as the main attack had succeeded, Descorps was ordered to take up the pursuit and occupy Bir Jemameh and Huj.

Ausdiv received orders at 16:00 hours to march to Bir Imleih and bivouac there, leaving 3rd A.L.H. Brigade to cover the Karm-Shellal railway. During the night, at Bir Imleih orders were received for Ausdiv to march at 02:00 hours on 7 November via Abu Irgeig to just south-west of Tel El Sharia. By 07:30 hours the whole division was concentrated in this position of readiness close to Descorps Headquarters.

Descorps was therefore in a position at 07:30 hours on 7 November, about 15 hours after the moment of XX Corps success, to take up the pursuit. Ausdiv was complete, but much tired after an 18 mile night march. ANZAC Div. was not complete. The whole of the N.Z.M.R. Brigade, two squadrons and eight machine guns of 2nd A.L.H. Brigade and Somerset Battalion R.H.A. were still absent. This Division, like Ausdiv, had been on the move all night and was also tired. 7th Mounted Brigade arrived after a night march from Karm.

Out of 11 brigades of Descorps, only 6 were present for the exploitation, and these toed the mark 12 hours late, and were not fresh.

To all concerned this result brought bitter disappointment. After years of disappointment in France, it really looked as if, at last, a real smashing example of cavalry exploitation was to be given to the world. The ideal to be attained would require that Descorps, entire, rested and in the best possible condition, should be assembled close behind the 'softest' spot at the moment of success of the main infantry attack. All that they could then ask was that the direction in which they were launched and the objectives given to them should be the most suitable.

The C-in-C was, and is today, the greatest believer in the power of mounted troops to exploit the success of the other arms. His mounted troops comprised a quarter of his force. His original plan was deliberately framed to include cavalry exploitation as its final decisive act. He knew, better than anyone else in the force, that cavalry exploitation, to attain its best, demanded perfect timing, maximum numbers, and that the troops should be fresh. None of these conditions were attained. It is clear that at least one factor that affected the situation was insuperable ; owing to shortage of water, it was impossible to assemble the whole Cavalry Corps fit and rested at the correct place and time. Further, his decision to continue with his decisive attack from the south-east against Sharia and Kauwukah, when the Karm-Shellal railway was so exposed to counter-offensive, and while the heavy counterattacks were threatening Beersheba from the north-east, was a most daring decision; and it is only to be greatly regretted that the mounted troops could not, apparently, be relieved earlier than they were from their protective roles on both flanks of XX Corps.

Pursuit from Sharia.
Descorps on 7 November consisted of Ausdiv, ANZAC Div., and 60th Div. The orders to the corps for 7 November were to push as rapidly as possible to the line Bir Jemameh-Huj, with a view to cutting off or pursuing the Gaza garrison. The enemy, however, succeeded in organising a rearguard, which resisted strongly.

(a) 60th Div. drove them from Tel El Sharia about 06:00 hours and advanced to a maximum distance of two miles to the north of the big Wadi Sharia.

(b) ANZAC Div. was detailed as advanced guard to Descorps, and given as first objective Kh. Umm Ameidat to a point two miles west of it, and ordered to send reconnaissances on Tel El Nejile and Bir Jemameh.

ANZAC Div. marched at 06:25 hours, in the dark, and moved at a fast pace on Ameidat Station. Hostile shell fire came from both flanks, persistent though not heavy. Ameidat Station was taken at 11:00 hours, with 400 prisoners, a very large ammunition dump and a hospital.

1st A.L.H. Brigade pushed out patrols to the east, to Tel El Nejile and towards Jemameh. The Turks, however, were holding Tel Abu Dilakh strongly, and shell fire was directed on the brigade from that place, as well as from east and west.

At 12:30 hours came news of the evacuation of Gaza, and orders to push on to Jemameh. At this time 1st A.L.H. Brigade were fighting heavily close to Tel Abu Dilakh, and were held up just east of it. They were also engaged in the direction of Tel El Nejile, and a small right flank guard was opposed to Turks about El Henu. The Brigadier had only two squadrons in hand. 2nd A.L.H. Brigade (less two squadrons and eight machine guns) alone remained as a reserve for the Divisional Commander. There was no sign of Ausdiv on the left or of any troops coming up in support. However, in view of the report that columns of all arms were retreating north from Gaza, the G.O.C. ordered forward the 2nd A.L.H. Brigade to attack Tel Abu Dilakh, shortly after 15:00 hours. The brigade advanced, with regiments in line of troop columns, covered by the fire of Ayrshire and Inverness Batts., and galloped straight at the hill. They met a very hot shellfire, and for part of the way rifle fire as well; but the casualties were slight. As the brigade came on, the Turks holding the hill went hurriedly back, and the lower slopes were taken. The hill was cut up by small wadis. The brigade left their horses under cover, and pushed on and, by 16:40 hours, took the hill. The Turks held the ridges behind in strength, and the brigade could not get farther forward.

The two reserve squadrons of 1st A.L.H. Brigade were the only troops remaining in ANZAC Div. available for any further action. The Division was quite out of touch with the rest of Descorps and it was growing dark, so the Divisional Commander decided to hold his position during the night and push for Jemameh at dawn. The Division had been almost continuously engaged since 31 October; there had been practically no sleep the previous night, and there was a limit even to the endurance of the Australians and New Zealanders of ANZAC Div.

2nd A.L.H. Brigade pushed on 1,000 yards beyond Tel Abu Dilakh after dark, but were then stopped by Turks in sangars and rifle pits.

After dark, contact was made with Ausdiv south-west of Tel Abu Dilakh.

(c) Ausdiv had concentrated at 07:30 hours in a valley three miles S.S.W. of Tel El Sharia. When it was seen that 60th Div. were unable to drive the enemy from the long ridge on the north side of the Wadi Sharia at Tel El Sharia, Descorps ordered Ausdiv to clear the enemy from the front of 60th Div., in order to enable the infantry to concentrate for a further advance. The line of advance of Ausdiv should probably have been directed further north than it was; as it turned out, instead of turning the left flank of the enemy, the 4th A.L.H. and 5th Mounted Brigades of Ausdiv struck the enemy's front, and met with no greater success than 60th Div. It was not until nearly dusk that Ausdiv was disengaged, when rapid progress was made past the enemy's left flank. 5th Mounted Brigade drew swords and cantered out into the open, but darkness fell before they were able to close with the enemy.

Descorps bivouacked for the night behind battle outposts on the general line railway north of Tel El Muleiha-Tel Abu Dilakh-Tel El Sharia. On this day very few troops of the corps obtained water.

8 November
The object of the operations on 8 November was to cut off the enemy who had now evacuated Gaza; El Atawineh redoubt, well to the south, still held out and it was thought that they, at least, could not escape us. XXI Corps was pursuing north along the coast from Gaza with the Imperial Service Cavalry Brigade and 52nd and 75th Divs. The XX Corps halted.

The objectives of Descorps were:
(a) ANZAC Div., with 7th Mounted Brigade attached-Bir Jemameh, thence towards Bureir.
(b) Ausdiv –Huj and to the east of it.
(c) 60th Div. –Huj.

ANZAC Div. was to endeavour to keep in advance of Ausdiv, so as to outflank opposition.

ANZAC Div.

1st A.L.H. Brigade occupied Tel El Nejile shortly after dawn, and reported that considerable bodies of Turks could be seen moving north. 2nd A.L.H. Brigade became hotly engaged west of Tel Abu Dilakh with a hostile flank guard. Both these A.L.H. Brigades advanced on Bir Jemameh, and by 08:45 hours were strongly opposed. 7th Mounted Brigade was put in between them and some progress was made. At 13:00 hours the Turks were apparently reinforced and counter-attacked heavily against the left of 7th Mounted Brigade. The 1st A.L.H. Brigade came up on the west, and drove back the Turks. Jemameh was captured about 15:45 hours, but fighting continued until dark. The Div. established a night outpost line covering Tel El Nejile and Bir Jemameh. Nearly all the horses were watered during the night; some had been 56 hours without a drink. During this day ANZAC Div. took 240 prisoners, four guns and much material, and the Turks lost heavily in their attacks; but the Turks held their own, and progress at this pace certainly did not hold out much promise of big results.

60th Div. advanced rapidly, and, after driving the enemy with great dash from three successive rearguard positions, were finally strongly held up and heavily shelled, with 2,500 yards of open slopes to cross to reach the enemy's last rearguard position covering Huj.

Ausdiv advanced at 04:00 hours, with 3rd A.L.H. Brigade on the right, and 5th Mounted Brigade on the left. 4th A.L.H. Brigade was not available, being held in Corps Reserve ready to march at 07:30 hours.

3rd A.L.H. Brigade met opposition throughout the day. They carried out the tactics of mounted riflemen most excellently, and met with great success, taking many prisoners and 15 guns.

5th Mounted Brigade advanced between 3rd A.L.H. Brigade and 60th Div. They were in comparatively close touch with 60th Div.

throughout the day. After midday it became apparent that the 60th Div. were pushing the Turk rearguard quicker than they liked, and their resistance began to stiffen, while a considerably increased gunfire was now hampering the advance. The following account is from the report of a senior officer present at the time:

> About 14:00 hours, the enemy were holding a ridge near Huj in considerable strength in front of 60th Div., whose leading lines were 2,000–3,000[12] distant, with absolutely bare ground in between. The enemy were also putting over a lot of shrapnel, and an infantry attack on this position would probably have been a slow and costly proposition. General Shea, commanding 60th Div., and himself a cavalry soldier, rode to a small hill on the flank of his division to make a personal reconnaissance and there met Lieutenant-Colonel Cheape, commanding the Warwickshire Yeomanry, to whom he suggested that the cavalry might endeavour to turn the hostile position and silence the guns which were inflicting casualties on the infantry.
>
> Lieutenant-Colonel Cheape had one and a half squadrons Warwickshire Yeomanry with him and at once decided to make a mounted attack; and Major Wiggin, who was in command of one and a half squadrons of the Worcester Yeomanry, close at hand, agreed to cooperate. A messenger was immediately despatched to inform the G.O.C. 5th Mounted Brigade of what was happening, but did not arrive in time to enable the Gloucestershire Yeomanry to be moved up soon enough to be of any assistance.
> Unfortunately the attack could not hope for support either from machine guns or Hotchkiss rifles. The previous night, when 5th Mounted Brigade had cantered out in the dusk to try and make a mounted attack, the Brigade Commander had considered that the situation promised no scope for fire support, and therefore ordered the Machine Gun Squadron

---

[12] The original doesn't say whether this is feet or yards, I suspect it was yards.

and all the pack horses, including the Hotchkiss rifles, to remain behind and find water. They failed to find water during the night, whereas the brigade did so. After dawn they were sent with guides to the place where the rest of the brigade had watered, with orders to rejoin as soon as possible. They had not rejoined at 14:00 hours, when they were most urgently required.

(See Plate VIII). From the south-west end of Ridge A, position marked (1), the hostile guns could not be seen, but were apparently firing from about 1,200–1,500 yards away, behind a small crest. Ridge A appeared to offer a covered approach for a flank attack, and accordingly the Warwickshire and Worcestershire Yeomanry moved round in line of troop columns under its shelter to position (2), from where it was seen that a hostile battery was in action at position (3), about 900–1,000 yards distant, with open ground in between.

The dust raised by this movement had drawn the attention of the enemy, and he swung two guns round to counter the attack. Fortunately he was rather rattled and his shooting was erratic and little harm was done. A halt was made for a moment at position (2), but the force came immediately under a heavy rifle fire from hostile infantry on ridge C, about 600 yards away.

The leading squadron of Worcestershire Yeomanry, under Major Albright, was at once ordered to form half squadrons, and to charge this position; the order was rapidly carried out, the enemy ceasing fire and retreating, leaving a good many men on the ground, killed by the sword. This squadron had been told not to pursue, as the guns were their real objective. The half-squadron formation was adopted because the frontage to be attacked was small, and numbers were limited.

Captain Valentine's squadron of Warwickshire Yeomanry

now formed column of half squadrons, extended and went straight for the guns, coming under a hail of shell fire, rifle and machine gun bullets immediately they topped the ridge A. They were closely supported, slightly in echelon, by the remaining two troops of Worcestershire Yeomanry, under Lieutenant Edwards.

The distance was about 800–1,000 yards down a steep slope and up the other side, with the last 100–150 yards very steep indeed. Major Albright had quickly and gallantly rallied and reformed his squadron and came on in echelon a moment later, the combined attack being completely successful, sweeping over the guns and reaching the top of the ridge in rear of them. The enemy, however, continued firing his guns, machine guns and rifles and casualties were heavy. Most of the officers were casualties and it was impossible to organise a pursuit, so that many escaped who should have been captured, had any body of organised supporting troops been available.

Just before position (2) had been reached, Turkish guns were seen retreating along the road to the north; Lieutenant-Colonel Cheape took the remaining two troops of Warwickshire Yeomanry with him in order to intercept them; this he successfully accomplished, taking a complete battery of 5.9 in. howitzers.

A large number of Turks were killed with the sword, and the captures amounted to one battery of 5.9 in. howitzers; one Austrian F.A. Battalion, served by Austrian gunners, who fought to the last; one Mountain Battalion, abandoned by its personnel on Ridge C; four machine guns, which did much damage; and about 70 prisoners.

Colonel Preston gives two battalions of infantry as composing the Turkish rearguard, besides the guns and machine guns.

Our casualties were very heavy, partly owing to the unavoidable

PLATE VIII.

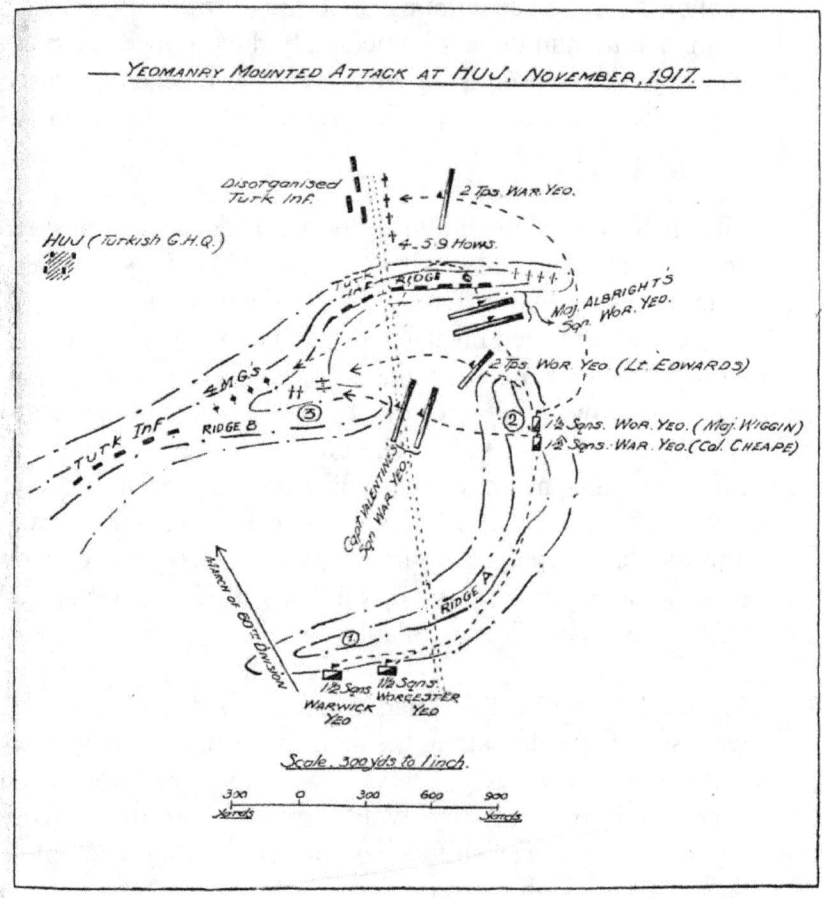

lack of any fire support. Out of 170 horses which took part in the charge, 100 were killed, i.e., 60 percent. Of horses. Out of about 12 officers, the 3 leaders, Albright, Valentine and Edwards were all killed; 6 other officers were wounded; casualties in officers, 75 percent. Out of 158 men, 26 were killed, 40 wounded; casualties in men 42 percent.

The operation was complete in a few minutes, and the 60th Div. marched into Huj without further casualties; if the infantry had had to continue the attack across such open ground, their casualties would almost certainly have been very heavy indeed.

This operation by a small force is a wonderful example of the power of the mounted attack to gain a rapid decision; and in a pursuit of this nature 'time' is the one thing that must be denied to the retreating enemy.

Comments on the Pursuit of 7 and 8 November
By the evening of 8 November it was apparent that the in direct pursuit of Descorps had in great part failed; the Gaza garrison and some of the garrisons of the works east of Gaza had made good their escape. Henceforward the pursuit by Descorps would be direct and consequently only limited success could now be expected.[13]

There were various factors that appear to have affected the result :
(a) During the two vital days, 7 and 8 November, Descorps was comparatively weak; Yeodiv, the N.Z.M.R. Brigade of ANZAC Div. and the I.C.C. Brigade were absent from the main operation, forming part of the right flank guard in the hills about Tel Khuweilfeh.
(b) The direction in which Descorps was launched, i.e. on Bir Jemameh-Huj, did not result in the pursuit being of a very 'indirect' nature. Rearguards and flank guards, put out by the Turkish forces retiring from Sharia, Hareira, et cetera, were met at every mile. It is probable that nearly all of this resistance might have been avoided if the whole of Descorps had been directed north along the railway to Tel El Nejile and thence across towards the sea near El Mejdel.

It is quite certain that the C-in-C realised better than anyone else that, within reason, the more indirect the pursuit, the greater would be the results; in fact, the instructions originally issued to Descorps, before the capture of Beersheba, enjoined that men and horses were to be kept as fresh as possible for the second and principal stage of their operations, in which their role would be to

---

[13] While this is not very clear, it is what the original text says.

pass round the enemy's left and establish the corps about Tel El Nejile-Wadi Hesi. It is presumed, therefore, that it was considered, in the light of later knowledge, that an advance by such a large force via Tel El Nejile was rendered impossible by the impracticability of supplying it; further, it is presumed that the Intelligence Branch of the General Staff at G.H.Q. considered that sufficient water could not be found east of Bir Jemameh and Huj.

(c) It is questionable as to whether the inclusion of a division of all arms in a Cavalry Corps is liable to interfere with the activity of the cavalry. 60th Div. could not hope to move fast enough to make an indirect pursuit, and necessarily had to be directed straight on Huj. Assuming that it was possible for the two mounted divisions of Descorps to pursue 'indirectly' via Tel El Nejile, the Corps Commander would have had considerable difficulty in controlling them and, at the same time, 60th Div. advancing in quite a different direction.

(d) Lastly, the writer considers that the corps was severely handicapped by the fact that four out of the six pursuing mounted brigades were mounted riflemen and not cavalrymen. The 5th and 7th Mounted Brigades had swords, and the 1st, 2nd, 3rd and 4th A.L.H. Brigades had not. The writer is firmly of opinion that the Australian Light Horse and New Zealand Mounted Rifles have no superiors in the world as offensive fighters, but in such an operation as this pursuit they were severely handicapped for want of an *arme blanche* weapon. The tactics of mounted rifles in pursuit necessitate turning movements, which are comparatively slow. The sword permits a far more direct line of attack and brings quick decisions.

With the conditions as they were on 7 and 8 November, the writer considers that, if all six pursuing brigades had had swords, the whole mounted portion of the corps could have been directed in depth on a narrow front, and the results would have been very different. If each of the six brigades had been able to bring off a mounted attack, as the 5th Mounted Brigade were able, the Turkish retreat would have been converted into complete rout.

It has been stated previously that General Grant, commanding 4th A.L.H. Brigade, became a confirmed believer in the power of the sword at the time of his brilliant mounted attack at Beersheba.

The events of 8 November, on which day the 3rd A.L.H. Brigade fought all day with great success, converted General Wilson, commanding 3rd A.L.H. Bde, to the same opinion.

He wrote the following over a year later, just after his own brigade had at last been armed with the sword.
> From my subsequent experience of the use of the sword, I consider it would have been invaluable here (i.e. on 8 November 1917). If we had had swords, I am sure we could have ridden on and captured thousands ; as it was, we stood off and shot hundreds only.

And again he writes:
> One of the chief values of the sword is the spirit of progress that it inculcates in the carrier. He does not allow himself to be bluffed by slight opposition. He rides on feeling that he has a weapon in his hand, and in nineteen times out of twenty, finds the opposition only a bluff. With mounted riflemen, on the other hand, his only course is to make wide turning movements to induce the opposition to retire, or to dismount and try to shift it by fire action. This all means time, or uncertainty, which is exactly what the enemy wants... Dealing with a pursuing foe, as we were in the Beersheba-Jerusalem operations in November,1917....
>
> There are numerous cases in these operations where the sword would have been ... invaluable. Take the operations about Huj, in November 1917. With my late experience I can see what we could have done with the sword there. We were in touch with large bodies of the enemy, somewhat disorganised, retreating, but still armed. We had no swords and could only deal with them by fire action. Their line was too broad to outflank. The regiments engaged them at a distance and, when practicable, raced in and cut out guns

and transport. They inflicted casualties and took prisoners, but did nothing really big. If they had had swords I am now confidant from my later experiences that they would have made wholesale captures. It is not reasonable to expect mounted riflemen to charge positions mounted, it is only bluff, and if the enemy stood to it the charge could end in failure only. Such bluffs, I know, have come off, but we cannot always expect to be lucky.

18. PURSUIT AND BATTLE

9 November
Orders were now issued for direct pursuit by as many troops as could be supplied in front of railhead.

Descorps, with ANZAC Div., Ausdiv, Yeodiv and I.C.C. Brigade (the two last-named formations having rejoined from the eastern flank), took up the pursuit, supported by the 52nd and 75th Divs. of XXI Corps. The objective was Junction Station.

It was obvious from the reports of the R.F.C., who throughout the 7th and 8th attacked the retreating columns with bombs and machine gun fire, that the enemy was retiring in considerable disorganisation, and could offer no very serious resistance if pressed with determination.

ANZAC Div., which had watered during the night 8–9 November, alone made any progress. Ausdiv, of which the largest proportion had not watered since 18:00 hours on 6 November, struggled all through the night 8–9 November, and during the 9th, trying to find water between Huj and Jemameh. Men and horses were rapidly growing exhausted. Yeodiv reached Huj, but was unable to proceed further, owing to water and supply difficulties.

ANZAC Div. (with 7thMountedBrigade attached in place of N.Z.M.R. Brigade, which had not rejoined from the eastern flank), pushed on through Bureir and Simsin to El Mejdel. Meeting shellfire at first, the pursuit became more rapid as the day went on, the Turks being greatly demoralised by their rapid retreat and for want of water.

At Kaukaba, just north of El Huleikat, a large number of prisoners were taken. In the village was a great mass of transport, the animals still in the shafts, either dead or dying from thirst and fatigue. By nightfall the 1st and 2nd A.L.H. Brigades reached Esdud and Suafirel Sharkiye respectively. The Turks in their retreat had left material, rifles and ammunition scattered all over the country; the Arabs and villagers were looting everything, and there was not time to deal with them. Prisoners were in a bad way, suffering from exhaustion, want of water and dysentery.

The brigades of ANZAC Div. were also badly in want of both water and forage. The wells in the villages were deep (100 to 200 feet) and of small capacity; the Turks in passing had cut all the well ropes, and thrown them and the buckets into the wells. The watering was much hampered by the inhabitants, who, mad with thirst themselves, rushed the nose bags as they were drawn to the surface. The horses were almost unmanageable; when they saw water they threw themselves on their knees, and upset as much as they drank.

10 and 11 November
ANZAC Div. most cleverly seized the bridge at Jisr Esdud and formed a bridge head there. The water question had now become so acute, that the division was compelled to halt. During these two days, 9 and 10 November, ANZAC Div. had done splendid work and captured 1,000 prisoners and 16 guns.

52nd and 75th Divs. of XXI Corps arrived on the line Suafir el Sharkiye-Esdud on the evening of 10 November, and took over the defence of those places.

On 11 November, 1st A.L.H. Brigade drove the enemy from the banks of the Wadi Sukerier and occupied Tel el Murre.

Ausdiv marched from Huj on the evening of 9 November, and found good water at Tel el Hesi ; reaching Arak el Menshiye, they gained contact with ANZAC Div. to the west. Well organised opposition was encountered on the line Zeita-Summeil. After considerable fighting the division, on the evening of 11 November,[14] were in possession of the line Zeita-Berkusie-El Jeladiyah; they connected with the right of 75th Div. at the last-named place.

Yeodiv left Huj early on 10 November and followed Ausdiv, on 11 November they moved across to El Mejdel.

Operations on the 10th and 11th showed a stiffening of the enemy's resistance on the general line of the Wadi Sukerier, with centre about El Kustine; the original Hebron group prolonged the enemy's line to about Beit Jibrin; this group appears to have been reinforced from the north, and consisted of III and XV Turkish Corps. It was obvious to G.H.Q. that the hostile forces opposed to us on this line were no longer only rearguards, but that all the remainder of the Turkish Army that could be induced to fight was making a last effort to arrest our pursuit south of the important Junction Station.

12 November
12 November was spent in preparations for the attack, which was ordered for 13 November. Yeodiv relieved ANZAC Div., and cooperated in a preliminary attack made on Burka by 52nd Div.

Ausdiv made preparations for its role of the following day, which was to protect the right of the attack, and draw the enemy's attention upon itself. The division was extended on a front of 11 miles, from Arak el Menshiye, through Balin to El Jeladiyeh. About 13:00 hours, the enemy suddenly flung a force of about 5,000 men against this line. These troops came by train and march route from the direction of Junction Station, and attacked through Balin on Summeil. The attack fell chiefly on 5th Mounted Brigade, which suffered heavily and, at one time, was almost surrounded. They were extricated, however, and the attack was held, and finally died away. There is reason to believe that this counterattack was directed by Marshal von Falkenhayn in person. Ausdiv bivouacked for the night on the line Arakel Menshiye-

---

[14] It is not clear if the author is referring to Ausdiv or ANZAC Div, or both.

Summeil-El Jeladiyeh, and this heavy Turkish counterattack had no effect whatever on the situation.

13 November
The situation on the morning of 13 November was that the enemy had strung out his force (amounting probably to no more than 20,000 rifles), on a front of 20 miles, on the line Beit Jibrin-Berkusie-Tel El Turmus-Katrah-El Mughar-Zernike-El Kubeibe.

The attack was to be made with the primary object of cutting the Jerusalem-Jaffa railway. XXI Corps (75th and 52nd Divs.) advanced with its right on the Gaza-Junction Station road, protected on that flank by Ausdiv, and with its left on the line Beshshit-Sidun.

Descorps (less Ausdiv) was to operate on the left of XXI Corps, with objective the railway from a point due west of Sidunto Naane. Yeodiv led with I.C.C. Brigade attached. ANZAC Div. was to follow Yeodiv closely, either to support them or to move through them to the final objective.

Narrative of the Battle.
75th Div. had a good deal of trouble with the Turks about El Mesmiye. The place was finally stormed from the south, and the division took 292 prisoners and seven machine guns. It also captured Yasur and pushed back Turkish rearguards towards Junction Station.

52nd Div. had launched several assaults the previous day, before Burka was taken late in the afternoon. On the 13th the enemy continued to fight stubbornly and severe opposition was met on the Katrah-El Mughar line. The attack against the south end of El Mughar (see Plate IX) had to cross over 4,000 yards of open ground swept by heavy shell and machine gun fire, and was held up, with its left in the Wadi Jamus at Y.12 central. The Divisional Commander thereupon requested Yeodiv to assist on the left.

PLATE IX.

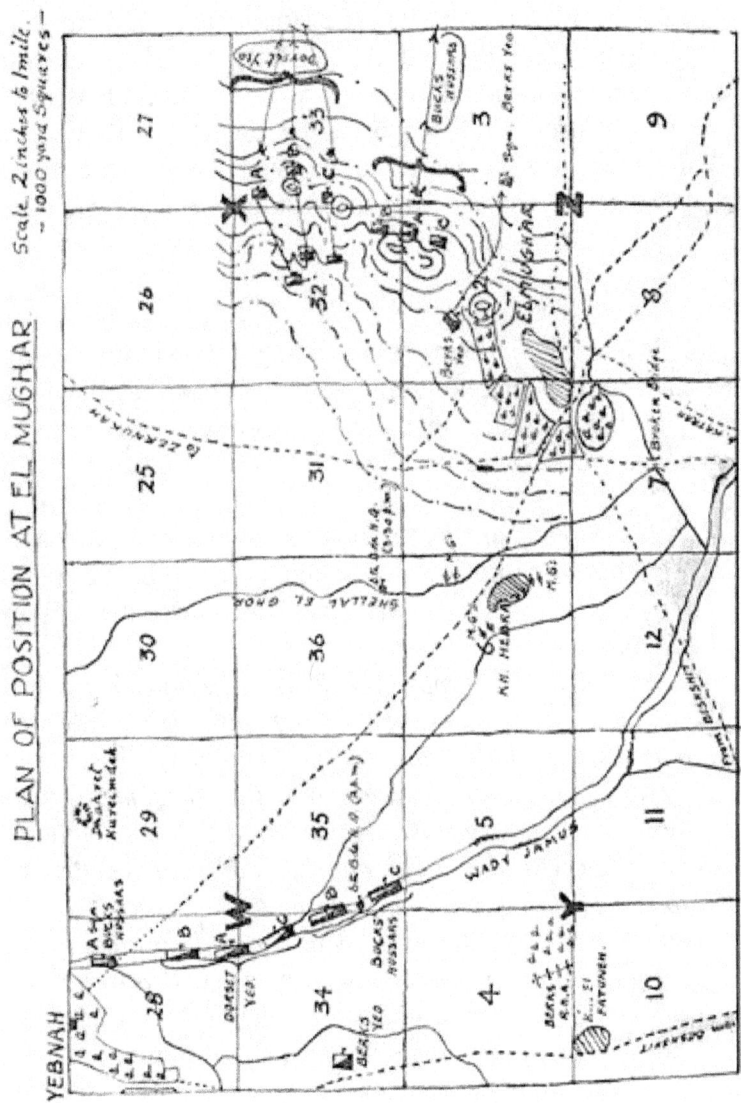

Yeodiv The following account is extracted from the official report on the action of Yeodiv (Ref. Plate IX):

By 12:30 p.m. 8th Mounted Brigade were in possession of Yebnah. 6th Mounted Brigade Hd Qrs and the Brigade, less the Bucks Hussars and Berks Battery R.H.A., assembled between Yebnah and Tel El Murre. The Bucks Hussars, less one squadron, and supported by the Berks R.H.A., were advancing via Beshshit into the Wadi Jamus. One squadron had entered Yebnah from the east, cooperating with the 8th Mounted Brigade.

Brigadier-General Godwin commanding 6th Mounted Brigade was called to the telephone and told verbally that the infantry attack was held up, and that the 6th Mounted Brigade were to advance and take El Mughar.

At 12:45 p.m., just as the brigade was moving off, and the Brigadier moving forward to reconnoitre a line of approach, this verbal message was confirmed by the following telegram:

I.C.C. Brigade will move on El Kubeibeh and Zernuka with the object of covering the left of our further advance on Akir, leaving half battalion in Yebnah until relieved by infantry. This half battalion will then become Divisional Reserve. When Zernuka is occupied I.C.C. Brigade will cooperate with the attack on Akir. 6th Mounted Brigade to move on El Mughar. 22nd Mounted Brigade to move east to a point midway between El Mughar and Zernuka and after the occupation of these places by us will advance to the attack on Akir. 8th Mounted Brigade will form up one mile east of Yebnah and come into Divisional Reserve.

Reconnaissance
Advancing through Squares W. 32–33, 6th Mounted Brigade Headquarters joined the Headquarters of the Bucks Hussars in the Wadi Jamus W.34. The Berks Battery was in position in Y.4d, shelling El Mughar and the ridge beyond.

Lieutenant-Colonel Hon. F. Cripps, commanding the Buckinghamshire Hussars, had been in communication with the C.O. of the infantry battalion of 52nd Div. on the right, who were also in the Wadi further to the east, their left being about Y.12 central. The Bucks Hussars were employed in pushing mounted patrols forward towards the position.

The Dorset Yeomanry, Berkshire Yeomanry andthe6thMounted Brigade field ambulance were halted in a depression, out of sight, about square W.33d and Y.3d.

The Brigadier reconnoitred the position, and Lieutenant Perkins, Bucks Hussars, was sent forward to the Wadi Shellal el Ghor to ascertain the cover there. He carried out a very good reconnaissance under very dangerous circumstances, as he became the focus of every description of fire from the ridge.

Captain Patron, commanding the 17 Machine Gun Squadron, did the same, with a view to getting a position for covering the advance of the Brigade with concentrated machine gun fire.

Preliminary Movements and Orders.
(a) It was decided to bring the Dorset Yeomanry at once into the Wadi Jamus and they trickled by squadrons into the Wadi in Squares W.34b. and d.

The Wadi is a narrow ravine, difficult to enter and emerge from, and broad enough to take a single rank of horses and men only. It afforded, however, excellent cover. The Dorsets came under rifle and shell fire while entering the wadi.

(b) Commanding Officers were assembled and verbal orders issued to the effect that :
   The Bucks Hussars would attack the ridge just north of El Mughar village, and the Dorset Yeomanry the hill on the

left of the Bucks. Both attacks to start simultaneously at 3 p.m. and to be carried out mounted. Regiments were ordered to advance in column of squadrons extended to about five paces. The artillery to open intense covering fire from their position in Y.4d.

Each regiment had two machine guns attached; the remainder, under Captain Patron, were to cover the advance from positions he had reconnoitred in the Wadi Jamus and in advance of it from the right flank in the Shellal el Ghor, near Khurbet Hebra.

The conformation of the ground aided this plan, as fire could be brought to bear for the longest time possible before being masked by the advancing troops.

The Berks Yeomanry were to be kept in support, but were to push forward into the Wadi Jamus directly the Bucks Hussars had vacated it.

(c) While these orders were being given out a message was received from the 52nd Division suggesting that a flanking movement by the cavalry to the north of El Mughar would enable the infantry to advance. A reply was sent to the effect that the brigade would advance at 3 p.m.

(d) The orders were issued at 2:30 p.m., which left half an hour for the battery to register certain points, and the Commanding Officers to issue their own orders.

The Mounted Attack.
(a) Punctually at 3 p.m. the Bucks Hussars, in column of squadrons extended to four yards interval, advanced at a trot directed on the ridge immediately north-east of El Mughar village.

The distance was 3,000 yards, swept by rifle and machine gun fire, and sprinkled with shells. The pace at the commencement was the trot, the last 1,000 yards being covered at a hard gallop.

At the foot of the hills Captain Bulteel, M.C. (B Squadron) leading, drew swords and charged. Captain the Hon. Neil Primrose, M.C. (C Squadron) came upon his right.

On reaching the summit the Turks in some instances threw down their arms, but a number retired, and finding the weakness of the cavalry, came back and got into the knolls on the flanks, and a fire fight ensued at close range. This prevented the succeeding squadrons from moving straight on, and Captain Primrose's squadron was attacked on his left flank. Captain Bulteel was now across the ridge and down on the eastern side, and putting a machine gun and Hotchkiss barrage on to the rear of the village. Captured Turkish machine guns were used for this purpose.

Captain Lawson (A Squadron) arrived from Yebnah and consolidated the position, and with his support the remainder of the ridge was finally taken.

(b) The Dorset Yeomanry advanced on the left of the Bucks according to plan. They had 4,000 yards to go and arrived at the foot of the hills with their horses much exhausted. Captain Dammers (A Squadron) dismounted (see plan) and fought his way on to the crest on foot. His led horses suffered heavy losses, while those of the other two squadrons, which remained mounted, were much less.

The remaining two squadrons, Major Gordon, M.C. (C Squadron) on the right and Major Wingfield-Digby (B Squadron) in the centre, led by Lieutenant-Colonel Sir R. Baker Bt, formed line on the left of the Bucks, and galloped at their objective.

Action of Reserves.
The Dorsets and Bucks having gained their objectives, the Berks Yeomanry, headed by Brigade HQ, crossed the Wadi Jamus and reached the Wadi Shellal el Ghor in W.36b,

where they came under machine gun fire from the village and cactus hedges west of it. Before proceeding further it was necessary to clear the village, which was carried out successfully by two squadrons of the Berks dismounted.

The remaining squadron pursued the enemy into the plain beyond, rounding up stragglers.

Machine Guns and R.H.A.
The machine guns attached to regiments moved with them. They arrived on the crest very shortly after the charge and quickly came into action against the retreating stragglers. The six guns furnishing the covering fire under Captain Patron were most effective. They pushed forward as soon as the troops advanced, and fired on distant targets from the summit of the ridge.

The Berkshire Battery R.H.A. supported with excellent and accurate fire, shooting 200 rounds at ranges from 3,200–3,500 yards during the charge.

Subsequent Action.
At 4p.m.thefollowingmessagewasreceivedfromDivisional HQ:

52nd Division unable to make progress. Cooperate and turn Mughar from the north.

This message was timed 2:45 p.m. and the operation ordered had been carried out by the time of receipt.

Mughar village was not completely cleared until 5:30p.m., the enemy hiding in the houses and hedges.

In the meantime 22nd Mounted Brigade had advanced on the left of 6th Mounted Brigade, and commenced an attack on Akir, which did not develop owing to a Turkish counterattack on their left.

The position was consolidated and patrols pushed forward and the Brigade bivouacked on the position for the night.

Results

The total number of prisoners handed over to the A.P.M. were: 18 officers, 1,078 other ranks;14 machine guns and 2 field guns were also captured.

Undoubtedly a larger number of prisoners could have been taken had not the finishing gallop up the hill completely exhausted the horses, added to which, the steep descent on the eastern side was most difficult.

The casualties in the 6th Mounted Brigade were as under:

	Officers		Other Ranks		
	Killed	Wounded	Killed	Wounded	Missing
Brigade Hd. Qrs				1	
Bucks Hussars		3	6	44	1
Dorset Yeomanry		3	8	42	
Berks Yeomanry	1			7	
17th M.G. Squadron			1	19	
Field Ambulance				3	
Berks R.H.A					
	1	6	15	107	1

Animals : Horses 265, mules 2, killed and wounded.

Remarks.

(a) This action is a good example of what can be effected by mounted troops, moving rapidly in extended formation.

(b) The value of personal reconnaissance on the part of all commanders; from the Brigadier downward, is clearly shown. The objectives were pointed out on the ground.

(c) The skill and enterprise shown by the officer commanding Bucks Hussars, in pushing forward into the Wadi Jamus and in initiating reconnaissances from there, prepared the way most efficiently for the subsequent attack.

(d) Machine guns played a large part, as is narrated above. The use of the captured Turkish machine guns is worthy of special notice. They prevented the enemy from escaping from El Mughar village and from launching a counterattack against the right of our position. Their action also contributed to the subsequent capture of the village with small losses, since they took in reverse the hostile positions in the cactus hedges on the north and north-west faces.

To the north of El Mughar the enemy was strongly posted at Zernuka and El Kubeibe, which places were not occupied till early on 14 November.

On the 14th, 22nd Mounted Brigade drove the enemy from Akir and Naane and the railway was destroyed as ordered. A railway guard of three officers, 69 other ranks and one machine gun were captured. Touch was established with 52nd Div. on the right and with ANZAC Div. on the left.

ANZAC Div., which had two brigades only, by midday 14 November reached the outskirts of Ramleh, in touch with Yeodiv, and the ridges about Khurbet Surafend. The N.Z.M.R. Brigade on the left were heavily counter-attacked, the enemy approaching within bombing distance. The New Zealanders completely repulsed him with a bayonet charge and he retired in disorder and with heavy loss. Unfortunately no mobile reserve was at hand to pursue.

15 November
(a) Ausdiv, on the right of XXI Corps, advanced three and a half miles east of Junction Station towards Latron.
(b) Yeodiv, with I.C.C. Brigade attached, found the enemy strongly posted at Abu Shusheh, a high rocky hill covered with boulders. After a stout resistance, including a determined counterattack against our right, the enemy was driven from the hills by 6th and 22nd Mounted Brigades and retired on Latron in disorder, leaving 360 prisoners in our hands; 400 dead were counted on the field. The main feature of this operation was once again a mounted attack by the 6th Mounted Brigade. This mounted attack at Abu Shusheh is considered by some authorities to have been a more brilliant exploit even than the charge of the same brigade at El Mughar, owing to the fact that the rocky hills up which the charge was made appear impassable for horses except at a walk.
(c) 1st A.L.H. Brigade of ANZAC Div. seized Ramleh and afterwards Ludd, taking 360 prisoners, and carried out railway demolition north of the town, as ordered.

16 November
On 16 November, the line was pushed forward to Latron (the mouth of the pass being still in the enemy's hands) – El Kubab-Ludd-El Yahudie-Jaffa. Jaffa was occupied by the New Zealanders at noon without opposition.

The Turks had by now broken into two distinct masses, widely separated by the physical formation of the country. Eighth Army (XX and XXII Corps), consisting of four damaged and one fresh division, retired into the plain of Sharon behind the Nahr el Auja, a river about 30 yards broad. This Army was based on the railway running down from the north. The remnants of VII Army (III and XV Corps), consisting of six shattered divisions and the 3rd Cavalry Div., were based on Jerusalem and the road running north from there. The Junction Station-Jerusalem railway was of no value to them, as it ended in a cul-de-sac at the latter place.

The only means of effective lateral communications between

these two armies was by road to the north, a circuitous route of 75 miles.

The C-in-C decided to contain Turkish VIII Army, to attack Turkish VII Army and occupy Jerusalem.

The decision to march into the mountains marks the conclusion of the great pursuit. Our mounted troops had been marching and fighting continuously since 31 October, and had advanced a distance of 75 miles in a straight line from Asluj to Jaffa.

Descorps had captured 5,720 prisoners, more than 60 guns and about 50 machine guns. The enemy had lost altogether about 11,000 prisoners and 100 guns, approximately one-quarter of his force ; he had been thoroughly defeated and was in a very broken condition. He had, however, managed to avoid complete annihilation, and had now reached comparative safety; our advance through the mountains to Jerusalem must necessarily be slow, for these narrow passes have seldom been forced and have proved fatal to many invaders. The winter rains had set in, and our troops were 40 miles in front of railhead.

All ranks of Descorps were disappointed that they had failed to annihilate the enemy. The suitability of the country and the demoralised condition of the enemy gave promise of such a result. Various factors, however, combined to defeat our object. If it had been possible to direct the whole corps on one suitable line of advance, and employ its whole weight in depth in a series of mounted attacks, it is considered that the enemy's rearguards could have been overwhelmed and that the corps could have reached vital points on the enemy's line of retreat. The extraordinary success of the various mounted attacks made during the pursuit by the Yeomanry showed clearly the value of this form of attack, and the writer, as stated earlier, considers that the corps was severely handicapped by the fact that half the mounted troops were not armed with the sword or lance.

The main handicap, however, was the lack of water in very hot weather. It was necessary to split up the formations on wide fronts, so that each unit could have a village well to itself and arrange its own watering. Lieutenant-Colonel Preston[15] tells of one occasion where large numbers of horses were 84 hours without water, and brigades frequently went without for 48 hours. Under these conditions it was impossible to assemble a really large force of cavalry for a decisive blow ; and the enemy's rearguards had only to deal with cavalry spread right across the plain, and comparatively weak everywhere.

---

[15] Lt-Colonel R. M. P. Preston, *The Desert Mounted Corps* (Boston: Houghton Mufflin, 1921)

19. PHASE IV.
THE ADVANCE INTO THE JUDE AN MOUNTAINS
Ref. Map A and Plate X.

The problem that faced the C-in-C on 16 November was a difficult one. He had decisively defeated his enemy, and had ultimately caused him to separate his forces.

The C-in-C had interposed a force of three cavalry divisions and two infantry divisions between these separated forces, and was determined, while holding off one force with a detachment, to continue the pressure on the other. A continuation of the advance up the maritime plain in pursuit of Turkish VIII Army would have given the cavalry their best chance, for the plain of Sharon, which lies north of a line Ludd-Jaffa, is as suitable for the action of large cavalry forces as is the Plain of Philistia, to the south of that line. But the communications would have been in danger from counter-offensive from the mouth of the pass at Latron or from the main road, which runs from Jerusalem south-westward to Beersheba.

The C-in-C was of the opinion that, before the position in the plain could be considered secure, it was essential to obtain hold, north of Jerusalem, of the one good road that traverses the Jude An range from north to south. He therefore decided to force his way into the Jude An Mountains. The difficulties were immense. The only troops available for immediate action were Descorps (three cavalry divisions, 7th Mounted Brigade and Imperial Camel Brigade) and XXI Corps (52nd and 75th Divisions), which had carried out the pursuit. XX Corps (53rd, 74th, 10th and 60th Divisions) was still back between Gaza and Beersheba, mainly for want of transport and lack of efficient communications. 54th Division of XXI Corps was gradually moving up from Gaza and had reached Julis. Transport had to be sent back from 52nd and 75th Divisions to enable 54th Division to march.

The leading divisions were tired; they only had their summer cotton khaki clothing; the winter rains had already begun to fall, and it was obvious that it would be very cold 3,000 feet up on the top of the mountains.

The difficulties of supply were very great. The advanced troops were about 40 miles in front of railhead; the broad gauge railway was advancing from Deir el Belah very slowly, and did not reach Deir Sineid, and so join up with the Turkish narrow-gauge railway (8 feet 6 inches), until 28 November. A certain amount of Turkish rolling stock had been captured at, and south of, Junction Station, and was used.

Once the rains broke, the mechanical transport lorries, working forward from about Gaza, quickly went through the one poorly metalled main road, and the camel convoys suffered severely in the mud, in which the camels slid and slithered and frequently broke their legs. Every opportunity was taken to land stores on the coast, but the work on this notorious coast was dependent upon a continuance of favourable weather, and might at any moment be stopped for several days together.

The supply of rations and other necessaries of life, such as clothing, fuel and tentage, was precarious, and the supply of forage to the large number of horses in forward areas was already inadequate.

Lastly, and most difficult of all, the attainment of the objective involved the forcing of the famous pass of Bab-el-Wad, between Latron and Kuryet el Enab; a pass which, throughout past centuries, has stopped army after army, and which was known to be fortified with field entrenchments. The agents working for the Intelligence Branch of the General Staff at G.H.Q. considered this pass impregnable to attack from the west.

The west side of the Jude An range consists of a series of spurs running down from east to west, and separated from one another by narrow valleys. These spurs are, for the most part, steep, bare and rocky; they are much terraced for the cultivation of the olive, and are in some places precipitous.

In the intended area of operations, i.e. the area Junction Station-Ludd-Bire-Jerusalem, only one good road, the Jaffa-Latron-Jerusalem road, traversed the mountains from west to east, and that road ran through the Pass of Bab-el-Wad (extends from the K to the l of Kuryet el Enab, Ref. Map A). The other routes, shown on Map A, east of a south and north line drawn through Sura, Latron and Annabe, were mere native donkey-pack and camel-pack tracks on the sides of the hills or up the stony beds of wadis, and were impracticable for wheeled transport without improvement.

In spite of the state of his leading troops and of the weather; in spite of the difficulties of supplying food, forage, clothing and ammunition; and in spite of the lessons of past history in this land, which counsel caution, the C-in-C decided to force his way at once into the Jude An Mountains and to Jerusalem, before sitting down to reorganise, re-equip and assure his communications.

His decision brought much discomfort and hardship upon his troops; but, in the sequel, all ranks thoroughly recognised that the one time to force the Jude An Mountains, and in particular the pass of Bab-el-Wad, is upon the heels of a demoralised enemy. Subsequent events showed clearly what procrastination would have cost; and the morale of the troops, in spite of their hardships, rose higher and higher as they realised that they were in the hands of a commander who made his decisions quickly, and apparently always soundly, and who certainly never wavered once they were made.

Plan
The task primarily allotted to Descorps was, without waiting for the infantry, to push forward in all directions so as to give the enemy no rest, and to allow him as little time as possible to bring up reinforcements. The two divisions of XXI Corps, preceded, if possible, by Yeodiv and Ausdiv, were to move into the mountains and, avoiding any fighting in or near the Holy City, to isolate it from the north.

18 November
Narrative
ANZAC Division advanced northwards up the plain with the object of containing that portion of the Turkish forces which had retired up the maritime plain; the division was ordered to establish a line south of the Auja from the foothills to the sea.

Yeodiv
with Hong Kong and Singapore Mountain Battery attached (camel-pack), started on a dash for Bire, situated on the main road north of Jerusalem, moving by the track from Ludd through Berfilya, Shilta and Ur el Tahta, which 19 centuries before had been a Roman road. The cavalry brigades had to wind their way along rock-strewn wadis, and over tracks, which, in November 1919, existed only on the map. Horses could only march in single file, and for the most part had to be led. Sniping opposition was encountered. With great difficulty, 8th Mounted Brigade reached Ur el Tahta by nightfall; 22nd Mounted Brigade reached Shilta.

Ausdiv
meanwhile, attempted to capture the mouth of the pass at Latron; 4th A.L.H. Brigade could make no progress against the opposition encountered; 3rd A.L.H. Brigade attempted to move north of Latron through the mountains and reach the main road between Latron and Kuryet el Enab.

The brigade pressed on throughout the day; two water carts and three ambulance wagons collapsed, and finally the guns and wheels had to be left behind.

Horses had to be led, as the hills became too rocky for riding, and many horses were lamed.

The advanced squadrons, however, penetrated well behind the enemy's right flank, and Notts Battery R.H.A. found good targets at Latron and shot 189 rounds during the afternoon at a range of 5,000 yards, and silenced a hostile battery. The Turkish gunners attempted to manhandle this battery away, but rapid fire was opened and the enemy was dispersed without removing his guns.

At 16:30 hours, Ausdiv was ordered to withdraw, presumably because the difficulties were too great, and 75th Division was to advance against the mouth of the pass next day.

The efforts of Ausdiv had not, however, been entirely unsuccessful; the threat against their right flank had been too much for the Turks, who abandoned the position during the night, leaving the four guns in position.

5th Mounted Brigade attempted to reach the rear of the enemy's position by moving from Junction Station up the Jerusalem railway, but found the country impassable for cavalry, and perhaps even for infantry, in face of only slight opposition.

19 November
Yeodiv
continued its advance. Imperative orders had been issued to the 8th and 22nd Mounted Brigades to take Bire on the 19th at all costs. Difficulties of the route, or fatigue of horses, or shortage of supplies, were not to be considered. Turkish supplies and water would be found at Bire.

At daybreak, 8th Mounted Brigade pushed on for Beitunia, while 22nd Mounted Brigade made for Ain Arik, thus protecting the left flank.

The 'going' was even worse than on the 18th. Not only had the horses to be led in single file, but the majority of the men had to lead two horses, as the heights on both flanks had to be picqueted. Vehicles simply could not advance further. G.O.C. 22nd Mounted Brigade sent Hants Battery, R.H.A., back to Ludd, and went on without it, reaching Ain Arik at dusk.

8th Mounted Brigade was not so fortunate, and finally the Brigadier decided it was absolutely impossible to push on further.

The Divisional Commander, however, was determined to obey his orders to the letter and count no costs, and at 2100 hours issued orders to the following effect for next day:

> 6th Mounted Brigade to advance at 0600 hours on Beitunia and Bire via Ur el Foka. 22nd Mounted Brigade to continue its advance on Bire via Ain Arik. 20th Brigade, R.H.A. (less Hants Battery, R.H.A.), to concentrate at Ur el Tahta under escort of one regiment, 8th Mounted Brigade. Hong Kong and Singapore Mountain Battery to be attached to 6th Mounted Brigade. Div HQ to follow 6th Mounted Brigade. 8th Mounted Brigade (less one regiment escort to guns) to withdraw to Tahta and follow Div HQ as divisional reserve.

On this day, the infantry continued its advance:75th Division, advancing through Latron, pushed on through the narrow defile against considerable opposition and reached within three miles of Kuryet el Enab. The experience of the Ghurkhas and 58th Rifles (Indian Army) in mountain warfare was of the greatest value.

52nd Division advanced from about El Kubab, parallel to and on the left of the 75th Division, and reached Beit Likia. Only six guns could be brought up, and these were extra horsed up to 10 and 12 horses per gun.

On this day, the real winter rains broke in a torrential downpour, and they continued all night.

The three divisions had reached a height of between 2,000 and

2,500 feet in winter, in mountains on which snow falls. When the rain fell, it turned very cold. The troops were dressed in summer clothing, i.e. khaki-drill; they had no blankets, greatcoats or tents, and there were no billets. Each man had a waterproof sheet to lie on, and in addition a canvas 'bivouac' sheet, which, when laced to the sheet of a pal and propped on sticks, formed a small bivouac for two men. Both of these things are cold comfort on mountain tops.

The men, in fact, were suitably dressed and equipped for the northern edge of the Sinai Desert in October, and suffered accordingly.

20 November
Yeodiv
6th Mounted Brigade struggled slowly forward through Ur el Foka, and in the vicinity of Beitunia met organised resistance, which they were unable to brush aside before dark.

22nd Mounted Brigade sent one regiment forward from Ain Arik, directed upon Ram Allah. It reached halfway and found that Beitunia was held by a strong force of Turks, who were now interposed between the leading regiment of 22nd Mounted Brigade and the 6th Mounted Brigade.

The Horse Artillery could not accompany the cavalry at all, and the 20th Brigade R.H.A. was sent back out of the mountains to Ramleh.

75th Division captured Kuryet el Enab with the bayonet, and 52nd Division occupied Beit Dukka. Rain fell heavily and continuously throughout the day.

21 November 21 (See Plate X and Map A)
Yeodiv made last desperate efforts to reach Bire. 22nd Mounted Brigade got to within two miles, but the opposition at Ram Allah was too strong; it then tried to assist 6th Mounted Brigade in its attack on Beitunia, but the combined effort failed. The troops

were exhausted and severely handicapped with led horses; the camel mountain battery comprised their only artillery support.

At 15:00 hours, the Turks commenced to counterattack, and forced a partial withdrawal of 6th Mounted Brigade. Thereupon the Divisional Commander at last admitted failure to reach Bire and decided to withdraw his division during the night to Ur el Foka and Ur el Tahta, where they would be within reach of reinforcement and help from 52nd Division. All horses were sent back to Ur el Foka soon after 15:00 hours.

The withdrawal of personnel commenced at 19:30hours, and was successfully accomplished. All wounded were got safely away, and their convoys had all passed Ur el Foka by 02:00 hours on 22 November.

The enemy apparently were unaware of the withdrawal during the night and made no effort to follow up.

The casualties of Yeodiv during 21 November, as officially reported, were about 800 killed and wounded.

The total number of rifles deployed in the line by Yeodiv was never greater than 1,200.

Subsequent intelligence disclosed the fact that Beitunia had been held on this day by over 3,000 Turks with four batteries of 77s and some camel guns, and that these troops were well trained and fresh from Aleppo.

Comments

Military writers – English, French, American and German – have described the success of the British cavalry in the Palestine Campaign, and in particular the final operations in 1918, as a wonderful cavalry achievement. It is often obvious, however, that, being without local knowledge, they are wondering how the armament and fighting qualities of the Turk, and the degree of opposition put up by them in this campaign, compare with the opposition met by English, French and German cavalry in other theatres, in mobile operations.

The writer suggests that the only just basis upon which to form a conclusion lies in a comparison of the percentages of casualties suffered in relation to the number of troops engaged in operations of like nature; in this case, in mobile operations, i.e. in movement or in temporarily arrested movement, and with horses held by horseholders and close at hand.

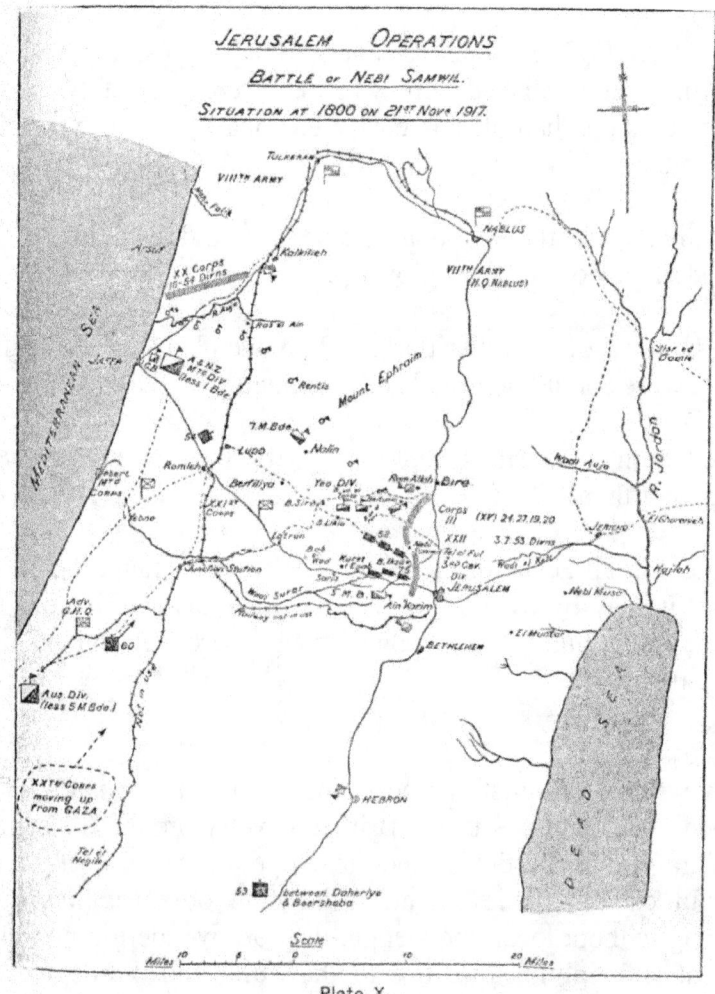

Plate X.

It may interest the reader to study the casualties of Yeodiv on 21 November from this point of view. Yeodiv, on that day, lost 800 killed and wounded out of 1,200 engaged. Is there any other example in the late war of a cavalry division – English, French or German – suffering such a high percentage of killed and wounded in one day in mobile operations?

In trying to find such an example, an officer will clearly come to realise the nature of the fight put up by Yeodiv on that day.

75th Division had secured Kustul by evening on 21 November, and Nebi Samwil, a position of the greatest importance because of the observation from it; from here, the eye can see the Mediterranean, Jerusalem and the Jordan valley.

During 22, 23 and 24 November, Yeodiv consolidated its position. On 25th all horses, except those required for machine guns, Hotchkiss rifles and packs, were sent back to Ramleh in the plain.

During these days, heavy fighting took place about Nebi Samwil. 75th and 52nd Divisions made two determined and gallant attacks on the hostile positions covering the main road to the north. The artillery, from lack of roads could not give adequate support to the infantry, and both attacks failed.

It was now evident that a period of preparation and organisation would be necessary before Jerusalem could be cut off from the north. The two worn out divisions of XXI Corps consolidated their positions and awaited relief by the fresh divisions of XX Corps.

Much had been accomplished. Had the passes from the plain into the mountains not been taken with a rush, the enemy would have had time to reorganise his defences in the western foothills, and the conquest of the plateau would have been slow, costly and precarious. As it was, positions had been won from which the final attack could be prepared and delivered with good prospects of success.

Yeodiv, however, was in a very critical position. Only 1,000 rifles were now available to hold more than 7 miles of front (one man to 12 yards). A gap of over 5 miles existed from its left at Ur el Tahta to the right of the outpost line of 54th Division about Shilta. The troops were exhausted with many days' hard hill-fighting and great physical exertions. The rocky precipitous ridges, separated by deep wadis, rendered the reinforcement of a threatened part of the line a matter of several hours, so that sectors, and even posts, had to rely on their own resources to repel attack.

On the afternoon of 27 November, the enemy commenced his offensive. He first attacked, with 400 men and a howitzer battery, a forward post of 6th Mounted Brigade at Zeitoun, held by two officers and 60 O.R.s. During the afternoon the garrison suffered 57casualties (92 percent.), but still held on. 25 men were sent up from Foka to reinforce Zeitoun, but, such was the difficulty of the country, they took 2½ hours to cover the distance.

Meantime 200 Turks attacked the left of 8th Mounted Brigade just north-east of Beit Dukka. A deserter reported at least 2,000 Turks at Beitunia prepared to follow up these attacks. At nightfall the situation looked so threatening that the Divisional Commander asked that the despatch of Descorps Reserve, 7th Mounted Brigade, which had already been detailed to relieve one brigade of Yeodiv next day, might be accelerated.

This Brigade was rushed up from the plain during the night, and 52nd Division, which had been relieved by 60th Division and was withdrawing out of the mountains for a well-earned rest, was hurried back to come upon the left of Yeodiv, but did not arrive until 09:00 hours next day, 28 November.

At 06:30 hours, 28 November, 800 Turks suddenly developed a strong attack against the left of Yeodiv at Ur el Tahta. Fortunately, the Sherwood Rangers and South Notts Hussars, of 7th Mounted Brigade, had arrived and were massed behind the left, and there is no doubt that their arrival saved Yeodiv from disaster. The Turkish rush was stopped at very close quarters, but not until the Turks had got temporary command of the communications to the rear and had exterminated a portion of the Brigade Ammunition Column, which was coming up with ammunition, but without escort. Two of the Mounted Brigade Headquarters fought all day at such close quarters that all their pistol ammunition was expended.

Heavy fighting continued throughout the day; the Turks overwhelmed the gallant post on Zeitoun, and 8th Mounted Brigade was forced out of Ur el Foka.

The horses of 7th Mounted Brigade were a great handicap in the mountain ravine, and the official report states that, in each of two regiments, 100 horses were killed by shellfire.

During 29 November, the Turks continued to attack, but reserves were arriving, and the crisis came to an end.

Arrangements were made for 74th Division and 52nd Division to relieve Yeodiv during the night of 29–30 November, while Ausdiv was hurried up from Mejdel, where they had been resting by the sea, and filled the gap on the left of 52nd Division by establishing a line Beit Sira-El Burj.

In the early hours of 30 November, Yeodiv left the line, after 10 days' very heavy fighting, intense exertion, and great discomfort. With never more than 1,200 rifles in the line, Yeodiv had suffered, during these days, 499 casualties.

The exceptionally fine behaviour of this division, and the importance of its achievement, were thoroughly appreciated throughout the force. The division marched back to bivouac in the plain at the site of its former great triumph at El Mughar.

Ref. Plate XI and Map A
Ausdiv worked hard to prepare a defensive position in

anticipation of attack. Big stones were collected and made into sangars, as it was too rocky to dig. The three R.H.A. Batteries covered the position. All the horses were sent down into the plain.

At 01:20 hours on 1 December, the attack fell on the junction of the 3rd and 4th A.L.H. Brigades; confused fighting resulted, but as dawn broke it was seen that the enemy was in a cup under crossfire and had suffered immense casualties. They were counter-attacked, surrounded and taken prisoner. 112 unwounded and 60 wounded prisoners were taken, and over 100 dead were buried. The casualties in Ausdiv were five officers and 47 O.R.s.

It was subsequently established that 190th Assault Battalion of the 19th Turkish Division, picked troops, 500 strong, had started out on this attack. Turkish deserters declared later that none ever came back, and that the mysterious and complete disappearance of a whole battalion had a very bad morale effect.

The Maritime Plain (Plate X)
ANZAC Division, during the fortnight 17 November to 1 December, were busily employed in containing the remnants of Turkish VIII Army, which had withdrawn north along the plain of Sharon.

The enemy allowed ANZAC Division to press them over the Nahr el Auja, but counter-attacked heavily to maintain the northern bank. The line (see Map A) Yahudie-Jerisheh-south bank of the Auja to the sea was consolidated in expectation of a general counter-offensive by the Turks in the plain, but the attack did not materialise. The 54th Division came up into the line, which stabilised across the plain.

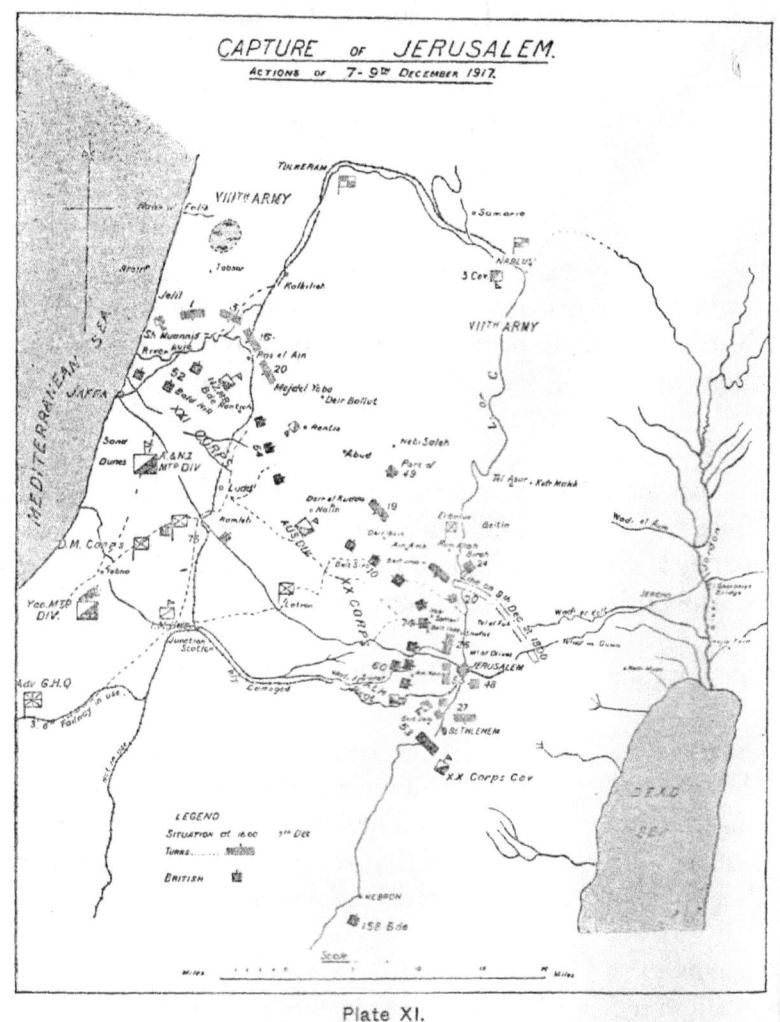

Plate XI.

Capture of Jerusalem (Plate XI)
During the first week in December, the final preparations for the taking of Jerusalem were completed.

The 60th, 74th and 10th Divisions of XX Corps, well rested, had relieved the war-worn XXI Corps. 53rd Division had advanced from Beersheba along the watershed to cooperate in the attack, and contact between it and 60th Division at Ain Karim was established by the 10th A.L.H. Regiment, detached from Ausdiv.

The assault commenced at dawn on 8 December. By the morning of 9 December, Jerusalem was isolated, with the roads cut on the south, east and north, and at noon, the enemy surrendered the city.

Stabilisation
During the last weeks of December the C-in-C attacked in the plain with XXI Corps, and astride the Jerusalem-Nablus road with XX Corps, in order to drive the enemy back out of gun range of Jerusalem and Jaffa, and of the main road joining those two places.

These operations were successful in both cases, and Von Falkenhayn's great counterattack in the mountains, intended to retake Jerusalem, was smashed to pieces most brilliantly by XX Corps, who buried more than 1,000 Turks.

The line now stabilised as follows (Plate XII and Map A):

XX Corps
53rd Division astride the Jerusalem-Jericho road; 60th Division astride the Jerusalem-Nablus road near ElJib;74th Division on the approximate line Foka-Tahta-Shilta; Ausdiv still in the mountains at Nalin, but about to be withdrawn to the sea.

XXI Corps
75th, 54th and 52nd Divisions on the general line Beit Nebala-Nebi Tari-in front of Mulebbis-El Haram (on the coast).

The Relief of Descorps (Map A)
Descorps
By the end of the first week in January the entire corps – Yeodiv, Ausdiv, ANZAC Division, 7th Mounted Brigade and I.C. Brigade –had been withdrawn from the line and had moved southwards to the sea to rest, re-equip and train; Yeodiv, Ausdiv and 7th Mounted Brigade at Deir el Belah, south of Gaza; ANZAC Division at Esdud, near the mouth of the Nahr Sukerier.

It was obvious that the front had stabilised. The fact that the Turkish right rested on the sea and its left in difficult mountainous country, with still more mountainous country away to the east across the Jordan valley (see Plate XII) gave little promise of facility for outflanking movements by large cavalry forces. The idea arose that cavalry exploitation in the future would be through a gap made in the enemy's front rather than round his flank. The training at Belah, consequently, dealt mainly with the exploitation of the action of the other arms on a battlefront, and with the passage of a defile.

Immediately on reaching Belah, the G.O.C. Ausdiv applied to the G.O.C. Descorps to arm the 3rd and 4th A.L.H. Brigades of his division with the sword, in addition to the rifle and bayonet. He expressed the firm conviction that his A.L.H. had been severely handicapped, during the cavalry pursuit from Beersheba to Junction Station, for want of an *arme blanche* weapon.

The Corps Commander decided to put the question to the vote.

The three brigade commanders of the 1st and 2nd A.L.H. Brigades and of the N.Z.M.R. Brigade of ANZAC Division voted against the sword; the writer presumes, but cannot be certain, that the regimental commanders of these three brigades held the same opinion as their brigade commanders. The two brigade commanders of the 3rd and 4th A.L.H. Brigades of Ausdiv (the other brigade being 5th Mounted Brigade, armed with a sword and not concerned in this voting) voted for the sword; the six Australian regimental commanders of these two brigades were in solid agreement with their brigade commanders.

The G.O.C. Descorps decided, as two Australian and one New Zealand Brigade had voted against, and only two Australian brigades for, the sword; that swords should not be issued.

The G.O.C. Ausdiv, of course, accepted this decision loyally. He realised, however, that pursuit might again come in the maritime plain, and that the most suitable form of attack might be the mounted attack. He therefore trained his division in the use of the bayonet as an *arme blanche* weapon.

Dummy-thrusting courses and dummy-charging scaffolds were built, and all the junior Australian officers were taught to use the bayonet as a sword. In the Divisional Sports, skill-at-arms competitions were held, and the Australians with the bayonet competed against Yeomanry with the sword, and they held their own. The Corps Commander attended these competitions and was most interested in the results.

20. PHASE IV, OPERATIONS ACROSS JORDAN
Ref. Map B and Plate XII.

Position in February 1918
Turkish XX Corps, with Headquarters at Jericho, held a strong position astride the Jerusalem-Jericho road, approximately on the line Kaneitera-Jebel Kalimum-Talat ed Dumm and joining up with the Turkish III Corps, which had its main strength just north of Bire astride the Jerusalem-El Lubban road. 60th Division was astride the Jerusalem-Jericho road, opposed by 5,000 rifles, while to the north another 2,000 rifles were in a position to act against the left flank of the 60th Division if it advanced.

Any advance northwards was out of the question for the time being. Roads and communications had to be constructed in forward areas; stores of supplies and ammunition had to be accumulated; the railways were advancing very slowly owing to spells of wet weather. Moreover, before a further advance northwards could be made it was necessary to drive the enemy across the river Jordan and so render the right flank secure. The possession of the crossings over the Jordan offered three advantages. These were:

(a) The enemy would be prevented from raiding the tract of country to the west of the Dead Sea.
(b) Control of the Dead Sea would be obtained.
(c) A point of departure would be gained for operations eastwards with a view to interrupting the enemy's line of communications to the Hejaz, in conjunction with the Arab forces based on Akaba, in the Red Sea.

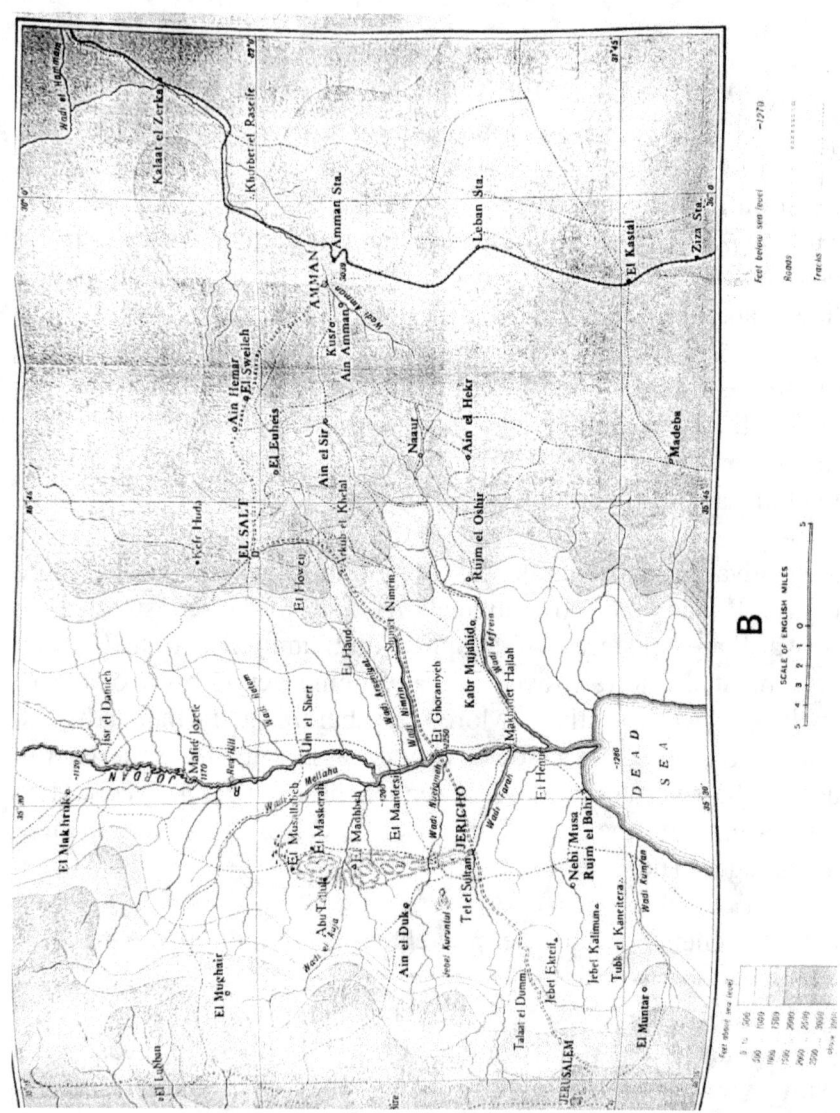

The Commander-in-Chief therefore decided to carry out the advance down into the Jordan valley, the limits of the advance being the Jordan on the east and Wadi el Auja on the north. This wadi joins the Jordan 8 miles north of the point where the Jordan enters the Dead Sea.

The chief obstacle to the advance lay in the difficulties of the ground. The descent from the vicinity of Jerusalem to the valley of the Jordan is very steep and the beds of the main wadis run from west to east. Their banks are often precipitous, rendering any crossing from one bank to the other impossible. The descent to the Jordan valley from the line then held by the 60th Division is not, however, continuous. It is interrupted by a series of ridges, which afforded the enemy strong defensive positions, and opposite the right of the 60th Division El Muntar formed a conspicuous landmark overlooking all the country in the vicinity. After a big fall down from Jerusalem, the ground again rose at Talat ed Dumm. This rise continued in a south-easterly direction to Jebel Ekteif and Nebi Musa, descending from there sharply to the Jordan valley; to the west of Jericho, at Jebel Kuruntul, the hill on which Christ was tempted, the ground falls in sheer cliffs to the Jordan valley.

Plan
The general plan consisted of a direct advance by the 60th Division to the cliffs overlooking Jericho. ANZAC Division, without artillery or any other wheels, was to cooperate on the right flank, with a view to entering the Jordan valley near Nebi Musa and cutting off the enemy's retreat from Jericho.

Narrative
19 February
The operations started. By 9 a.m., 60th Division had captured El Muntar, which enabled ANZAC Division to concentrate behind it, preparatory to operating against the enemy's left.

20 February
60th Division captured Talat ed Dumm. After a pause to enable guns to be brought forward, a further advance of 2,000 yards was made. On the right, about Jeb el Ekteif, great opposition was met. Moreover, the ground over which the attack had to take place proved the most rugged and difficult yet met with in Palestine; however, soon after midday, Jebel Ekteif was stormed. In the meantime, ANZAC Division, on the right, had encountered considerable opposition, and had been much hampered by the difficulties of the ground. The N.Z.M.R. Brigade struggled forward all day, but they were finally checked by heavy fire from Nebimusa; but, in the meantime, 1st A.L.H. Brigade had been reconnoitring down the Wadi Kumran, and a troop had got through to the edge of the Dead Sea, the whole brigade following; by 1800 hours they were concentrated at the mouth of the Wadi Kumran. The chief feature of the enemy's resistance during the day had been the volume of machine gunfire.

21 February
1st A.L.H. Brigade, advancing north along the plain, entered Jericho at 08:20 hours, the enemy having withdrawn during the night. 60th Division advanced to the cliffs overlooking Jericho. Meanwhile patrols from 1st A.L.H. Brigade reconnoitred north to the Wadi el Auja and to El Ghoraniyeh bridge. The enemy was found to be holding the high ground north of the Auja and a bridgehead on the right bank of the Jordan covering the Ghoraniyeh bridge, with guns on the left bank. As a direct attack on the bridgehead would have involved heavy losses without compensating advantages, it was not attempted.

60th Division was withdrawn to a line running north and south through Talat ed Dumm, leaving outposts on the cliffs overlooking Jericho. ANZAC Division, leaving one regiment to patrol the Jordan valley, returned to Bethlehem. On no previous occasion had such difficulties of ground been encountered. As an instance of this, a Field Artillery Battery took 86 hours to reach Nebi Musa, a distance, as the crow flies, of only 8 miles. The Royal Air Force rendered very valuable service throughout the operations, but mist and low-lying clouds interrupted their work to a great extent.

Improving the Position.

This operation had rendered the right flank secure, but the base thus obtained was not sufficiently broad to permit of operations being carried out across the Jordan against the Hedjaz railway. Before such operations were possible, it was necessary for the XX Corps to capture Abu Tellul, a strongpoint in the Jordan valley, and to push north along the backbone of the mountains to a point 10 miles north of Bire. This was successfully accomplished by 11 March.

The Amman Raid
The Jordan valley had now been sufficiently cleared of the enemy to enable operations to be carried out against the Turkish line of communications to the Hedjaz, in conjunction with the Arab forces under Feisal, which were operating in the country to the south-east of the Dead Sea and under Lord Allenby's control.

Feisal, since January 1918, had met with a great deal of success, and had drawn large Turkish forces south along the Hedjaz railway. The situation to the east of the Jordan thus presented a favourable opportunity for a raid towards Amman against the enemy's communications with the Hedjaz. The C-in-C therefore decided to carry out such an operation in February. To really assist Feisal, it would be necessary to damage the railway seriously, and the object of the raid was to destroy the viaduct and tunnel at Amman. Even if the railway was only temporarily interrupted, the threat would compel the enemy to maintain considerable forces to cover Amman; the Turkish troops available to operate against the Arabs would be reduced, and possibly the enemy might transfer a portion of his reserves from west to east of the Jordan, thereby weakening his ability to make, or meet, an attack on the main front. Amman is 80 miles east by north of Jericho as the crow flies. The nature of the intervening country varies to a marked degree. From the bank of the Jordan to the ridges, 1 mile east of the river the ground is flat, and after rain, becomes marshy. Beyond these ridges, the country is covered with scrub and intersected by numerous wadis; but for 5 miles east of Jordan, until the foothills are reached, the valley is comparatively flat and good going for cavalry. In the next 12 miles, the ground rises some 8,500 feet, till the edge of the plateau of Moabis reached about Naaur and Aines Sir. The hills are rugged and steep, and the main wadis descend from the plateau to the Jordan in deep valleys.

The plateau itself is undulating and the lower portion of it marshy after rain. Immediately west of Amman there lies a cultivated plain extending 2 miles west and 4 miles north-west of the town. The Turks had constructed a metalled road from Ghoraniyeh bridge to Es Salt and Amman, which winds up through the hills from Shunet Nimrin, supported by embankments, in places 20 feet high. This main road was the only real road east of Jordan, and was in bad repair. At Es Salt, a town of some 15,000 inhabitants, it was joined, according to agents, by tracks leading from the fords over the Jordan at Mandesi, Um es Sher and Jisr ed Damieh, and by a track from the north. To the south of Es Salt various tracks follow the wadis to the plateau, and are now known to be unfit for wheeled traffic. One passes to Amman through Naaur; another from Shunet Nimrin through Ain es Sir.

Narrative
The force detailed to carry out the raid, under the command of the G.O.C. 60th Division, consisted of 60th Division, ANZAC Division, Imperial Camel Brigade, a Mountain Artillery brigade, a Light Armoured Car brigade, and a Heavy Battery. 60th Division was to force the crossing over the Jordan and advance astride the metalled road to Es Salt, which it was to hold, its left flank being protected by 1st A.L.H. Brigade. The remainder of ANZAC Division and the Imperial Camel Brigade, following 60th Division across the Jordan, were to move direct on Amman through Ain es Sir and Naaur. On reaching Amman the railway was to be destroyed and the viaduct and tunnel demolished. This

having been accomplished, the mounted troops were to withdraw on the 60th Division, the whole force then withdrawing to form a bridgehead on the east side of the Jordan.

The Passage of the Jordan

The crossing of the Jordan took place during the night of 21–22 March. The attempt to cross at El Ghoraniyeh failed owing to the strength of the current, which prevented all attempts to cross both by swimming and by means of rafts and pontoons. At Makhadet Hajlah the swimmers succeeded in reaching the opposite bank at 01:20 hours on the 22nd, and by 07:45 hours the leading battalion was across. Until dawn, this crossing was unperceived by the enemy, but subsequently troops had to be ferried across and a bridge constructed under fire. The bridge was completed at 08:30 hours and further troops crossed, but it was found impossible to enlarge the bridgehead until dark owing to the enemy's fire and the thickness of the scrub. A further attempt to cross at El Ghoraniyeh during the night of the 22–23 was again frustrated by the current and the enemy's fire.

Early in the morning, however, the Auckland Mounted Rifle Regiment, having crossed at Hajlah, charged and captured a Turkish post opposite that place. They then turned north, swept up the east side of the river, and galloped to Ghoraniyeh, capturing various parties of infantry and machine guns, which had prevented our infantry crossing. One troop moving northwards nearer the hills, encountered 60 Turkish cavalry making for Kabr Mujahid. The Turks tried to charge the troop, and in the hand-to-hand combat that ensued the Turks lost 20 killed and 7 prisoners, and fled in all directions. Two squadrons of this regiment attempted to rush Shunet Nimrin, but were met by heavy artillery and machine gun fire and had to withdraw and form a bridgehead east of El Ghoraniyeh.

Three bridges were constructed during the day, and the whole force crossed, but owing to the swollen state of the river valuable time had been lost.

On 24 March, 60th Division forced the entrance to the pass at Shunet Nimrin, and by the evening of 25 March, had occupied Es Salt without further opposition.

In the meantime, at about 15:00 hours on 24th, 2nd A.L.H. Brigade had started up the hills by the track to Naaur accompanied by Ayrshire Battery, R.H.A., and all the Brigade wheels, including L.G.S. wagons with explosives; ANZAC Division Headquarters and Divisional Troops, including Somerset Battery, R.H.A., with the Imperial Camel Brigade in rear, followed the 2nd A.L.H. Brigade. It was just dark, and the road was already becoming difficult, when a message came back from the 2nd A.L.H. Brigade to say that wheels could go no further. This was a serious blow. A French priest, who had lived in Madeba, had previously stated that he had driven his carriage by this road, but his information was now proved to be quite false. A long halt therefore took place while explosives were transferred to the emergency camels, which had been provided against such an eventuality. The batteries and all wheels had to be left with an escort, with orders to march to Shunet Nimrin as as soon as it was light enough to see.

The march of the column continued up the mountain; the track became more and more difficult; for the men on foot and leading their horses it was bad, for the camels it was far worse. At 16:20 hours it began to rain, and it became intensely cold with a strong wind. This increased and as the column climbed higher, a gale began. The path, bad enough in fine weather, became very slippery. A tone point it went up the face of a rocky cliff up which the camels were only got with the greatest difficulty.

In the early part of the night large bodies of friendly Arabs had joined the column, but as the conditions grew worse they gradually disappeared.

At 04:00 hours the moon went down, just as the head of the column reached the top of the hills. In the pitch darkness no movement was possible, and the whole force stood in a storm of wind and sleet strung out in single file for about 8 miles along the face of the mountains; the gale never ceased for a moment, and although the head of the column had reached the top at 04:00 hours, the last camel was not up until 19:30 hours.

At 09:30, the head of the column started on again, still in the pouring rain. The country was a morass in many places, and many of the camel-drivers collapsed with the cold, several being brought in dead on their camels.

At 21:30, Naaur was passed. A thick fog came on, and at 05:00 hours on 26 March the column by chance ran into the N.Z.M.R. Brigade at Ain es Sir. The 2nd A.L.H. Brigade pushed forward across the Es Salt-Amman road about El Swileh, and captured 170 prisoners and a number of motor-lorries. It was intended to push on to Amman at once, but the men were completely worn out by three days and nights without rest under appalling conditions. Orders were therefore issued for a night's rest, followed by an advance on Amman next day.

During the night, parties with explosives were sent out north and south of Amman to cut the railway. The southern party was successful in carrying out minor demolitions, but the northern party encountered the enemy and was driven off.

By the evening of 27 March, N.Z.M.R. Brigade had reached the railway south of Amman; in the centre and on the north respectively, the Imperial Camel Brigade and 2nd A.L.H. Brigade failed to reach the railway, being heavily counter-attacked, but during the night a demolition party succeeded in blowing up a small bridge north of Amman.

On 28 March, a brigade of the 60th Division arrived from Es Salt, accompanied by Mountain Artillery. The so-called metalled road was too soft to admit of field guns being brought up; in fact, 22 Turkish motor-lorries and other vehicles found along the road were so embedded in the mud that they could not be removed, and had to be destroyed.

On its arrival this brigade attacked astride the Es Salt-Amman road, the 2nd A.L.H. Brigade attacking on its left and the Imperial Camel Brigade on its right, while the N.Z.M.R. Brigade attacked Hill 8089, just south of Amman. The attack failed, and the enemy launched a counterattack. On 29 March, Turkish reinforcements arrived, and the counterattacks were renewed, but without success. During the afternoon two more battalions of 60th Division and a battery of R.H.A. arrived from Es Salt, after a long and arduous march.

The attack on Amman was renewed on 8 March and the N.Z.M.R. Brigade captured part of Hill 8089; parties of New Zealanders entered the village, but were fired on from the houses; elsewhere the attack met with only slight success. It was apparent that, without greater artillery support, further attacks would only succeed at the cost of heavy losses.

Meanwhile, Turkish forces from Jisred Damieh and from the north had begun to make their presence felt against the remainder of the 60th Division at Es Salt. Orders were therefore issued for a withdrawal to take place during the night. This was carried out without interruption after all the wounded had been evacuated.

By the evening of 2 April, the whole force had recrossed the Jordan with the exception of troops left to hold the bridgehead on the east bank.

Results of the Raid
Although no permanent damage had been done to the Hedjaz railway, the raid had succeeded in drawing northwards, and retaining not only Turkish troops which had been operating against the Arabs on the eastern shore of the Dead Sea, but, in addition, a portion of the garrison of Maan, further to the south. Before the raid was carried out, the enemy's strength in the Amman-Es Salt-Shunet Nimrin area was approximately 4,000; by the middle of April, it had increased to over 8,000.

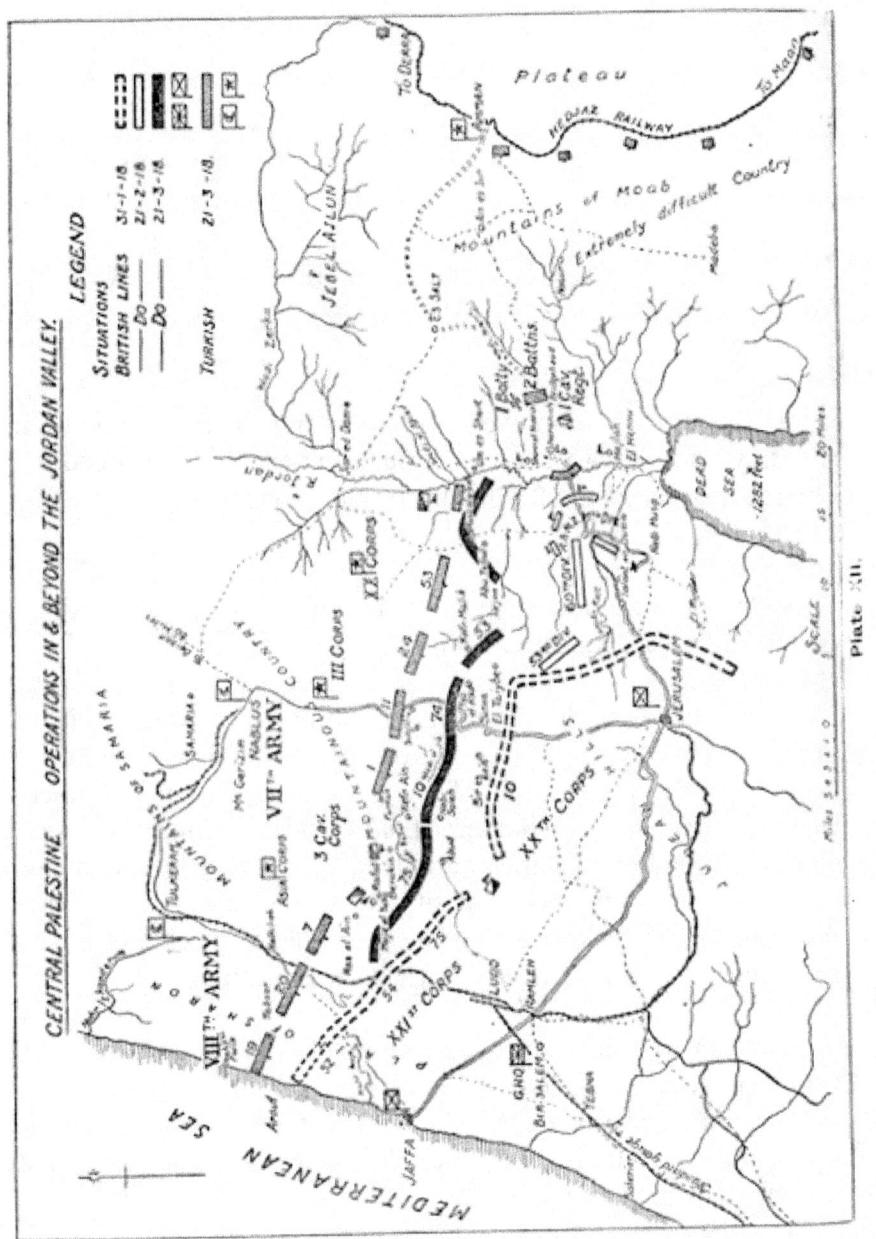

21. THE ES SALT RAID.
(Map B)

After the troops employed in the Amman raid had been withdrawn to the east bank of Jordan, the enemy reoccupied the Shunet Nimrin position, which they now held with some 5,000 rifles.

These troops were under the command of the G.O.C. Turkish IV Army, with its Headquarters at Es Salt.

The main position ran along the foothills from Kabr Mujahid through Shunet Nimrin and in front of El Haud, with its right resting on the wadi south of the Um es Shert-Es Salt track. Cavalry covered the southern flank, and the 2nd Caucasian Cavalry Brigade maintained an outpost line across the plain east of the Jordan from the right of the defensive position in the foothills to Um es Shert, at which, on the western side of the river, the Turkish 3rd Cavalry Division was located.

Turkish IV Army was comparatively isolated, and the Commander-in-Chief determined to seize the first opportunity to cut off and destroy the enemy's force at Shunet Nimrin, and, if successful, to hold Es Salt until the Arabs could advance and relieve the British troops.

Towards the end of April a deputation from the Beni Sakhr tribe arrived from over the Jordan, stating that the tribe was concentrated near Madeba ready to cooperate with any advance, provided it took place before 4 May, after which date their supplies would be finished and the tribe would have to disperse.

The troops available to carry out this raid were Descorps (less Yeodiv), 60th Division (less one Brigade), and the Imperial Service Cavalry and Imperial Service Infantry Brigades.

The 60th Division was to assault the enemy's position at Shunet Nimrin while the mounted troops, moving northwards from El Ghoraniyeh, were to turn east along the tracks leading from Um es Shert and Jisr ed Damieh and seize Es Salt.

In the previous raid, the only route found fit for wheeled transport between Amman and Shunet Nimrin had been the metalled road passing through Es Salt.

If the mounted troops could reach Es Salt, the main line of communications of the force at Shunet Nimrin would be severed, and this force would be dependent for its supplies on the track further south through Aines Sir.

This track was exposed to attack by the Beni Sakhr tribe. There appeared every chance, therefore, of the Turkish force at Shunet Nimrin being compelled to retreat under very difficult conditions, and a fair chance of its being captured.

Narrative
60th Division
On the morning of 8 April, 60th Division captured the advanced works of the Shunet Nimrin position, but were unable to make further progress in face of the stubborn resistance offered by the enemy.

Ausdiv, with 1st A.L.H. Brigade of the ANZAC Division attached, had one regiment, on 29 April, holding a thin extended outpost line facing the enemy's outpost, which ran from Um es Shert eastward to the foothills.

During the night the whole Division advanced from Jericho, crossed the bridges at Ghoraniyeh and assembled, in the darkness, 5 miles north of Ghoraniyeh, and just south of the wadi running into the Jordan, 2½ miles south of Um es Shert.

The Division lined up just before dawn in massed formation close behind its outpost regiment. This was a dangerous experiment, but successfully accomplished.

At dawn, 04:30, as soon as 50 yards could be seen, the 3rd and 4th A.L.H. Brigades started to gallop, and swept over the enemy's outposts.

The 5th Mounted Brigade, following close behind, turned east almost at once to try and find the way up the track, which had been reported as running from Um es Shert to Es Salt.

The 4th A.L.H. Brigade was to take up a position about Jisr ed Damieh to prevent the Turks crossing at that place and interfering with the operations.

The 3rd A.L.H. Brigade, on reaching Jisr ed Damieh, was to turn south-east and climb the mountainside to Es Salt, up the only track, which was known with certainty to exist.

The Horse Artillery Brigade accompanied the 4th A.L.H. Brigade. This Brigade, because it was not to leave the Jordan valley, took its wheeled transport and ambulance with it. The other brigades took only pack transport and camel and mule pack mountain guns (2.75 and 8.75).

The 3rd and 4th A.L.H. Brigades maintained a very rapid pace although shelled all the way. They reached the track near Jisr ed Damieh at 05:50 hours, i.e. they went 18 miles in one hour and 20 minutes, which is probably a record for a cavalry formation of such a size. The going the whole way to Jisr ed Damieh is quite good.

After the 3rd and 4th A.L.H. Brigades had passed, a regiment of the 1st A.L.H. Brigade attacked Red Hill, and, after considerable fighting, captured it.

Further Operations of Ausdiv
At 15:30 hours, the 4th A.L.H. Brigade was removed from the command of the G.O.C. Ausdiv, and came directly under the command of G.O.C. Descorps. G.O.C. Ausdiv retained command of the 3rd and 1st A.L.H. Brigades and 5th Mounted Brigade.

Throughout the day the 5th Mounted Brigade struggled up the track from Um es Shert to Es Salt. It was only suitable for donkeys; the men could not only not ride, but could not even lead their horses, and in the majority of cases the men held on to the tails of their horses, which pulled them up. The camels, carrying *cacolets* for evacuation of wounded, had to be sent back.

By nightfall 5th Mounted Brigade had reached the plateau, but was held up about 2 miles west of Es Salt.

Ausdiv Headquarters, 1st A.L.H. Brigade (less one Squadron, which stayed behind as garrison of Red Hill), and 2nd A.L.H. Brigade of ANZAC Division, which had now been put under G.O.C. Ausdiv, followed up the track behind 5th Mounted Brigade and bivouacked on the side of the mountain during the night.

Meanwhile the 3rdA.L.H.Brigade,advancing up the Jisr ed Damieh-Es Salt track, and accompanied by the Hong Kong and Singapore Battery, commenced to climb the mountain. This track proved to be a rocky mountain track impassable to wheeled traffic of any sort, but passable with difficulty for horses and camels in single file.

For the whole way the track was dominated by hills on either side, and a few determined riflemen and machine guns could have held up the column with the greatest ease.

No enemy was observed until the advance guard arrived almost at the top. Here, a scout noticed a saddle horse near the track; creeping up towards the horse, he came on three men and observed a troop of 15 cavalry some three hundred yards further on. The three-man post was evidently the advanced post of the cavalry troop.

Two Australian scouts got to within 25 yards before they were observed; finally one of the Turks was killed and the other two captured.

The scouts then fired on the cavalry troop; six of the Turks abandoned their horses and escaped on foot, the remainder escaping on their horses.

Two miles from Es Salt the enemy was found in occupation of a sangared position astride the track.

The advance guard had now climbed over 4,000 feet in 10 hours.

The enemy's position consisted of a high ridge about 1,000 yards long, and was held with rifles and machine guns.

The Australians opened fire with rifles and machine guns against this position but without apparent effect.

The Brigadier saw that immediate action was essential, and decided on a frontal assault. Time was getting on, and the camel guns were particularly slow in movement, and any flanking movement would have to be dismounted, as horses could not leave the track. He now intercepted a wireless message from Descorps to Ausdiv saying that Es Salt must be taken that evening.

Finally, the Brigadier managed to emplace 12 machine guns and 3 mountain guns. The enemy's lines could he enfiladed, and, under cover of this fire support, the 9th and both A.L.H. regiments made their attack.

The 8th A.L.H. regiment was retained, mounted, on the track, to dash through immediately the two leading regiments had got into the enemy's position.

The guns and machine guns opened rapid fire, and the stormers sprang forward down the steep rocky slopes and up similar slopes towards the enemy.

The conformation of the ground presented an unusually favourable opportunity for covering fire, allowing the men to get within 15 to 20 yards before it had to cease.

Many of the enemy bolted to the rear as the assaulting troops neared them, but a good number, amongst whom were German officers and men, fought to the last, and were bayoneted on the spot.

As the assaulting troops arrived on the crest of the enemy's position, the Brigadier ordered the 8th regiment to pursue. This they were able to do at the gallop, as the track improved very much as the plateau was reached.

The 8th regiment came upon a party of 50 Turks in sangars. A troop was at once despatched to get behind them, and the enemy fled. The 8th regiment then galloped on to Es Salt, which was entered at 18:30 hours.

A German staff officer, who spoke English, was endeavouring to organise resistance in the streets.

Lieutenant Foulkes Taylor, 10th A.L.H. Regiment, commanding the Advanced Troop, raced up to the German officer and demanded his surrender and that of his men. Lieutenant Taylor put 14 rounds from his own automatic and 2 clips from the German officer's pistol into the hesitating enemy and then smashed the pistol over the head of one of them.

The Brigadier reported as follows:
> The men of Lieutenant Taylor's Troop were using their bayonets as swords. One Sergeant got two on the point (sword in line). The general opinion was that they were not good for melee fighting – too blunt. They used them for striking. Swords would have been invaluable here. The men with revolvers, Hotchkiss gunners, were using them freely.

The streets and roads were full of mounted and dismounted enemy – 800 cavalry, 200 infantry, and all the miscellaneous personnel to be found in an Army Headquarters.

Lieutenant Taylor's troop raced on after lorries and limbers for two miles, causing great consternation, until he was finally held up by organised resistance of machine guns.

It was not possible to support this leading troop quickly, as it was only practicable to pass through the town in single file. This rapid pursuit by one troop, however, resulted in 200 prisoners, and Es Salt was firmly secured, with 860 prisoners and a motor-lorry company.

A senior German staff officer has stated that the Army Commander and Staff escaped in motors, with one minute to spare.

1 May
On 1 May, Ausdiv consolidated its position at Es Salt and sent out strong reconnaissances towards Amman; 5th Mounted Brigade, supported by 2nd A.L.H. Brigade, moved down the main road in an endeavour to attack the enemy's position about El Haud and Shunet Nimrin.

Meanwhile, in the valley, 4th A.L.H. Brigade had taken up a position facing the ford at Jisr ed Damieh, and at 08:00 hours on 1 May the Turks attacked in force, bringing their guns forward. Heavy Turkish reinforcements were observed coming up, and B

Battery, H.A.C. was withdrawn southwards. During its withdrawal one gun fell over a precipice and had to be abandoned.

At 10:00 the enemy attacked further to the south about Red Hill, and at 10:30 the Turks again attacked and drove in the northern flank.

At 11:30 hours, the Turks were only 200 yards away, and the situation had become critical.

The batteries still in the line, A Battery, H.A.C. and Notts Battery, R.H.A. continued in action, firing point-blank into the enemy.

The 4th Brigade, with its artillery, was, in fact, pinned with its back against the rocky foothills of the mountains, facing west.

The 4th A.L.H. Brigade fought stubbornly in withdrawal, but was in great difficulties owing to the steep gullies and gorges, down which many animals fell and perished.

The Brigade finally fought their way out, but the eight guns and a considerable number of L.G.S. wagons could not be got away, and the Brigade field ambulance was also captured.

By noon the Brigade had, by stubborn fighting, stopped the enemy just north of the Um es Shert-Es Salt track, but that track was under the enemy's rifle fire.

The situation was obviously serious, because this track was now the only means of supplying, reinforcing, or withdrawing the four Brigades of Ausdiv at Es Salt.

The N.Z.M.R. Brigade and 6th Mounted Brigade were rushed up to support 4th A.L.H. Brigade, and prevent the enemy from actually getting astride the track. This they succeeded in
doing, but the enemy still remained within rifle range of it.

Meanwhile, the enemy was bringing up large reinforcements from Amman and Jisr ed Damieh against Ausdiv at Es Salt, and the Beni Sakhr tribe had failed to take the action that had been expected.

This left the Ain es Sir track open to the Turks, and the Shunet Nimrin garrison, instead of being an isolated body of troops, formed the south claw of a formidable pair of pincers, with which the enemy threatened to cut off Ausdiv at Es Salt.

60th Division made several gallant attempts to relieve the situation by capturing the Turkish position at Shunet Nimrin, but failed completely, as the position was of great strength.

After having cleared their way of advance from Jisr ed Damieh towards Es Salt, the Turks made an attack at 20:00 on 2 May, against 8rdA.L.H.Brigadenear Kefr Huda.

In spite of constant repulses, the Turkish 66th Regiment came on again at 20:30 hours,againat03:00, and again at 04:00.On the failure of the last attack, the Turks were chased down hill by both A.L.H. regiments with bombs, and retreated nearly a mile.

The 8thA.L.H.regiment, covering the main road from Es Salt to Amman, was attacked at dawn by fresh troops from Amman. These Turks were vigorously counter-attacked by the 8th A.L.H. regiment, and lost 819 prisoners.

The 5th Mounted Brigade found their line of advance from Es Salt down the main road to Shunet Nimrin so rough as to be impassable in the face of opposition.

During this day it became obvious that Ausdiv at Es Salt was surrounded by strong enemy forces, and it appeared that it would be difficult to withdraw them without serious loss.

Towards evening G.O.C. Ausdiv was told to try to withdraw.

Immediately after dark the withdrawal commenced, regiment leap-frogging back through regiment, brigade through brigade. One regiment of each brigade remained out in their forward position in touch with the enemy until 01:00.

Soon after dawn on 4 May, the entire four brigades were out of danger. The pack convoys and wounded on camels, had been successfully evacuated, only two moribund cases being left in Es Salt.

The enemy followed up early next morning, but the system employed, that of each body in rear leap-frogging through a fresh body behind, completely defeated the enemy's infantry. As the column wound its way down the mountain tracks, it was shelled, and attacked by five aeroplanes, two of which were shot down by the troops.

By the evening of 4 May all the troops had recrossed the Jordan, bridgeheads being left to cover the bridge at El Ghoraniyeh and the ford at the mouth of the Wadi Mellaha, just north of Mandesiford.

Although the destruction of the Turkish force at Shunet Nimrin had not been effected, the enemy's losses were heavy, Ausdiv capturing about 900 men.

The raid had undoubtedly rendered the enemy apprehensive of further operations east of the Jordan, and compelled him, therefore, to maintain considerable forces in the Amman-Shunet Nimrin area, thus reducing the forces available to meet the Arab menace to the south or British activity in the maritime plain.

There is little doubt that his fear of Lord Allenby's 'Long Arm,' i.e. his Mounted Corps, was not lessened.

The enemy thoroughly appreciated the achievement of Ausdiv in these operations.

The enemy reported to Yilderim Headquarters by wireless, 'Es Salt was captured by the reckless and dashing gallantry of the Australian Cavalry.'

Comments on the Action of Large Cavalry Formations in Hill Warfare

The achievements of Descorps in the hills and mountains are interesting and important.

The value of cavalry in such country was not previously recognised, and the Turks learnt by the three big mounted raids – Yeodiv into Jude An in November 1917, and ANZAC Division and Ausdiv into Moab in March and April 1918 – that the more difficult the country the more dangerous became Lord Allenby's Mounted Corps.

The Turks had little fear that large infantry forces would come up these tracks. If they did come, they must necessarily come slowly owing to the difficulties of transport and supply, and time would be available in which to meet them.

The Turks themselves could not well maintain protective troops on all these tracks because of the difficulties of supplying them; but they now learnt that British cavalry, if unopposed, could scramble somehow up the mountains, and scramble up so quickly that the blow had fallen before it was even suspected.

The difficulties of supply did not stop them; the horse is a strong animal, and three days' supply for man and horse could be carried on the saddle.

It became obvious to the Turks of the ability of large cavalry forces to move quickly over ground which no other arm can cross except infantry, and they but slowly, opened up the possibility of a serious disaster.

If Yeodiv, in November 1917, had succeeded in getting astride the Turkish lines of communication at Bire on the Jerusalem-

Nablus road, and in taking up a defensive position there, the Turks to the south would have been hard put to it to shake them off.

ANZAC Division failed by very little to destroy the Amman Viaduct. Success would have had most serious results to the Turkish forces operating far to the south.

The sudden appearance of Ausdiv, and their capture of Army Headquarters at Es Salt, came as a thunderbolt. The Um es Shert-Es Salt track had been considered impassable by the Turks, and was not even guarded.

Lord Allenby's employment of large cavalry forces in such a country has clearly shown that not only is cavalry the most valuable arm for such operations but that it has not, nor will have, any competitor.

Their future in this role, and incidentally in all others, lies in close cooperation with the air. The cavalry is the 'Long Arm,' the aeroplane the 'Long Eye,' and probably the method of supply. At Es Salt, Ausdiv was supplied with medical comforts by air. In Palestine, aeroplanes succeeded in picking up written messages from cavalry without landing, by means of grappling hooks.

Lord Allenby has written:
> We used to hear, especially in peace manoeuvres, that such and such a tract of country was suited to cavalry action. The truth is that cavalry can, and will, fit its tactics to any country. This has been shown repeatedly during the war just ended; in the rocky hills of Jude An .... and the mountains of Moab.

The success of these raids into Moab must not be judged only by their material results.

Liman von Sanders was himself a cavalry soldier; this fact probably proved to his own disadvantage and led him to overestimate the power of Descorps to obtain material results. He began to fear a raid on Deraa, 50 miles north of Amman, the most vital point of all his communications, and through which his entire force was maintained. He appears to have been convinced that Lord Allenby intended to break through via Amman to Deraa.

He reinforced his IV Army in its main position astride the road at Shunet Nimrin, making it practically equal in strength to VII and VIII Turkish Armies west of the Jordan.

In doing so he stretched his force on a front of 62 miles, thus weakening it everywhere; to maintain such a front he lowered his G.H.Q. reserves to a more than dangerous minimum, as the sequel proved.

Judged in the light of their influence on subsequent events, these raids into Moab illustrate, in a unique way, the ultimate possibilities of the strategic cavalry raid.

Despatch of Troops to France
The despatch of troops to France, and the consequent reorganisation of the E.E.F., prevented further operations on a large scale being undertaken, and rendered necessary the adoption of a policy of active defence.

The 52nd and 74th Divisions sailed for France, and the 8rd (Lahore) and 7th (Meerut) Divisions came from Mesopotamia to replace them.

In addition, Yeodiv was broken up, and nine Yeomanry regiments, five and a half siege batteries, ten British battalions, and five machine gun companies were withdrawn from the line preparatory to embarkation for France.

The British battalions were replaced by Indian battalions from India, without war experience.

The Yeomanry regiments were replaced by Indian cavalry with war experience, from France.

After the reorganisation Descorps was certainly no weaker than before, and consisted as follows :

ANZAC Division.
1stA.L.H.Brigade,2ndA.L.H.Brigade,N.Z.M.R. Brigade; no change.

Ausdiv
3rd A.L.H. Brigade, 4th A.L.H. Brigade, 5th Mounted Brigade (now to consist of one Yeomanry regiment and two Indian cavalry regiments).

4th Cavalry Division.
10th Cavalry Brigade, 11th Cavalry Brigade, 12th Cavalry Brigade, each consisting of one Yeomanry regiment and two Indian cavalry regiments.

5th Cavalry Division.
14th Cavalry Brigade, 15th Cavalry Brigade; the former consisting of a Yeomanry regiment and two Indian cavalry regiments; and the last-named Brigade of three Imperial Service Indian cavalry regiments.

Imperial Camel Brigade (about to be broken up).

The Corps, as can be seen, now consisted of two cavalry divisions and two mounted divisions; the Ausdiv and ANZAC Division being mounted rifles; the 4th and 5th Cavalry Divisions being cavalry.

The operations in this country proved conclusively how much greater value has the cavalry division of three cavalry brigades and divisional troops than have three independent cavalry brigades, even though each of those brigades be well found with battery R.H.A., field ambulance, field troop, mobile veterinary section, et cetera. It is hoped that those responsible for the organisation of our cavalry in future will not fail to realise this fact.

The British, during the late war, at one time maintained nine cavalry or mounted divisions; but in Mesopotamia, even up to the end, the value of the cavalry divisional organisation, as compared to the system of unallotted brigades, does not appear to have been understood.

During this stationary warfare, even after the reorganisation was complete, the young troops, especially those from India, had to be trained.

Owing to the necessity for training, and to the fact that the serious situation in France did not admit of active operations elsewhere, the E.E.F. consolidated its position during the summer.

XXI Corps in the maritime plain was deeply dug in, with its left about Arsuf.

XX Corps linked up with the right of XXI Corps and, with many gaps in the line owing to the impassability of the country in many places, held strong 'localities across the Jude An Mountains, the positions consisting mostly of stone sangars.' The right of XX Corps rested on the cliffs looking down into the Jordan valley just south of the Wadi el Auja.

The task of holding the Jordan valley and of containing IV Turkish Army east of the Jordan was given to Descorps.

The frontage maintained, from the Dead Sea northwards, up the Wadi Mellaha and thence westward through El Musallabeh, and from there thrown back by Abu Tellul to the Wadi Auja, amounted to 25 miles. Opposite that front, both east and west of Jordan, the enemy disposed approximately 8,000 rifles, 2,000 sabres and 90 guns.

Throughout the summer, while two cavalry divisions were holding the valley in the blazing heat and suffocating dust, the other two were resting either on the cool tops of the Jude An Mountains or in the coastal plain near the sea.

Ausdiv and ANZAC Division alternately held the northern sector, from Mandesi, up the Mellaha and through Musallabeh to the foot of the mountains, where the Wadi Auja came out through precipitous cliffs.

The 4th and 5th Cavalry Divisions alternately maintained bridgeheads on the east side of Jordan, covering the crossings at El Henu, Hajlah, and Ghoraniyeh.

The sectors were held by a minimum of dismounted personnel and a maximum of automatic weapons, strongly dug in in defended localities. Each defended locality was small in extent, but strong.

The greater proportion of each Division was kept well in the rear with its horses, and mobile ready to move, mounted, at the shortest notice to counterattack.

The gaps between the defended localities extended to as much as 2or 3 miles in many cases. It was recognised that the enemy could penetrate into these gaps with comparative ease if he wished.

It was intended that the defended localities should hold fast, and that the mobile reserves should pivot on them in carrying out their counter-offensive.

It is thought that, in the defence of such a big frontage by two cavalry divisions, this system of defence was the most powerful that cavalry can employ. In addition, it is a system under which a cavalry corps can hope to maintain a big sector for a long period in stationary warfare without serious deterioration.

Deterioration of mounted troops increases with the number of men placed in defended localities, and consequently away from their horses, but where the great majority of the men and officers are continually considering and practising mounted movements with a view to counterattack, the deterioration is comparatively small.

Some officers have said that cavalry should not be employed in the line in stationary warfare.

The cavalry arm would be very unwise to support such an idea. The cavalryman should be, and can be, the handyman of the army, to whom nothing comes amiss. The remainder of an army is bound to lose confidence in an arm, which states that it will deteriorate unduly if employed in stationary warfare. It is not true, and Lord Allenby proved it in the Jordan valley during the months of May, June, July, August and September 1918.

The maintenance of so many horses in the Jordan valley, supplied by motor-lorry down the steep mountain road from Jerusalem, was most expensive from every point of view. Without doubt, the Jordan front could have been maintained more economically by using infantry, but it is presumed that the Commander-in-Chief maintained that front with cavalry for a specific purpose.

There can, anyhow, be no question that the presence of the Descorps on that front, with its nose always pointed through Amman to Deraa, continued to convince Liman von Sanders that he was in danger on that front.

During these months the most formidable Turkish attacks fell upon the Descorps sector, made in the hope of retaking Jerusalem. In spite of the fact that the enemy did succeed, at least once, in penetrating a considerable distance between the 'defended localities,' the latter were held most gallantly and were always relieved ultimately by the success of the counterattacks of the mobile reserves, which, owing to the fact that the men came forward mounted, always reached the scene of action in a minimum of time.

On the northern front Ausdiv and ANZAC Division alternately were holding some very rough country unsuitable for forward mounted patrol work.

In the southern sector, from Ghoraniyeh southwards, the Indian cavalry rode daily across the plain and spent the whole summer in carrying out offensive operations against any Turks who ventured forward from their main position in the foothills, 5 miles from the river. Time after time they laid up under cover for the enemy and got into him with the lance.

During July the Indian cavalry had one brilliant success after another with the lance in patrol encounters east of Jordan.

An account of their doings and the lessons to be drawn from them were circulated throughout the Corps, including Ausdiv and ANZAC Division. The G.O.C. Ausdiv replied that if his men were armed with an equally suitable weapon, they would do equally well, but as such a weapon had been denied them he must respectfully request that accounts of the undeniably brilliant exploits of the Indian cavalry with the lance should not be sent him in future for issue to his Division because they could only result in dissatisfying them with their own comparatively inferior armament. He asked, moreover, that the question of arming his Division with the sword might once more be reconsidered.

The Corps Commander was now able to send back the delightful answer, 'The Australian Mounted Division may have the sword.'

The Division was relieved from the Jordan plain on 23 August and went back to the maritime plain about Ludd; and there, for two weeks, all ranks including Brigadiers and Regimental Commanders, spent morning and afternoon learning the sword.

On the Divisional Staff two officers were British regular cavalry officers. During the first week they put the Commanding Officers, who volunteered, Squadron Leaders, Troop Leaders and Squadron Sergeants-Majors through sword training, mounted and dismounted.

During the second week regimental officers taught their men.

At the end of a fortnight the Division was thoroughly competent to take on any troops in the world with the sword.

This is a point of the greatest importance. Before the war the Yeomanry were denied the sword, and a hybrid book called *Yeomanry and Mounted Rifles Training*[16] was produced, because it was feared that it would take a long time to teach the sword and that the Yeomanry had not time to learn it.

The fact that the entire Ausdiv was taught to use the sword effectively in a fortnight proves conclusively that the pre-war decision as regards the Yeomanry was based upon a misconception.

In view of the history of Ausdiv and Yeodiv in Palestine, and the fact that the writer's conclusions are thoroughly endorsed by every experienced cavalry officer in the Empire who has had any experience of the sword, it is greatly to be hoped that this question will never again arise as regards the Yeomanry, and that the *Yeomanry Training* manual[17] will disappear forever.

When the writer commenced to write these articles he was informed on good authority that the two Australian Light Horse Divisions, now being formed in Australia, were to be armed with the sword. He has, however, just received a letter from a senior officer in Australia, who is in a position to know, saying that the question as to whether they are to have the sword or not is still *sub-judice*.

---

[16] *Yeomanry and Mounted Rifle Training* manual (London: HMSO, 1912).
[17] *Yeomanry and Mounted Rifle Training* manual (London: HMSO, 1912).

The writer wishes to repeat what he said before: that, in his opinion, the Australian Light Horse, by reason of their wonderful natural military characteristics, are at least without superiors amongst mounted troops.

If, however, they are denied an *arme blanche* weapon (or pistol), they cannot hope to attain to a first-class standard for offensive war. The question is of great imperial importance. Australia and South Africa, in the future, are likely to supply the major portion of the Empire's mounted troops; if the Australian Light Horse do not now realise the value of the sword in offensive war they never will, for in Palestine they had every opportunity of forming an opinion.

In South Africa, there are already many regiments of mounted rifles; but in that country the sword and lance are only remembered for the ridicule their failure drew upon them in the South African War[18]. If the Australian military authorities arm the A.L.H. with the sword, and the writer feels confident that they will, it is thought probable that the South African military authorities will consider the advisability of following suit.

The mounted arm of all belligerents earned high praise during the late war for their conduct of defensive war. The arm has been, however, severely criticised as regards its comparative lack of offensive power.

As things stand today, two aids are essential in offensive war: the first, an *arme blanche* weapon; the second, tank support.

---

[18]Now better-known as The Second Boer War, 1899–1902 – Ed.

22. PHASE V
CONSIDERATION, IN JULY 1918, OF OFFENSIVE OPERATIONS ON A GRAND SCALE.
(Map C.)

Throughout the first half of 1918 Lord Allenby had kept in view the possibility of offensive action on a grand scale, and had steadily prepared for it.

When, in the main theatre, after months of great trial, the tide began to turn in our favour, the question arose of a counter-offensive on all the fronts of the worldwide battle line.

In July, Lord Allenby informed the C.I.G.S. that, when the time came for him to attack, he hoped to break through and secure the line Nablus-Tulkeram-Mouth of the Nahr Iskanderuneh; he stated that he hoped for decisive success, which suggests that success in securing the objective named, although only an advance of 15 miles, was expected to lead to bigger things.

The general plan, in its main strategic outlines, may be regarded as a reversal of the plan of the third Battle of Gaza; then, the C-in-C had turned the enemy's left flank, after having convinced him that the main blow would fall on the coast at Gaza. Now, his intention was to break through on the coast, having already induced Liman von Sanders to believe that it was his left flank which was the danger point.

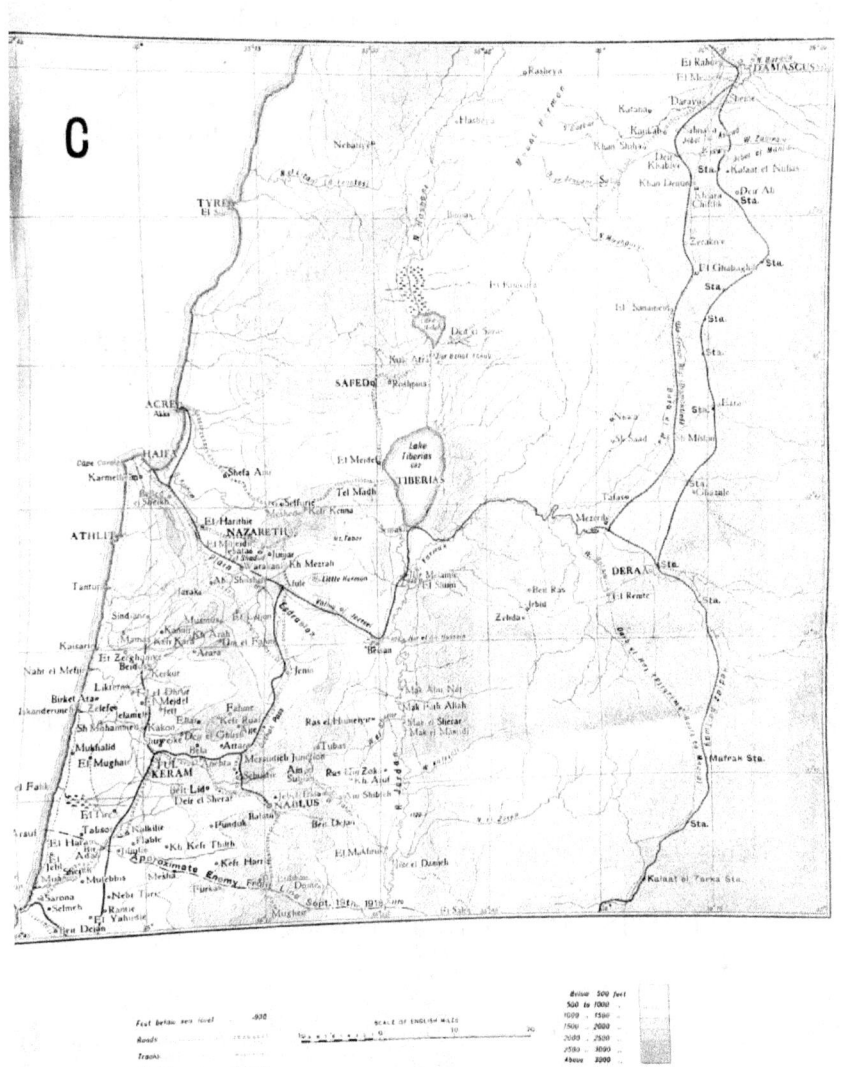

To mystify, mislead and surprise twice running is a very remarkable achievement in the art of generalship.

Reasons for the Selection of the Maritime Plain as the Front of Decisive Attack.

The two main instruments of offence on the ground at the disposal of the C-in-C may be termed: (a) hitting power and (b) mobility. As regards the first, his infantry and artillery; as regards the second, his large cavalry force. The one, without the other, could not attain decisive results.

East of Jordan supply difficulties would throttle movement. The Turkish positions in the Jude An Mountains for 10 miles east and west of the Jerusalem-Nablus road were of great natural strength; progress would be slow, not more than five miles in one day; far more rapid advance was necessary. In the maritime plain alone were the necessary conditions fulfilled. Here the maximum power could be developed in the infantry and artillery attack; the Royal Navy could cooperate, and here the ground was most suitable for rapid exploitation by the Desert Mounted Corps.

Turkish Situation Early September 1918. Strength and Disposition (See Map C and Plate XIII)

The Turkish Army was situated as follows:
VIII Army: from the sea at Arsuf to Furka, 21 mile front; 10,000 rifles and 157 guns.

VII Army: in the mountains astride Jerusalem-Nablus road, 19 mile front; 7,000 rifles and 111 guns.

IV Army: Jordan valley, front of 21 miles; 6,000 rifles and 74 guns. (See Plate XIII)

Maan Garrison and along the Hedjaz railway to the north of Maan; 6,000 rifles and 80 guns.

General Reserve: in area Sea of Galilee, Tiberias-Nazareth-Haifa; 8,000 rifles and 80 guns.

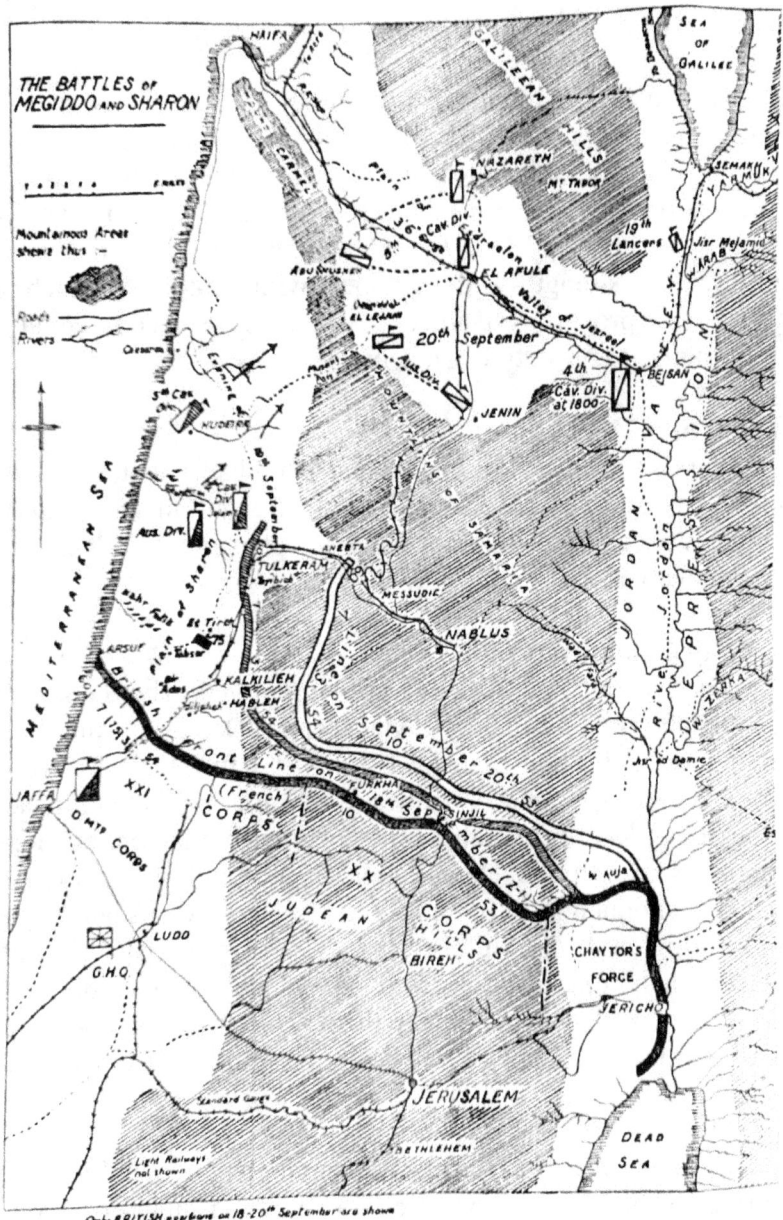

Plate XIII.

Total: 82,000 rifles, 4,000 sabres, 402 guns. The ration strength is believed to have been approximately 104,000.

The British had gradually gained great air superiority over the German aviators, mainly from morale rather than material reasons. The British aviators, including many brilliant Australian officers, proved superior to the German. It is a fact, however, that in early September 1918, the Turco-German Air Force was in considerable strength and equipped with up-to-date machines, which, if properly handled, would have been equal in performance to our artillery machines.

Health and Morale.
The Turkish medical arrangements were inefficient; the whole force was seriously weakened by malignant malaria, and its morale was consequently growing lower and lower, desertions continuously increasing.

Railway Communications (Map C)
The Turkish railways had not been improved. The Turks were supplied from Constantinople via Aleppo, Damascus and Deraa. From Deraa, the line Semakh-Beisan-El Afule-Jenin-Messudieh supplied the VIII and VII Armies; the former by the continuation through Tul Keram to Kalkilieh; the latter by the continuation to Nablus. The sections Deraa-Semakh and Jenin-Messudieh ran through mountainous country, and had necessitated great engineering skill in building; many bridges existed in these sections that, consequently, were exceptionally vulnerable to any hostile attack that could reach them. IV Army, on the Jordan valley front, was supplied by the Hedjaz railway from Deraa to Amman.

The Germans had taken over the running of the railways; but shortage of fuel and rolling stock rendered the supply of 100,000 men a precarious performance.

Road Communications
The Turks had no compunction in impressing the entire native

population for road-making, and stone was always at hand in the mountainous districts. As a result, the Turkish roads were comparatively efficient, especially in view of the primitive nature of the Turkish horsed transport. The German lorries, as also the British, proved their capacity to move over almost any track, provided the surface was not soft.

The Turkish armies relied principally on the following roads and tracks (see Map C and Plate XIII):

Behind VIII and VII Armies
Metalled road Damascus-Bridge over Jordan at Jisr Benat Yakub-Tiberias-Nazareth-Afule.

Behind VIII Army
(a) Metalled road Afule-Musmus Pass-Tul Keram-Kalkilieh
(b) Metalled road Tul Keram-Messudieh
(c) Many unmetalled tracks in the maritime plain; including one from Liktera over the pass at Jarak to Abu Shusheh, and one from Liktera along the coast to Haifa

Behind VII Army
(a) Metalled road Afule-Jenin-Messudie-Nablus and south along backbone of Jude An Mountains.
(b) Metalled road running from Nablus down the Wadi Farah to the Jordan at Jisr Ed Damie.
(c) Unmetalled track down the valley Tiberias-Semakh-Beisan and thence over the mountains via Tubas to Nablus.

Behind IV Army (Plate XIII and Map C)
(a) Metalled road Ghoraniyeh Bridge-Es Salt-Amman; thence unmetalled north along the plateau to Deraa (pilgrim route).
(b) One unmetalled track west, and one east of the Jordan from Semakh southwards along the valley.

Turkish Formations Headquarters
    G.H.Q. - Nazareth.
    VIII Army - Tul Keram.
    VII Army - Nablus.
    IV Army - Es Salt.

Description of Turkish Position and Country behind (Map C)

(a) Maritime Plain Sector of VIII Army.
There were two main systems of trenches and a third line in rear.

1st System: From the foothills south of Hableh, through Jiljulie and Bir Adas, passing south of Tabsor to the sea just north of Arsuf.
These defences were 2,000 to 8,000 yards deep, practically continuous and wired, but weakly. There were many dug-outs and some very strong points, particularly at Jiljulie and covering the approaches to Tabsor.

2nd System: From Et Tireh to the coast, along the north bank of the Nahr Falik. These defences were formidable, but believed to be unwired.

3rd line: A partially dug, unwired and unoccupied line close behind the Nahr lskaneruneh.

In this maritime plain sector of VIII Army the main topographical features were :

The Nahr Falik: A marsh, forming a considerable obstacle, bridged in two places and passable at the mouth on the sand of the sea shore.

The Nahr lskanderuneh: A considerable obstacle, which contains deep water pools throughout the year.

Hills of Samaria: From Messudieh these hills run north-west, separating the maritime plain from the Plain of Esdraelon and ending in an abrupt cliff at the west end of Mount Carmel; though lower than the Jude An Mountains south of Nablus, they were of considerable military importance; the road over the Musmus Pass was the only one fit for wheels north of the Tul Keram-Messudieh-Jenin road, and it and the track via Jarak and Abu Shusheh (Map C) could be easily defended. These hills, therefore, by nature and location, were suitable as a defensive position supporting the Turkish right, and covering the railway communications back to Deraa.

(b) Foothill Sector of VIII Army and VII Army.
The foothill country north of the Turkish line from Hable to Furka was very difficult; the valley running in from Tul Keram to Messudieh and Nablus, and thence north to Jenin, was about 1,000 yards broad and the most suitable line of operations into the mountains from the west.

At Jenin the road enters the Plain of Esdraelon, which is almost entirely flat and without obstacles to movement.

The Plain of Jezreel, approximately 2 miles broad, runs from Esdraelon down to Beisan in the Jordan valley.

British Situation, Early September 1918
(approximately shown on the German Intelligence Map, Plate XIV, see also Map C)

The Army was situated as follows:
XXI Corps (four Divisions): From the sea at Arsuf to Furka (Furcha), 21 mile front. (11 miles open plain; 10 miles of lower slopes.)

XX Corps (three Divisions): Extending across the mountains to the cliffs overhanging Jordan; 15 mile front. The last 5 miles at the east end of this line was lightly held, being impassable for formed bodies.

Descorps (four cavalry divisions): 22 mile front (on the north front, 7 miles of plain; on the east front 15 miles of river with three bridgeheads.)

Note. One or two cavalry divisions were always out of the valley resting; usually one near the sea, and one on the top of the mountains near Jerusalem.

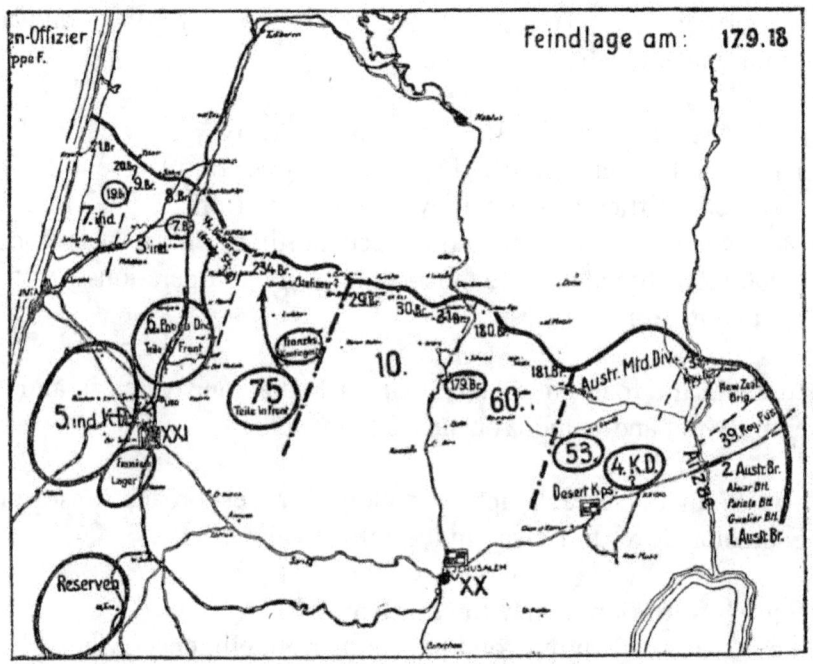

BRITISH DISPOSITIONS AS SHOWN BY ENEMY INTELLIGENCE SERVICE.
Plate XIV.

Strength

7 divisions, 4 cavalry divisions, 1 Indian infantry brigade, 1 French infantry brigade.

Total rifle strength, 57,000; sabre strength 12,000; heavy and siege guns 94, mountain guns 42; total guns 512 (approx.)

Health

XXI Corps was in a Mediterranean climate, warm but healthy, though the malaria was bad in the marshes of the Nahr el Auja.

XX Corps lived in a splendid mountain climate, and the troops were very fit.

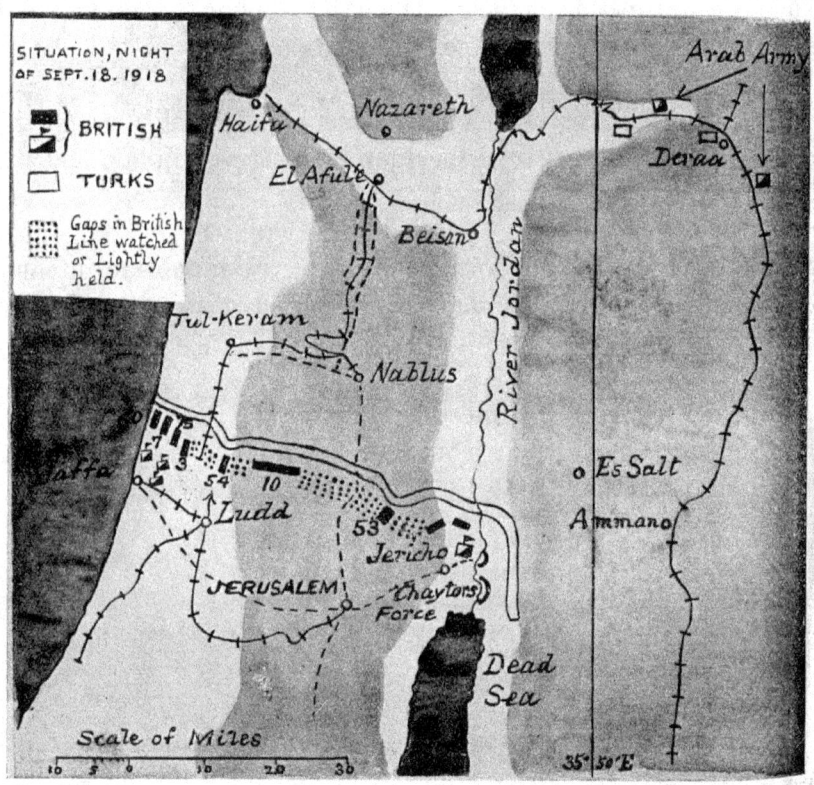

Plate XV.

Descorps had spent six months in Jordan, 1,200 feet below sea level, in equatorial climate and vegetation. No white man had ever spent a summer there, and the few natives who remained during the hot weather were coal black; the dust was suffocating; malignant malaria was rampant, but was kept in check by the splendid preventive measures of the R.A.M.C. By September, however, in spite of everything that could be done, Descorps was seriously full of malaria. The horses, on the other hand, got through without serious deterioration; for, although they got no shade, the water supply was excellent and abundant.

Original G.H.Q. Plan (Plate XV and Map C)
The C-in-C timed his attack for the third week in September. The following is a statement of the original plan:

(a) XXI Corps (five Divisions) to attack and break through the enemy's defences between the foothills east of Jiljulieh and the sea.
(b) As soon as the enemy's resistance should be broken, three cavalry divisions of Descorps were to pass through the infantry and take Tul Keram, and subsequently to advance on Messudieh by the Tul Keram-Anebta road.

Note, it will be seen that, in order to assemble this striking force, three cavalry divisions and one infantry division would have to move across from the east flank to the sea. (cf Plate XIV and Plate XV)

(c) XXI Corps then to wheel to the right; two Divisions to fight their way through the hills to Anebta, while a third was to follow Descorps.

(d) XX Corps, with two divisions, to advance astride the Jerusalem-Nablus road after the main attack of XXI Corps had been launched.

(e) Chaytor's Force, i.e. ANZAC Mounted Division, 25th Indian Infantry Brigade (I.S. Infantry), the Composite Infantry Brigade (two battalions Jews; two battalions W.I. Regiment), to form a defensive flank to guard the crossings over the Jordan and to be prepared, on receipt of orders, to cooperate in the advance and seize the crossing at Jisr Ed Damieh.

Comparative Strengths, Frontages, et cetera
If the foregoing statement of strengths are compared, it will be seen that the British preponderance consisted in:

Cavalry   -   a superiority of 3 to 1
Infantry   -   a superiority of 7 to 4
Artillery -   a superiority of 11 to 8

It is suggested that the superiority in infantry was no greater than that of the Allies over Germany on the Western Front during the major part of 1916 and 1917; it was realised by the C-in-C that, if completely decisive success was to be attained, his great superiority in cavalry would have to be the final factor in attaining it.

His first necessity, therefore, was to ensure making an effective gap through which Descorps could issue; and it appears that he considered that completely decisive success on a 5 mile front would fulfil this requirement.

On the main (XXI Corps) front of attack extending 15 miles (actually 8½ miles attacking front) he concentrated 35,000 infantry and 883 guns, against 8,000 Turkish infantry and 130 guns ; i.e. a superiority of 4½ to 1 in infantry, and of 3 to 1 in guns.

He skinned slimmed down the remainder of the line and maintained 45 miles with 22,000 rifles and 157 guns, holding Turkish forces numbering 24,000 infantry and 270 guns.

He kept no G.H.Q. reserve; every available man was put in the fight, including Corps cavalry, Pioneer battalions, and details from reinforcement camps.

Measures Taken to Mystify, Mislead, Conceal, and Surprise.
The greatest care was necessary to conceal the heavy concentration in the coastal sector; the C-in-C continuously and personally supervised the measures taken by the General Staff to secure surprise; the arrangements were elaborate and nothing was left to chance.

In a country with few wooded areas, superiority in the air is almost essential if moves are to be concealed; and the R.A.F., during the final days of assembly, almost attained (a temporary) command of the air.

Enemy agents were always able to move with impunity through certain gaps in the line around the open eastern flank. As they could not be prevented from seeing things, the General Staff used various stratagems to make it appear that all preparations were for an attack eastwards of the Jordan sector.

The move of three cavalry divisions from the Jordan valley, where they were in full view of the enemy's observation posts in the surrounding hills, was very difficult to conceal, but it was essential to conceal it, as the location of the cavalry mass during an offensive operation is a sure indication as to the decisive point of attack.

During the first fortnight of September troops marched down from Jerusalem to the Jordan valley, arriving after daylight, so that their arrival could be seen by the Turks. New camps were pitched in the valley; troops marching westward did so by night, leaving all camps standing.

Lastly, as the cavalry marched out of the valley, in place of their horses they left behind them dummies made of wood and canvas. Great numbers of these were elaborate, and would deceive at a few hundred yards, but our airmen reported that stuffed sacks lying on the ground threw a deep shadow in that bright sunlight, and were quite effective enough to deceive from the air.
As a result of all the precautions taken, the heavy concentration on a 5 mile front by the sea was effected unknown to the enemy.
At the last moment the Turkish air service reported: 'No essential changes have taken place in the distribution of the British forces.'

On 18 September, the day before the attack, when all our dispositions had been completed, the Turkish Intelligence Service issued a map (Plate XIV) showing three cavalry divisions still in the Jordan valley on17 September, and 60th Division still in the right sector of XX Corps. Their information was remarkably accurate as to the situation before the final concentration moves took place, but these had been successfully concealed.

23 THE FINAL PLAN

Comparatively late in the day, on August 22, the C-in-C suddenly announced to Corps Commanders his intention to extend the scope of the forthcoming operations.

The tasks of XXI Corps and XX Corps remained much the same: their final objectives were respectively the high ground north of Anebta and the high ground north and north-east of Nablus; but, after reaching their objectives, they were to be prepared to pursue, XXI Corps towards Jenin, XX Corps towards Beisan.

The main alteration in the plan concerned Desert Mounted Corps. Its original role had been to operate on the same line of advance as the left wing of XXI Corps, and supported by it. Its task was now enormously increased; and the writer well remembers the expression of astonishment on the faces of the Cavalry Brigade and Regimental Commanders when they heard, two days before the operation, the scope of the role allotted to them. The G.H.Q. orders to Descorps were, as follows:
> As soon as the crossings over the Naher Falik, and the marshes to the east, have been cleared of the enemy by the advance of XXI Corps, Descorps [Fivecav, Fourcav, and Ausdiv less 5th A.L.H. Brigade], passing round the left of XXI Corps, will advance to El Afuleh and Beisan to cut the enemy's railways communications, and to block his retreat in a north and north-east direction. First objective : the line Kakon-Jelameh-Tel El Dhruh-Hudeira (Plate XIII).

The advance of Descorps will be continued [i.e., from the first objective] as soon as possible and with the utmost speed to El Afuleh by the road Kerkur-Musmus-El Lejjun, and by the road crossing by Jarak to Abu Shusheh. Every effort will be made to prevent the escape of Turkish rolling stock by cutting the railway lines from Jenin and Haifa to Afuleh at the earliest possible moment.

The G.O.C. Descorps, retaining sufficient troops in the Afuleh-Jenin-El Lejjun area to close the Turkish lines of retreat to the north and north-west, will push on to close the roads which converge on Beisan from the Jordan valley and Nablus.

In amplification of the G.H.Q. Operation Order, Sir Harry Chauvel received special instructions, of which the following is an extract:

> 1. G.O.C. XXI Corps has been entrusted with the task of breaking the enemy's resistance in the coastal plain and opening a way for your Corps to cross the N. Falik and Zerkiyeh Marsh [source of N. Falik. Map C]. In view of the long marches which you have to make and the necessity of conserving your full strength to carry out the important role assigned to you in the enemy's rear, you must on no account allow your troops to be drawn into the infantry fight south of the N. Falik, nor, after the passage of this stream, to be diverted from your objective by the presence of hostile troops in the Tulkeram – Et Tireh area, which will be dealt with by XXI Corps.
>
> The advance of your Corps from its positions of readiness will be regulated by the progress of XXI Corps, and you will be responsible for arranging that the line Zerkiyeh Marsh-mouth of N. Falik is crossed at earliest possible moment. In your approach march, care must be taken that there is no interference with the movement of units and formations of XXI Corps engaged in the attack; it is particularly important that the fire of the Corps Artillery

should not be masked.

2. Should any portion of the enemy's forces retreat in direction of Haifa, you will detach only sufficient troops to keep touch with it and protect your L-of-C, as it is vital that as large a proportion of your force as possible should be available to carry out the role assigned to you, which is to place your troops about Afuleh and Beisan where the enemy's railway communications can be cut at their most vital point, and whence you will be in a position to strike his columns if they endeavour to escape in a northerly or north-easterly direction.

The action of your troops must be characterised by the greatest vigour and rapidity, as it is essential that they should reach Afuleh and Beisan before the enemy can withdraw his rolling stock and material or assemble troops for the defence of the railway.

3. On arrival at El Lejjun you will detach a Brigade to block the roads and railway passing through Jenin and to gain touch with the Cavalry Brigade attached to XXI Corps [i.e. 5th A.L.H. Brigade of Ausdiv], which will be directed on Jenin from the south if the situation permits.

4. From Afuleh a detachment will be sent to seize the road and railway bridges over the Jordan at Jisr Mejamie. The railway bridge should be prepared for demolition, but not destroyed so long as we are able to hold it.

5. Demolitions on the railway should be limited to such as can easily be repaired.

Comments on the Final Plan.
1. The cavalry plan was astonishingly bold. It seems clear that, even to the C-in-C himself, the idea came as a second thought. It is probable that it originated entirely in his own head, and it is not thought likely that any appreciation and proposed plan, put up to

him by his staff, contained any idea of a cavalry task of such magnitude.

Frequently during past centuries cavalry officers have complained that the cavalry has suffered through being handled by commanders who did not understand how to get the maximum out of the arm (e.g. see Lord Haig's introduction to his book[19]). Is it probable that any C-in-C, other than a cavalry officer, would have conceived a cavalry plan of such magnitude? The writer personally thinks that very few would have done so.

General Ludendorff appears to agree with Lord Haig that, at the end of March 1918, he himself had much the same opportunity to launch a cavalry mass in front of Amiens; but, great General though he was, he completely failed to seize it, because he had not prepared for it.

It is not contended for one moment that every cavalry commander would have conceived such a plan possible. Lord Allenby's opponent, Liman von Sanders, himself a cavalry soldier, certainly did not; and, as stated earlier, many of the best informed of Lord Allenby's subordinate cavalry commanders could hardly believe their ears when they heard the scope of their task. The fact remains, however, that the cavalries of all nations in future will say that this, the greatest cavalry achievement for at least a century, was mainly due to the fact that the C-in-C happened to be a cavalry soldier.

The cavalry, unfortunately, is comparatively an isolated arm. In peace it is organised and trains in formations of its own, which makes it a thing apart. In war, the eyes of the entire army are levelled at close range at the slow moving formations; but the work of the mobile forces is usually comparatively far afield, is seldom seen in detail by the other arms, and remains a mystery to them. For these reasons the cavalry know more about the other

---

[19] Earl Doulas Haig, *Cavalry Studies : Strategical and Tactical*, (London: H. Rees, 1907)

arms, than the latter know of them.

There is a moral. If an officer of any of the slower-moving arms aspires to command a force of all arms; and if he hopes to be capable, when the time comes, of conceiving a plan such as that conceived by Lord Allenby, then he must go out of his normal way to make a very special study of the handling of mobile forces.

Final, Assembly of Descorps.
The concentration of Descorps (less ANZAC Division), by night marches, behind and in XXI Corps area, was successfully hidden, not only from the enemy but also from the inhabitants. It was completed by17 September, when the Corps was disposed as follows:
Fivecav, in orange groves north-west of Sarona (8 miles behind the line).
Fourcav, in orange groves east of Sarona (10 miles behind the line).
Ausdiv, in olive groves about Ludd (17 miles behind the line).
Adv. Descorps HQ, in close touch with XXI Corps HQ, north of Sarona.

It had originally been intended that, during the night of 18–19 September (XXI Corps' zero hour being 0430 hours 19 September), Fivecav should move across the River Auja and be formed in depth and superimposed upon the area of the 60th Division on the coast; and Fourcav formed in depth and superimposed upon the area of 7th (Ind.) Division (Plate XIII).

It was later decided however, that, in the final assembly, no part of either of the two leading cavalry divisions should be farther forward than a line (called Brown line) which demarcated the southern boundary of XXI Corps gun positions.

The bombardment by XXI Corps began at 04:30 hours, 19 September, and the infantry attack was launched at 04:45 hours.

The two leading divisions of Descorps were timed to complete their final assembly in the early morning of 19 September, as follows:

(a) Fivecav, at 04:00 hours, in rear of and in close liaison with 60th Division; formed up in depth with its head west of Jelil (approximately 8 miles behind front line).

(b) Fourcav, at 07:30 hours, in the rear of and in close liaison with 7th (Ind.) Division; formed in depth with its head at Cromarty Hill (i.e. about 2 miles east of Fivecav).

Ausdiv marched during the night from Ludd to Sarona, with orders to be prepared to cross the River Auja at 07:00 hours.

Plan of Descorps (as stated in Descorps official report) :

The role assigned to Descorps was, as soon as the way had been cleared by the infantry assault, and the 60th Division had swung to the east towards Tul Keram, to move at greatest possible pace and cut in on the enemy's communications well behind the enemy divisions and reserves from the River Jordan at Beisan to the coast, thus blocking all possible chances of the Turkish Army west of the Jordan being able to escape northwards from the pressure of XX and XXI Corps' attacks.

With this in view, Fivecav was assigned the task of reaching Nazareth with all possible speed, moving on its first objective, the line Tel El Dhrur-Liktera-the sea; thence via …. [this is blank in the original] and Jarak on Nazareth. It was hoped that the German C-in-C would be captured in Nazareth.

Fourcav was assigned the task of moving inside Fivecav via the Musmus Pass on Afuleh, with the final objective Beisan, linking up with Fivecav on the first objective, from Kakon to Tel El Dhrur.

Ausdiv was to follow Fourcav, in Corps reserve.

Adv. Corps H.Q. to move with Ausdiv.

Comments on Final Assembly of Descorps
This cavalry problem of passing large cavalry formations through infantry and artillery, after the success of the latter in a deliberate attack, had been continuously studied in France since the battle of Neuve Chapelle, early in 1915.

No real success had been achieved until the attack in front of Amiens on 8 August 1918; but most definite lessons had been learnt.

The main lesson learnt is that the opportunity for cavalry
to pass through is usually a fleeting one, and that it will be missed unless the responsibility for the selection of the moment is delegated to the most forward cavalry commanders, working in close conjunction with the most forward infantry commanders; further, that those cavalry commanders and their advanced troops must be very far forward, in fact, in close touch with the forward fighting infantry.

There may be various methods of applying this rule;
but usually every forward cavalry formation should have an advance guard maintaining closest touch with the attacking infantry – even to the extent of dismounted patrols in the infantry trenches at zero hour, and going forward dismounted with them.

The commanders of these advance guards are best placed
for bearing the responsibility of choosing the moment to pass through the infantry; and they have the troops immediately at hand for making the initial effort.

Sir Harry Chauvel strongly urged some such arrangements, but the G.O.C. XXI Corps was afraid that cavalry in such large numbers might interfere with the infantry attack and, in particular, might mask the fire of the guns; and he strongly urged that no cavalry should be allowed, until he himself gave permission, in front of a line which demarcated the southern boundary of XXI Corps' gun positions.

It is believed that the C-in-C himself supported the view that a forward assembly of cavalry advance guards was most desirable; but he was probably quite confident that the operation, in this particular case, would be successfully carried through whether the forward cavalry lined up behind the guns or close behind the attacking infantry; and as the G.O.C. XXI Corps was the individual most responsible for the success of the final assembly and the initial breakthrough, the C-in-C must have been most anxious to allay his anxieties as far as possible.

As a result, the cavalry had no option but to submit to staff arrangements that a long and bitter cavalry experience had proved to be unsound.

The orders of Fourcav read as follows:
> Fourcav (plus 11th L.A.M. Battalion and No.1 Light Cav Patrol) will be assembled on Z day [approximately at 07:30 hours] in a position of readiness in Column of Brigade Masses, in a position in rear of the 7th Division, and will be prepared to move forward directly the front is cleared. The order to move will come from the Division. (i.e. from Cavalry Division HQ) .... No mounted man is to pass north of the Brown line [the line which demarcated the southern boundary of XXI Corps' gun positions], shown on the attached plan, on any account, without permission from Divisional Headquarters.

The great emphasis laid on the last sentence suggests that the Divisional Commander, in view of his orders, was forced to deliberately forbid his leading troops from doing what they knew was the correct procedure, i.e., to keep close up behind and in touch with the attacking infantry.

It should be noted that :
(a) The order to move forward was to come from the Divisional

Commander; and it is known that he himself had first to obtain permission from the G.O.C. 7th (Ind.) Division.
(b) Some of the heavy artillery of XXI Corps, in front of which no mounted cavalryman might pass, was in position 5,000 yards behind the line.

In the opinion of the writer, all cavalry experience had proved such arrangements unsound from a cavalry point of view; and if, in the sequel, the cavalry opportunity had been a fleeting one, it would have been lost. As a fact, the cavalry divisional commander actually went ahead himself to Headquarters 7th (Ind.) Division, at Tabsor beyond the enemy's front line, and met the G.O.C. 7th(Ind.)Division there at 08:40 hours. It was then decided that the cavalry could pass through. G.O.C. Fourcav then went back to meet the head of his Division, which had then arrived within one hundred yards of the gap made for it in our own front line wire.

The fact that such arrangements were successful constitutes a positive danger for the future. The future generation of cavalry soldiers, in studying the staff arrangements of this successful movement of cavalry through infantry, in exploiting the success of the latter in a deliberate battle, will probably copy these arrangements, which would be a tragedy.

The writer suggests that the cavalry should take steps, as soon as possible, at staff rides, manoeuvres, et cetera, to demonstrate to the commanders of other arms, that cavalry formations can guarantee to make every arrangement they wish to, in such an operation, without in any way interfering with the infantry or masking the guns; that a cavalry division, without interfering, can assemble at zero hour, superimposed upon the area of the Division with which it is cooperating, with advanced elements, dismounted if necessary, accompanying the attacking infantry.

The secret of success seems to lie in detailing one infantry formation and one cavalry formation (neither ever larger than a Division) to work together in cooperation – leaving them to work out together the details of their joint plan.

The writer has strongly emphasised his point that the tactical disposition of the cavalry in assembly was faulty, as he considers it so important. The difficulties, which arose from it, were greatly lessened by the exceptional sympathy and assistance given to Descorps by the Commander and B.G.G.S. of XXI Corps – an assistance very necessary for cavalry when attempting this peculiarly difficult operation.

The Morale of the Cavalry.
It has been stated previously that Descorps was malaria riddled; and it was only to be expected that, consequently, the morale of the Corps would be reduced.

On 17 September, the C-in-C came to see all the unit commanders in Descorps. He staggered them by his optimism; he stated his confidence that we should have a success of great magnitude. His bearing had a magnetic effect upon all.

All cavalry divisions were fortunate in their commanders, and the training, which they pumped into their divisions just prior to the operation, was of a high order – it dealt principally with the conduct of attack and pursuit. Fourcav and Fivecav had always been armed with swords or lances as well as rifle and bayonet; Ausdiv had just been issued with the sword.

In the training, the *arme blanche* weapon was not forgotten. Ausdiv had two weeks' intense training in its use. Previous experience in Palestine had proved that, in pursuit, it is the weapon par excellence.

The G.O.C. Fourcav, Sir George Barrow, issued a paper entitled *Fighting Instructions* to his Division just before the attack. It shows the spirit that animated Descorps throughout, a wonderful spirit in which to go into battle after four years of war. It is not contended for one moment that others could have produced anything so inspiring or so full of knowledge. It is a wonderful example of the art of command.

The paper is based upon the experience of four years' war. Any reader will see that the General believed that what he said was true; it carried conviction to his troops; and the sequel proved him right. The paper is reproduced in full below; it should prove a great inspiration to all cavalry soldiers who read it, in particular to those called to fight in the Middle East.

FIGHTING INSTRUCTIONS.
4th Cavalry Division

I. Introduction.
The principles of war are unchanging, but the manner in which these principles are applied varies according to the nature of the warfare in which we are engaged, the character of the enemy and his armaments, the climate, the lie and lift of the ground, and above all, the respective morale of the opposing forces. For this reason, the Divisional Commander considers it desirable to issue Fighting Instructions, which are largely based on experiences gained during recent operations against the Turk in Palestine.

II. The Nature of the Country and its Influence on Movement and Manoeuvre.
The country affords nearly every facility for the movement and manoeuvre of large bodies of cavalry. It invites mounted action, whether the scene be set on the maritime plain of Sharon or whether it be on the table-land of Amman and Es Salt. While the undulations, the low hills of 200 feet to 800 feet high, the patches of cultivation and trees favour cover and concealment, there is little to impede movement. The only obstacles are the wadis and plantations, which break up formations without constituting barriers to mounted men. Direction and command are simplified by the numerous points of observation which are to be found on the low hills and from which an extensive view can often be obtained; and by the clear definition of the villages and

plantations. The wadis present the only surprises, as they are often difficult to see until one is 'on the top of them.' At the same time, when sufficiently broad and deep, they are valuable for purposes of concealment and covered movement. The 'going' is sound and good, except after rain.

From the foregoing brief description, it is evident that the country is singularly suited to that articulate formation which is the most favourable for cavalry, and which it is safe to adopt owing to the cavalry's mobility. An articulate formation implies one in which the various parts of a force have room to move, and in which, although all the parts are well linked together, the joints are perfectly supple; each part of the force has room in front and rear and on the flanks to move freely and take advantage of ground and to deploy rapidly. The limiting factor is cooperation. All the component parts of a unit moving in an articulate formation must be in a position to participate in an action in which its unit engages.

Regiments and brigades should constantly practice this formation and the rapid concentration there from for action.

Although the theory is simple, it can only be efficiently worked when all ranks are accustomed to it and when the system of intercommunication is in thorough order.

III. Mounted Action.
The country being, as we have seen, favourable for mounted action, are the other factors equally favourable? What are these other factors?
They are:
(a) Our own ability to carry out a mounted attack when opportunity offers.
(b) The degree of efficiency of the Turkish soldier.
(c) Morale.

As regards-
(a) Training, tradition and inclination are on our side. Leaders and

men have been constantly trained in the drill and technique of the mounted attack against hostile infantry, cavalry and guns; the traditions of ages culminating in the experiences of the present war give us the necessary confidence; the natural inclination is strong. The ability therefore exists.

(b) The Turk has the reputation of being a stubborn fighter behind trenches. But in open warfare his efficiency is seriously impaired by his indifferent marksmanship. He rarely hits anything that he aims at, even at close ranges. Our recent experiences in the Jordan valley are all in support of this assertion. And since fire effect is the only effect, which the mounted attack has to fear, we are able to gallop the Turkish infantry with a light heart on occasions when we might hesitate in the face of a better shooting enemy.

The Turkish artillery is to be respected. It is often taken up accurately and effectively. But, in open warfare, the enemy is not in a position to bring very great weight of metal against us. In 99 cases out of 100, there is nothing in his artillery or rifle and machine gun fire to stop a determined charge.

(c) We have established a great moral superiority over the Turk. He has suffered severe defeat, and has been constantly forced to retire. He has been defeated in every mounted attack that we have undertaken and in frequent patrol encounters. He dislikes our cold steel, and the sight of it makes his fire erratic. He cannot stop us from reaching him, and when once we reach him his fate is sealed.

Every factor, therefore, when the tactical situation permits, is in favour of the attack mounted. And it must be borne in mind that not only does a mounted attack bring about a decision much more quickly than a prolonged fire fight, but its results are more decisive and the after-effects are more far-reaching and much more lasting.

Troops who have fought afire action, even when forced to retire, are generally prepared to fight again next day or even earlier; troops who have once been ridden over by cavalry will rarely face a second charge throughout the course of the same campaign.

In the element of surprise, rapidity of action is the complement of concealment. Especially is this so when dealing with the Turks. A sudden and rapid attack, carried through with determination, will always be more effective than wide turning movements and elaborate tactics, once we have arrived within striking distance.
To sum up-
(a) Whenever there is a choice between mounted and dismounted action, it is the mounted attack, which should be adopted, because
(i) All the factors requisite for a successful charge are present.
(ii) The results are more quickly attained, more decisive and more lasting.
(b) The attack should be based on a simple plan, put into execution as rapidly as is consistent with proper preparation.

IV. Preparatory Formations.
Although it is not out of the question that we may be called upon to meet Turkish cavalry, it is infantry that we shall generally be up against.

The procedure for the attack against infantry and artillery is laid down in Section 208 of Cavalry Training. The most suitable formations from which to launch the successive lines of attack should be considered and practised by Regiments and brigades, so that there may be no delay or confusion when the time for action arrives. These formations may vary according to the time available for preparation, the frontage, the plan and other circumstances; but the variations must be simple and few and known to all, in order that the one selected by the commander at the time maybe adopted readily and without risk of misunderstanding.

V. Hotchkiss Rifles.
A mounted attack must be assisted by all the fire power available.(The question of the employment of artillery and machine guns is dealt with later.)
When the mounted attack is decided upon, Hotchkiss rifles must

fall out automatically and be grouped under squadron and regimental arrangements in charge of officers previously detailed for the purpose.

Their duties will then be-
(a) To look out for and deal with flank attacks;
(b) Make good a captured position;
(c) Cover a retirement.
For (a) and (c) they must be prepared to occupy tactical points and come into action with great rapidity. And their skilful handling will demand, on the part of the officers who are commanding them, alertness and quick decision.

VI. Ground Scouts.
In front of the attacking line, when once it has deployed, ground scouts are of very little use. Their information arrives too late, and in any case the time is past for modifying one's dispositions. In the majority of instances, a certain period elapses before the launching of the attack from the preparatory position, during which the commander explains his plan and the preliminary dispositions are being made. This period should be utilised to send forward officers for the purpose of reconnoitring the ground over which the advance will take place. These officers should work in pairs. If the number of available officers does not permit of this, each officer should be accompanied by a N.C.O., who can bring back information in the event of his officer becoming a casualty and to meet the case of an accident to a horse. This precaution is all the more necessary in this country, where small wadis are frequent and cannot be seen even at a distance of a few yards.

VII. Dismounted Attack.
Dismounted action will only be resorted to when a mounted attack is out of the question.

The rules for dismounted action are to be found in pages 283 to 298 of *Cavalry Training*, and it only remains to consider the question of the employment of Hotchkiss rifles, with which the cavalry has been armed since the commencement of the war.

Hotchkiss rifles are an addition, and, in the case of the comparatively weak rifle strength of a cavalry force, a very important addition to our fire power. We obtain a valuable clue as to their role and proper method of employment in the 'Notes on Recent Fighting,' issued by the General Staff, April 1918, and from which the following is extracted, substituting 'Hotchkiss' for Lewis gun and 'dismounted' for infantry attack:

'The Hotchkiss rifles form, owing to their great mobility and concentrated fire power, the framework of the dismounted attack. They can carry on the fire fight, if necessary, without any groups of riflemen. If the fighting strengths do not permit of special groups of riflemen being formed, the Hotchkiss groups can be correspondingly strengthened.'

We cannot do better than base our experience on these latest experiences. The result of the firefight depends on the volume and accuracy of the fire and not on the numbers of men engaged. And although the Hotchkiss rifles cannot replace bayonets in the final charge, they can supply the necessary volume of fire to enable the bayonets to get forward to within charging distance and with the minimum number of casualties.

Situations will occur when the fire zone can be crossed at the gallop, although the position itself must be assaulted with the bayonet. When this is the case, it will be the quickest and least costly method of approach. The only proviso of a 'mounted approach' is cover for the act of dismounting and the led horses. The moral effect on the enemy bears a distinct ratio to the pace at which the attack advances. If the time in which the attackers can succeed in arriving at assaulting distance becomes a matter of minutes instead of hours, the moral effect on the enemy will be such that he will rarely stand to face the bayonet assault.

Given, therefore, the conditions which we may expect to find at my time in Palestine, viz.:

(i) A position from which it is necessary to drive the enemy and which cannot be galloped.
(ii) The approach to the position leading over ground favourable to the rapid movement of mounted men.
(iii) Shelter of some sort in the vicinity of the position, or dead ground at its foot, the approach should be made extended at the gallop. A painful and prolonged fire fight will thus be avoided.

VIII. Artillery.
As to the artillery, there is nothing in the local conditions to call for any modifications in the instructions given in pages 297–308 of *Cavalry Training*, and pages 265–276.

Field Artillery Training. These instructions can be accepted in full.

Normally, when the Division is working in the field, batteries will group with the brigades to which they are affiliated. They must always be prepared, however, to be brigaded at any time under the direct command of the C.R.A.

There is one thing, which the experience of this war has brought out, and that is the importance of close association between the artillery and the arm, which it supports. An exchange of liaison officers between the cavalry and the artillery for the period of operations is not sufficient. What is required is personal touch between regimental and battery officers. It is too much to expect good cooperation between strangers. It becomes a duty, therefore, for regimental and battery officers of a Brigade Group to get to know each other well before coming into the presence of the enemy.

IX. Machine Guns.
At the commencement of the war, machine guns were integral parts of the squadron and company. The tendency has since been to organise them into independent formations, and now we have the machine gun company and the machine gun battalion, and at last the machine gun has come to be recognised as 'an

intermediate weapon with tactics of its own.' This being so, the machine gun squadron, like the regiments and battalions of a Brigade Group is disposed of directly by the Brigade Commander. He gives to it its own place in his operation orders. He will aim at keeping its fire value in his own hands. In other words, the temptation to break up the machine gun squadron by allotting sections and sub-sections to regiments and squadrons must be resisted. It is not meant by this that guns are never to be detached from the machine gun squadron. It will often be necessary and advisable to do this, for protective and for special purposes, in the same manner as a section of guns is often detached from a battery of artillery. But such detachment should be looked on as a temporary measure, and the guns should return to their squadron immediately on completion of their special task. Only in this way will their great firepower be directed towards the attainment of big results.

In a mounted attack the machine guns will normally be massed on a flank of the artillery.
In dismounted action their duties will be:
(a) In attack to concentrate their fire on the part of the line against which our main attack is directed.
(b) In defence, to concentrate on whatever hostile bodies of attacking troops are at the moment most threatening or dangerous; and to cover a counterattack.
(c) In both attack and defence, to provide overhead fire for the support of the rifle and Hotchkiss groups.
(d) To protect the flanks against outflanking movements and counterattacks.

For these purposes, the machine guns should not be disposed in one line, but be distributed in depth; by which they can make better use of the ground, offer a much more difficult target to the enemy, and are much better able to meet the contingencies referred to in (d).

It is concentration of effort, as opposed to dispersion, which wins battles, and this rule applies to the machine gun, as much as to any of the other arms.

X. Security.
Allusion has been made to the inferior moral of the Turks. This does not justify the slightest relaxation in the measures we must take for our security. Contempt for the enemy, bringing with it carelessness in the matter of protection, has been a constant source of disaster throughout the history of war. We must be as careful in face of the Turk as we should be if opposed to the most skilful and enterprising foe.

Protective dispositions must not be contracted, and patrols must be sent out to a distance of 4 to 5 miles at least from the main body. And when once touch with the enemy has been gained, he must be picquetted.

Massed formations on the march must be avoided. Death loves a crowd. By making every possible use of cover, and by the adoption of suitable formations, the opportunities for hostile artillery and aircraft will be reduced to a minimum.

XI. The Pursuit.
All pursuing troops should act with great boldness, and
be prepared to accept risks, which would not be justifiable at other times (F.S.R., I., sec. 112, 4). When the enemy is beaten and we are on his heels, a methodical progression, as is adopted in the approach march, is out of place. Reconnaissance and protective bodies must still be employed, but we cannot afford to wait too long on their movements. The only objective to be given at this time should be the enemy. Everyone should be animated with the desire to get forward as fast as possible, to kill and take prisoners and to capture guns. By these means, the enemy's demoralisation will be increased, and he will fall an easy prey. The pursuit, carried on in this fashion, will entail a good deal of dispersal of units, and it is here that good discipline, good training and a good system of communication and command will come in. If the men 'see red,' so much the better; but the leaders must keep their heads and constantly endeavour to maintain touch with

neighbouring units and with the formation to which they belong. Every formation must endeavour to keep a reserve in hand to meet unforeseen contingencies, and on which the leaders of the pursuing troops must rally on every occasion after they have dealt with the enemy in their own immediate sphere of action.

XII. Moral.
'The moral is to the physical as three is to one.'
No military maxim has been more often quoted; none so little understood.

The sight of a determined mounted advance and the fear of cold steel have far greater and more lasting effect than many bullets. The terror inspired by a cavalry charge extends far and wide, and is not confined to the troops immediately attacked.

Officers should try and realise that morale is something more than an abstract quality. For you it is a tangible asset. If you have confidence in your men, and they have confidence in you; if they are well trained and, above all, leavened through and through with discipline of the right sort, and if you yourselves have the tactical knowledge and insight to manoeuvre your men into suitable positions for dealing with the enemy – then one of your troops becomes the equivalent of three troops, one squadron the equivalent of three squadrons, and one regiment the equivalent of three regiments. Then you can venture much and greatly dare.

24. PHASE V
PRELIMINARY OPERATIONS

While the concentration of XXI Corps and Descorps in the coastal plain was nearing completion, various preliminary operations were undertaken.

Feisal's Arabs, coming in from the east, blew up the railway south, west and north of Deraa onv16, 17 and 18 September; as a result, all through traffic to Palestine ceased, and Turkish reserves (probably one battalion) were sent east from the Plain of Esdraelon to meet this menace. The R.A.F. cooperated by bombing Deraa.

Chaytor's Force carried out active patrolling on the nights of 17 and 18 September, and made a demonstration to induce the enemy to believe that a movement eastward over Jordan was intended.

XX Corps, during the night 18–19 September, swung forward its right on the east of the Bireh-Nablus road; heavy hand-to-hand fighting resulted, in which over 400 prisoners were taken.

On the night of 18–19 September a Handley-Page machine, which had flown from England, dropped 1,200lbs of bombs on Mule aerodrome, railway station and signal exchange.

The Main Attack
At dawn on 19 September the attack of XXI Corps began.

During the night the attacking infantry had deployed on taped lines in No Man's land, behind a weak line of outposts; No Man's land averaged about 1,000 yards in width on the front of attack.

At 04:30 hours, the artillery opened an intense bombardment lasting 15 minutes, under cover of which the infantry moved forward from their positions of deployment; the enemy's artillery barrage came down on our front line trenches, and consequently passed over the heads of our infantry.

The attack was a complete success, and went through with unexpected rapidity. On the extreme left 60th Division, attacking on a front of two battalions and in depth, had crossed the Nahr Falik by 07:00 hours, and had established a bridgehead to cover the debouching of Fivecav (Note. 60th Division had advanced 7,000 yards in 21 hours.)

In the centre, 75th Division had more difficulty, especially at Et Tire; but by 11:00 hours both systems had been taken and the Turks were in full retreat.(75th Division had advanced 11,000 yards in 6½ hours.)

The Pursuit on the Battlefield
By 11:00 hours disorganised bodies of the enemy were streaming across the plain towards Tulkeram, pursued by 60th Division and 5th A.L.H. Brigade.

This cavalry brigade, belonging to Ausdiv, had been temporarily detached from Descorps and attached to XXI Corps for local and immediate exploitation.

Tulkeram, a fortified area at the entrance to the important pass into the mountains, contained the Headquarters of Turkish VIII Army; the pass would be the only suitable line of retreat for the Turks from the maritime plain in case of defeat. 5th A.L.H. Brigade was, therefore, directed by XXI Corps to move as rapidly as possible by the north of Tulkeram and to drop down into the pass east of that place and to cut the railway there. It was hoped they might, perhaps, cut off and capture VIII Army Headquarters.

This Cavalry Brigade had a remarkable origin. At the end of June 1918, three months before these operations, the Imperial Camel Corps Brigade was re-organised as a cavalry force, which was to be named 5th A.L.H. Brigade, and which consisted at first of two A.L.H. regiments and a New Zealand machine gun squadron. The officers, N.C.O.s and men had fought as camelmen throughout the campaign; many had never ridden a horse before. Not only were they confident that they could become efficient mounted soldiers in three months, but they insisted on being armed with a sword; they were, in fact, the first Australians to enlarge their role from that of mounted riflemen to that of cavalrymen.

After three months of intensive training, under Brigadier-General C. L. Gregory, 19th Lancers, they succeeded in what they had set out to do, and became by September an efficient Cavalry Brigade. The C-in-C paid them the compliment of especially selecting them for attachment to XXI Corps, for carrying out the first desperate venture of the pursuit, the capture of Tulkeram. The Brigade had been completed by the inclusion in it of a French regular cavalry regiment named *Régiment Mixte de Cavalerie*; it consisted of two squadrons of *Chasseurs d'Afrique* and two of Algerian *Spahis*. This regiment was well equipped with everything, including automatic weapons; and was mounted on barbs, which were efficient and could stay forever; being small, however, they could not be expected to carry the weight or go the pace of our much bigger horses.

Such was the unique composition and origin of 5th A.L.H. Brigade. It did all its work well in the subsequent operations, and much of it most exceptionally well.

Cavalry is an arm which takes a long time to make; and it is sometimes assumed that military organisers would not attempt to create new cavalry formations during war; but the 5th A.L.H. Brigade showed that it can be done, given the highest class of instructor produced in the Empire, and such personnel as can be found on the sheep and cattle stations of Australia and New Zealand.

As stated above, 60thDivisionand 5thA.L.H.Brigade, at 11:00, were in full pursuit towards Tulkeram, where great confusion reigned. Bodies of troops, guns, motor-lorries and transport of every description were endeavouring to escape along the road leading to Messudieh Junction and Nablus. This road, which follows the railway up a comparatively narrow valley, was already crowded with troops and transport. The confusion was added to by the persistent attacks of the British aeroplanes, from which there was no escape; great havoc was caused, and in several places the road was blocked by overturned lorries and vehicles.

Brigadier-General Onslow, commanding 5th A.L.H. Brigade, reached Tulkeram about midday and succeeded during the afternoon in getting one regiment and some machine guns round by the north of Tulkeram, and so cutting the main Turkish line of retreat. Owing to the large numbers of enemy in Tulkeram and the strength of the defences, 5th A.L.H. Brigade was unable to do more than hold the enemy and prevent him withdrawing pending the arrival of 60th Division. The leading brigade of 60th Division arrived by dusk, having advanced, against opposition and over sand,16½milesin12½ hours; it assaulted the town from the south-west. As a result of the combined action of air force, cavalry and infantry, about 3,000 prisoners, large quantities of transport and many guns fell into our hands.

Simultaneous with this wheel of 60th Division and 5th A.L.H. Brigade on Tulkeram, the centre and right of XXI Corps also wheeled eastwards and pressed forward in pursuit into the hills.

The positions reached by 22:00 hours on 19 September by the 60th, 7th, 75th, 3rd and 54th Divisions and the French detachment of XXI Corps are shown on Plate XIII.

Exploitation by Desert Mounted Corps.
(The Order of battle of Descorps on 19 September 19 is shown in Appendix A, below)

Fivecav

About 06:30 hours on 19 September, Fivecav began to pass through the enemy's entrenchments on the seashore; under protection of the bridgehead formed by 60th Division, 18th Cavalry Brigade (Advance Guard) and 14th Cavalry Brigade (both less wheels) had crossed the Nahr Falik at its mouth at about 08:30 hours.

The rapidity and ease with which the cavalry division passed through the infantry was largely due to the fact that the narrow strip of sand on the sea shore was hidden from view and fire from inland by cliffs.

The enemy could only hope to stop the mounted column by actually holding the strip of sea shore and shooting southward along it; the British destroyers firing offshore effectively dissuaded the enemy from any activity on the beach and, as a result, Fivecav made its exit in column of troops through the trench systems and battle front down what was in effect a deep and broad communication trench – an ideal covered route.

The sand, however, on the beach, except at the water's edge, was deep, heavy and holding; eight miles of such going was a bad preparation for the hard work to follow.

Almost immediately after crossing the Nahr Falik, small parties of Turks were met by 9th Hodson's Horse (the advance guard of 18th Cavalry Brigade). This regiment at once squashed all opposition with great dash, by riding straight at the enemy. All Turks, who did not actually stand across the line of advance, were allowed to melt away, as strict orders had been passed down from the C-in-C that the cavalry were to avoid being involved in any fighting while breaking away.

18th Cavalry Brigade

By 11:00 hours, 18th Cavalry Brigade (less wheels) had occupied their first objective, Liktera, having taken 250 prisoners and 4 guns, and having done 22 miles in about 4 hours over heavy going. The remainder of Fivecav arrived by 15:00 hours.

Brigadier-General Kelly, commanding 18th Cavalry Brigade, had received instructions approximately as follows :

    1. The distance from the mouth of the Falik to Liktera is roughly 15 miles, and this place should be reached four hours after crossing the Nahr Falik.

    2. A halt until 18:15 hours should be made on the line of the Wadi Hudeira (Liktera) to water, feed and rest.

    3. At 18:15 hours your Brigade will move on Nazareth, a distance of 80 miles. It is calculated that the leading regiment should reach Nazareth by 08:00 hours [20 September]. It is of the utmost importance that Nazareth is surrounded before daylight. All roads will be barricaded so as to make it impossible for a car, by rushing the posts, to enter or leave Nazareth. All individuals moving to or from Nazareth are to be made prisoners.

    4. The town of Nazareth will be captured, but it is not to be bombed or shelled. Hostile G.H.Q. is situated in the town, and all Commanders, Staffs and documents are to be seized and taken care of.

    6. Should, for unseen reasons, the march of the Brigade be so delayed that it cannot reach Nazareth before daylight, the leading regiment must be pushed on and followed as rapidly as possible by the remainder. If the fighting wheels are unable to keep up, the advance of the fighting troops is on no account to be delayed.

    7. 14th Cavalry Brigade will follow 18th Cavalry Brigade as closely as possible, and will be responsible for the fighting wheels of 18th Cavalry Brigade, should they be unable to keep up.[Note. No wheels were taken by 18th Cavalry Brigade.]

At 18:15, 18th Cavalry Brigade left Liktera to cross the hills at Jarak and surround Nazareth before daylight (approximately 04:30). The country was unknown, the track over the hills impossible for wheels, the map a small scale one and inaccurate, and men and horses were tired, as this was the third successive night the Brigade had been on the move. The General Staff had not provided the Brigade with guides.

Fortunately the Brigade Commander spoke Arabic and he spent the afternoon questioning local Arabs and Jews concerning the track over the mountains, and finally bribed two Arabs to lead the way. The chief difficulty lay in finding in the dark the opening into the hills, and the guides alone made this possible. On getting into the hills about 22:00 hours, innumerable goat tracks were found to be running in every direction; in many places horses could only move in single file and much credit for keeping up is due to the pack leaders of the Hotchkiss gun sections and of the machine gun squadron.

At Jarak a squadron was dropped to guard the pass as a protection to the left flank of main force of Descorps which was to cross the mountains further south through the Musmus Pass. This detachment was made under Corps orders; it is surprising, however, that the G.O.C. Fivecav did not order the detachment to be made from 14th Cavalry Brigade, which was closely following 18th Cavalry Brigade through the pass, as every detachment from the latter Brigade would handicap its chances at Nazareth.

The mountain range was successfully crossed, and when the Brigadier at the head reached Warakani near the railway about 02:15, a halt was called and the Brigade ordered to close up. It was then found that no one was present except Brigade Headquarters, Signal Troop and F Troop. Guides were sent back, and after waiting an hour, two regiments arrived, but not the third.

The Brigade trotted on and began to climb the lower slopes of the Nazareth Hills. About 04:15, the head of the Brigade reached a village, which the guide declared to be Nazareth. The Brigadier, however, interrogated a small boy asleep in the street and found that the place was El Mujeidel, the boy stated there were a lot of Turks in the village. These could not be left, as they might have telephoned a warning on to Nazareth; as they had to be located and disarmed, more delay occurred. On proceeding again, the Brigade reached Yafa, 1½ miles short of Nazareth. Here again 75 Turks had to be rounded up, causing delay and forcing the Brigadier to detach escorts from his already much depleted strength.

Daylight was fast approaching as the head of the Brigade trotted on from Yafa towards Nazareth. The road had become very narrow, with a precipitous drop on the south-east side and high hills on the north-west side.

On reaching the forked roads just south of Nazareth, a squadron 18th Lancers was sent as right flank guard to watch the Mule road. This squadron almost at once found the road crowded with lorries and an escort of about 400 Turks heading up the hill to Nazareth; these were taken completely by surprise, could not well extend in the difficult stony country, and, after putting up some fight, surrendered.

The last remaining squadron of 18th Lancers was sent up the hill on the north-west side of Nazareth, where a large barrack full of Turks was in a dangerously dominating position.

The Brigadier, left with only the Gloucestershire Yeomanry, tried to push on and reach the branch roads north of the town, which remained the only road by which motor-cars could escape.

It was after 05:00 and light; Turks and Germans could be seen running about in the town in every direction, and very soon they were found to be manning fire positions.

Nazareth lies in a saucer with hills on all sides; the Turks quickly got into positions on these hills and the Gloucestershire Yeomanry did not succeed in pushing through to block the northern exit. They attacked many occupied buildings, which were stoutly defended, principally by Germans, and some hundreds of prisoners were taken in this street fighting.

Many inhabitants and prisoners stated that Liman von Sanders had left the night before and this, no doubt, influenced the Brigadier, for it would be questionable as to whether it was worthwhile to continue to struggle to reach the northern exit if the C-in-C had already escaped. Especially so, as it was long since evident that Nazareth was strongly held, and our troops were already heavily handicapped with the necessity of safeguarding and evacuating 1,200 prisoners scattered in many directions.

Between 10:00 and 11:00 a heavy counterattack, directed by Liman van Sanders himself, developed from the high ground to the north-west of the town against the rear of the Brigade. Towards midday the Brigade was recalled to join Fivecav at Afule.

The Brigade had failed to capture the C-in-C, but certain definite results had been gained. The railway between Haifa and Afule had been cut, 1,200 prisoners had been taken and the enemy's Commander-in-Chief was a fugitive; his staff and communications had been broken up. He took to flight and so became unable to direct the retreat of his defeated armies.

For many reasons this cavalry raid has appealed to the imagination of cavalry soldiers. The idea of riding straight at hostile G.H.Q. and capturing the enemy's C-in-C is an engaging one; it very nearly succeeded. The reasons for the failure have been actively discussed among the regiments of Descorps.

The raid appears to have been an afterthought; there is no mention of it in the G.H.Q. Operation Order, nor in the G.H.Q. special instructions to G.O.C. Descorps.

The Descorps order to Fivecav, to whom it gave as its final objective 'a position north of Afule,' deals with it in these words: 'In advancing on the El Afuleh road, the Haifa railway should be cut and dispositions should ensure a detachment visiting Nazareth, with a view to capturing influential prisoners and confidential documents.'

The instructions on which 18th Cavalry Brigade acted (given above) weredated18 September; they give to 18th Cavalry Brigade quite a different ride to that given it by Fivecav Operation Order dated 17 September. It therefore appears that the decision to raid Nazareth with one Brigade was made after the Operation Order was issued on 17 September. This probably explains why the Brigadier was not provided by General Staff (Intelligence) with guides, nor with a plan or aerial photographs or an adequate map of Nazareth. Some such aid should have been within the power of General Staff (Intelligence) to provide, and would appear essential to success.

The Brigade had halted at Liktera from 11:00 until 18:15 and was not allowed to leave Liktera until then.The distance from Liktera to Nazareth is 80miles,and had to be reached by 08:00hours – that is,80milesin8¾hours. Such going would be possible by day, but seems very overoptimistic for night over one mountain and up another, with the columns practically always at a walk and often in single file.

The difficult nature of the task of surrounding Nazareth before daylight, owing to the rough nature of the hillsides surrounding the town.

The march of the Brigade (even though without wheels), under the exceptional difficulties, remains a remarkable performance – it covered 50 miles in under 22 hours.

4th Cavalry Division (Fourcav)
At 09:00, 19 September, Fourcav passed through the clearings, which had been made in our own trench systems, and, moving east of the marshes of the Nahr Falik, headed for El Mughair. The leading Brigade, 11th Cavalry Brigade, reached it about 18:00, up to this point practically no opposition had been met with. The R.A.F. during the march reported that large numbers of the enemy were moving northwards on all roads and that tents and stores were burning.

It will be seen, by comparing this performance with that of Fivecav, that the head of the latter had reached Liktera with a lead of about 8½ hours, presumably owing to the fact of the fear that the Turks had of our Navy resulted in their collapsing more quickly on the sea shore than inland; and also due to the fact that the sea shore, protected by cliffs, had given Fivecav a covered way.

After passing the Nahr lskanderun, the advanced guard came under slight rifle fire from the Kakon-Liktera switch line. The enemy's position was promptly galloped at by the 36th Jacob's Horse and 250 prisoners taken.

Fourcav reached its first objective, the line Jelameh-Tel ed Dhruh, by 16:30 and halted for 5 hours.

At 18:00, orders were issued for the advance of the Division to begin at 22:00 and to continue right through the Musmus Pass on El Lejjun, with 10th Cavalry Brigade acting as advanced guard. From this Brigade 2nd Lancers and 11th L.A.M. Battery moved off at 20:45 to 'make good the crossroads at Kh Arah.' This small force came up on the rear of a column of Turkish transport and stragglers and had collected, without fighting, 500 prisoners before Kh Arah was reached. Fourcav report states:

> At 2140 hours the Divisional Commander arrived at Headquarters 10th Cavalry Brigade at railway station Kerkur. Owing to some delay in watering 10th Cavalry Brigade was not ready to move at 2200 hours; they were ordered to move as soon as possible. The Divisional Commander then motored on to the 2nd Lancers who had by then made good Kh Arah. The 2nd Lancers were ordered to move on El Lejjµn at once, and the remainder of 10th Cavalry Brigade instructed to leave at 2800 hours. No.11 L.A.M.B. pushed two cars down the pass as far as Musmus, which was reported clear at 2850 hours. On returning to the entrance to the pass, the G.O.C. found that the 10th Cavalry

Brigade had taken the wrong road. As some considerable delay ensued in getting the head of the column back on to the right road, the 12th Cavalry Brigade was ordered to follow 2nd Lancers through the Pass; 2nd Lancers came under orders of G.O.C., 12th Cavalry Brigade, which entered the Pass at 01:00 hours on 20/9/18.

12th Cavalry Brigade was further instructed to push as rapidly as possible through the pass and gain, before dawn, the heights at El Lejjun, commanding the northern entrance to the pass.

At 03:30 2nd Lancers reached Lejjun, followed by 12th Cavalry Brigade at 04:05, and the remainder of the Division at 06:00.

The successful securing of this vital pass was entirely due to the energetic personal action of the Divisional Commander, who throughout a long and anxious night squashed every difficulty as it arose. In his motor-car, ahead of his Division and only protected by the advance guard on the road in front of him, he did his work at great personal risk, for the country was full of Turks.

It is interesting to note that the L.A.M. Battery preceded the cavalry through the pass; the road was fit for lorries and there was a moon. The L.A.M. Battery, by going on in front, did a big service to Fourcav, and enabled 2ndLancersto move at a greatly increased pace.

The Attack by 2nd Lancers
At 0530, 2nd Lancers, with No.11 L.A.M.B. and one section 17th machine gun squadron attached, moved forward towards Afule.

The advanced troops soon came under fire and it was apparent the enemy was in some strength astride the Lejjun-Afule road. One squadron, with No. 11 L.A.M.B. and a machine gun section, held the enemy in front, while two squadrons made a converging attack on the enemy's left flank. Although the enemy fired to the last and had three machine guns in action, the charge went home. 46 Turks were killed or wounded and 470 taken prisoners; none got away. 2nd Lancers had one man wounded, and about a dozen horses had to be destroyed.

In the opinion of the writer the importance of this brilliant attack cannot be overestimated. The C-in-C had said to the G.O.C. Descorps: 'The action of your troops must be characterised by the greatest vigour and rapidity.' The Divisional Commander had issued his stirring *Fighting Instructions*.

But such exhortations from superior commanders are of no value whatever unless their regiments have got the courage.

The hour was 05:30, just after dawn; the last hour that one would choose in which to be asked such a question. Officers, N.C.O.s and men had been on the move for three successive nights, which in itself alone is enough to lower the vitality of men to freezing point. The feat itself is remarkable; a cavalry regiment assisted by a L.A.M. Battery taking on in single combat an infantry battalion; a battalion which was fresh, which had not fought and which was not, and had no reason to be, demoralised. The attack was well handled, and from every point of view is well worthy of study in all cavalry regiments.

The writer well remembers the exhilarating effect the news of this victory had on the remainder of Descorps. It was clear by now that the Corps would have to meet enemy forces in huge superiority, and this action gave to all complete confidence in the method adopted; everyone determined to try and do likewise when the time came.

By 08:00, 12th Cavalry Brigade had occupied Afule, capturing large quantities of war material, including 10 locomotives, 50 rolling stock, and three aeroplanes. No.11 L.A.M. Battery captured 12 lorries driven by Germans who were trying to escape by Beisan. A German aviator, not knowing anything, landed at the aerodrome. Discovering his mistake he tried to get away; the observer was killed, the pilot wounded.

By 09:00 all railway lines bifurcating from Afule were cut with guncotton slabs.

At 12:00, the whole Division was concentrated at Afule and moved on Beisan at 18:00, leaving one regiment to guard the place until Fivecav, which was close at hand, assumed control.

The advanced troops occupied Beisan at 16:30, and the whole Division concentrated there by 18:00. Slight opposition was met with, but the place was at once attacked at the gallop, about 100 prisoners being taken. During the advance from Mule to Beisan some 800 prisoners were taken. Three 5.9 inch howitzers were captured at Beisan; they were at once manned by the horse gunners and put into action to command all roads leading into Beisan from the south.

From Afule, the 19th Lancers had started at 19:00 on a difficult march over almost impassable country to seize the big railway bridge over the Jordan at Jisr Mejamie, 5 miles south of Lake Tiberias. By 08:00, 21 September, they had prepared it for demolition, but it was not to be blown as long as it could be held. This was their fourth consecutive night on the move.

During the night the line Afule-Beisan was picquetted to catch any Turks trying to pass north between those two places. 700 prisoners were taken during the night; it was gathered from them that the Turkish Commanders and troops to the south were quite unaware that the British cavalry was across all their lines of retreat on the west side of Jordan.

The Division had marched 70 miles in 34 hours and had lost 26 horses, the first 20 miles being over a road-less country with sandy soil. The Americans, both of the north and south, in the Civil War, covered, with equal or greater numbers, bigger distances in shorter time. But the hitting power of their formations was small compared with that of Fourcav, which disposed of 108 Hotchkiss guns, 86 machine guns and 12 thirteen-pdr guns, in addition to its mounted men armed with rifle, sword, and bayonet.

In the past, fast paces over long distances have only been attained by cavalry at the expense of hitting power, and vice versa; though mechanical transport may easily provide a different experience. It is probable that this march of Fourcav is at least a British record up-to-date, as regards pace and distance for a formation of such power.

Australian Mounted Division
At 10:00, 19 September, Ausdiv (less 5th A.L.H. Brigade), having marched from Ludd during the early hours of the night, was ordered to follow Fourcav through the trench systems about Tabsor. From this hour onwards a hostile aeroplane observer, if one had been available, flying over the plain of Sharon would have seen a remarkable sight in the open plain – 94 squadrons, disposed in a great breadth and in great depth, hurrying forward relentlessly on a decisive mission – a mission of which all cavalry soldiers have dreamed, but in which few have been privileged to partake.

Ausdiv was in Corps Reserve; it reached the Nahr Iskanderun at 17:30 hours and halted.

At 01:00, 20 September, the march was resumed, but 4th A.L.H. Brigade was left behind as escort to the many supply and ammunition columns, which were still struggling in rear in the heavy sand. Practically all the G.S. wagons of all three divisions had fallen behind, and were in danger from any counter-stroke, which might come from the direction of Haifa down the coast road; which suggests that G.S. wagons, even when four-horsed, are unsuitable as transport to cavalry formations.

On reaching the summit of the Musmus Pass a regiment and machine gun section were dropped, with orders to occupy the high ground commanding the pass on each side; what remained of Ausdiv reached Lejjun about 10:00.

Advanced Descorps Headquarters reached Lejjun at 12:00; information began to come in from all directions.

At 15.35 hours the 3rd A.L.H. Brigade (less 8th A.L.H. regiment) with Notts Battery R.H.A. and 11th L.A.M. Battery attached, was ordered by Descorps to push on with 'all speed and greatest possible boldness' and occupy Jenin, which was known to be an important centre on the Turkish lines of communication. Situated on the only railway and metalled road behind the enemy's centre, it was considered certain that the main Turkish columns would attempt to escape that way. Additionally, it had already been reported by the R.A.F. that columns from the south were moving north from Mesudieh.

By 16:30, the Brigade began its march. 10th A.L.H. Regiment (six machine guns attached)was the advance guard; a troop of 9th A.L.H. Regiment, right flank guard. The writer had lately had the great privilege of teaching the 3rd A.L.H Brigade how to use the sword, and he could not resist the temptation of going with them to see what they would do with it on this, their first opportunity.

From the start, it electrified them, and the extraordinary pace of 10 miles an hour was maintained – the Brigade, including Notts Battery R.H.A., covering the 11 miles in 70 minutes.

Halfway to Jenin, a small enemy outpost was captured by the flank guard. As the advanced guard approached Jenin, a large enemy force was seen camped among the olive groves in the foothills immediately to the right of the line of advance. The right flank troop of the vanguard immediately charged them with drawn swords. The enemy promptly surrendered. A few minutes later the right flank guard and two additional troops sent out from the main body arrived, and together they rounded up the enemy scattered through the olive groves. The enemy was apparently astounded at the sudden appearance of our men, coming, as it did, from their rear. The prisoners amounted to 1,800, including many Germans; 400 horses and mules were also taken.

This episode, however, did not delay the general advance of the column. The advance guard pushed on rapidly, leaving the railway station about half a mile on its right, so as to get astride the Jenin-Afule road and a track, which led east to Beisan. By 17:40 the vanguard had reached Jenin, the remainder of the column, including the guns, being close in rear; by 18:00 all exits to the north and east had been closed.

Once astride the roads and railway the 10th Regiment turned south and drove back in towards the village and station. By this energetic action, the enemy were driven into confusion and our men, riding in among them with drawn swords, made prisoners of about 3,000.

This is the modest report by the Brigadier of an action full of brilliant dash. Later, in referring to this, the first experience of his Brigade with an *arme blanche* weapon, he made the following remarks:

> As the Brigade approached Jenin on the afternoon of 20 September, a party of 1,800 of the enemy were observed on our right front. They were promptly charged with drawn swords and surrendered. If we had had no swords the procedure would have been a careful approach, then probably a firefight, and we could not have got into Jenin that night. Probably the 6,000 extra prisoners that we got [later that night] would have evaded us, or had time to organise. Later on the same evening our men, galloping up the streets of Jenin, demoralised the enemy much more quickly than a dismounted approach with fire would have done. The quickness of it meant practically no casualties to us.

By now it was dark, and pressing on to clear the town the Light Horse were held up by rifle and machine gun fire from a party of Germans concealed in houses and gardens. Later this party tried to break away, and there was some confused fighting in the darkness. The Germans were caught by the fire from a section of machine guns as they tried to break for the road and a number were killed; they then surrendered without further opposition. Prisoners were collected, troops assembled, and dispositions made for the night.

The left flank troop of the advance guard captured 27 lorries, and a further 29 lorries were found abandoned.

10th A.L.H. Regiment moved through the town and took up a position astride the main road from Nablus, where it passes through the pass about one mile south of Jenin. The following occurred:
> Lieutenant Patterson, with his sub-section of machine guns, was sent to support them in the poor light, and got ahead of the squadron that they were to join. Some little distance down the Nablus road at about 2100 hours they saw a large body of enemy approaching in the moonlight – 2,800 in fact – with four guns. The officer thought it rather a big order for his troop of 28 to take on, but his Corporal (Lance Corporal B. George) proffered the advice that it was safer to bluff it out than retire. The officer agreed. He put a burst of M.G. fire over the heads of the leading troops and called upon them to surrender. At first they demurred. It was their first suspicion that there were any hostile troops in front of them. In fact, the Germans afterwards railed against the Turks for the latter's failure to keep them posted as to the situation; but the Turks themselves were equally ignorant. This column now found itself in a narrow gorge, wide enough for the road only, with steep hills on either side, over which single men could climb with difficulty. They were aware that they were being followed from the south. Their advance was blocked by a party of enemy whose strength they could not gauge in the moonlight, and machine gun bullets were whistling over their heads to expedite their decision. There was at the head of the column a German nurse who spoke English fluently. Lieutenant Patterson told her that there was an overwhelming force just to his rear. She passed his information on, and, after a short conference between the enemy leaders, the whole party surrendered.'

By morning, over 8,000 prisoners, including many commanders of high rank, had been captured by a cavalry brigade, less one regiment. Many German and Turkish officers admitted being taken completely by surprise at the unexpected appearance of our troops in their rear; they stated that they thought our troops must have been landed by the 'wonderful British Navy' at Haifa, as they did not believe it possible that such rapid progress could have been made up the coast.

Thus, by the end of the second day, General Allenby's hopes as to the success of his cavalry had been fulfilled. Within 36 hours of the commencement of the battle, all the main outlets of escape remaining to Turkish VII and VIII Armies had been closed, and about15,000 had already been taken. The remainder could only avoid capture by using the tracks which run south-east from the vicinity of Nablus to the crossings over the Jordan at Jisr ed Damieh. The first phase of the operations was over.

APPENDIX A
Order of Battle of Desert Mounted Corps, 19 September 1918
Commander. Lieutenant-General Sir H. G. Chauvel, K.C.B., K.C.M.G.

Australian Imperial Forces.
4thCavalry Division.
Commander. Major-General Sir G. de Symons Barrow, K.C.M.G., et cetera.
10th Cavalry Brigade (Dorset Yeomanry, 2nd Lancers, 38th C.I.H., 17th machine gun squadron)
11th Cavalry Brigade (County of London Yeomanry, 29th Lancers, 36th Jacob's Horse, 21st machine gun squadron)
12th Cavalry Brigade (Staffordshire Yeomanry, 6th Cavalry. 19th Lancers, 18th machine gun squadron).
20th Brigade R.H.A. (1/1st Berkshire, Hampshire and Leicester Batteries).

5thCavalry Division.

Commander. Major-General Sir H.J. M. MacAndrew, K.C.M.G., et cetera.
13th Cavalry Brigade (Gloucestershire Yeomanry, 9th Hodson's Horse, 18th Lancers, 19th machine gun squadron)
14th Cavalry Brigade (Sherwood Rangers Yeomanry, 20th Deccan Horse, 34th Poona Horse, 20th machine gun squadron)
15th Cavalry Brigade (Jodhpur, Mysore and 1st Hyderabad I.S. Lancers; I.S. machine gun squadron).
Divisional Artillery (B Battery H.A.C., and Essex Battery R.H.A.)

Australian Mounted Division
Commander, Major-General Sir H. W. Hodson, K.C.M.G., et cetera
3rd A.L.H. Brigade (8th, 9th & 10th A.L.H. Regiments, 3rd Australian machine gun squadron)
4th A.L.H. Brigade (4th, 11th & 12th A.L.H. Regiments, 4th Australian machine gun squadron)
5th A.L.H. Brigade (14th & 15th A.L.H. Regiments, *Régiment Mixte de Cavalerie*, 2nd New Zealand machine gun squadron)
19th Brigade R.H.A. (A Battery H.A.C. and Notts Battery R.H.A.)

Australian and New Zealand Mounted Division (temporarily detached from Descorps to Chaytor's Force)
Commander, Major-General Sir E. W. C. Chaytor, K.C.M.G. et cetera, N.Z.I.F.
1st A.L.H. Brigade (1st, 2nd & 3rd A.L.H. Regiments, 1st Australian machine gun squadron).
2nd A.L.H. Brigade (5th, 6th & 7th A.L.H. Regiments, 2nd Australian machine gun squadron)
New Zealand Mounted Rifles Brigade (Auckland, Canterbury and Wellington Mounted Rifle Regiments, 1st New Zealand machine gun squadron)
18th Brigade R.H.A. (Inverness, Ayrshire and Somerset Batteries, R.H.A.)

25 PHASE V

XX Corps.
By the evening of 20 September, XXI Corps had completely broken Turkish VIII Army, and Descorps, standing astride the enemy's retreat at Beisan, Jenin and Afuleh, had already taken several thousand prisoners.

Turkish VII Army, occupying strong defensive positions in the mountains south of Nablus, had been able to maintain a stout resistance to XX Corps, which only consisted of two divisions, supported by a comparatively weak heavy artillery. As a possible line of retreat, down the Wadi Farah to Jisr ed Damie, still remained open for Turkish VII Army, the G.O.C. XX Corps called on his troops for a special effort to drive in the enemy's rearguards and reach the high ground N.E. of Nablus and so cut off the last remaining line of retreat (Plate XIII).

The troops responded most gallantly, broke down the enemy's resistance, reached their objectives, and sent forward detachments in pursuit. The performance of the 10th Division was a very fine one; it fought and marched continuously for two days over more than 20 miles of difficult mountain country.

R.A.F.
Large columns of the enemy, particularly of transport, attempted to escape down the Wadi Farah. Reconnaissance machines

reported this to Air Force Headquarters. All available aeroplanes were mobilised for attack; the departure of machines from the aerodrome was so timed that two machines should arrive over the objective every three minutes, and that an additional formation of six machines should come into action every half-hour. These attacks were maintained for four hours, until troops of XX Corps arrived on the scene. The enemy's troops fled in all directions and the road was completely blocked and was strewn with a mass of debris of wrecked wagons, guns and motor-lorries, totalling in all 87 guns, 55 motor-lorries, four motor-cars and 932 wagons.

No eyewitness of the results of this disaster is likely ever again to underestimate the awful danger of heavy aerial attack against troops whose anti-aircraft defences have broken down. Complete and continuous efficiency of anti-aircraft measures is, henceforth, a vital necessity.

Desert Mounted Corps
Although the enemy's troops retreating northwards were much broken, yet many of their commanders, especially the Germans, were striving hard to restore discipline and organise the retreat. Lord Allenby gave orders that his Cavalry Corps, which was in position on all the enemy's lines of retreat, was not to remain sitting in those positions, but was to move southwards and meet the enemy and attack the heads of his columns.

5th Cavalry Division
It was known that Haifa was held by troops of Liman von Sanders' Army Reserve, which had not yet been engaged in the battle. At midday on 22 September, Fivecav was ordered to move at 05:00 on 23 September from about Afule and Nazareth, and to occupy Haifa and Acre.

The attack was most brilliantly conceived and carried out; it achieved the apparently impossible; no cavalry action in the campaign is more worthy of close study.

4th Cavalry Division

By 22 September, all eyes were turning towards the Jordan valley. Reports showed that the remnants of the Turkish VII and VIII Armies were moving towards Beisan and the several fords over the Jordan to the south of that place. Starting from Beisan early on September 28, 11th Cavalry Brigade of Fourcav moved down both banks of the Jordan with the object of closing the crossings over the river.

The following is extracted from the report of G.O.C. Fourcav on the action of 11th Cavalry Brigade (see Map C):

> About 0330 hours the left patrols were fired on from the direction of Mak Abu Naj. Reconnaissance disclosed the fact that a strong advance guard of about 1,000 infantry, and some 30 machine guns, with a few mounted men, were holding an advanced position covering the ford. The position ran through dense scrub, with its centre occupying a mound and a few houses. The mound was garrisoned by some 800 infantry with 15 machine guns. Captain Jackson, M.C., with 2 squadrons 29th Lancers, was detailed to clear up the situation in this direction. He very gallantly charged the mound, capturing some 800 prisoners and all the machine guns.
>
> Meanwhile the Middlesex Yeomanry had been ordered south to turn the rear of the hostile advance guard. It was then discovered that the enemy were in large numbers at the ford, and that also portions of the enemy were attempting to cross the river lower down.
>
> As two attacks on the ford by 36th Jacob's Horse on the east bank were unsuccessful, and the retreating enemy were in large numbers, the Brigadier wired to Fourcav at Beisan for Hants. Battery R.H.A.; it arrived about 1100 hours and came into action against the enemy holding the ford.
>
> It was not until the battery had fired its first round that the enemy disclosed his own batteries, of which he had

apparently two, posted on the east bank of the river and about 1500 yards south-east of the ford. The enemy's artillery quickly got on to Hants Battery, which, owing to the nature of the ground, was compelled to come into action in the open. Every gun of the battery was hit, but no damage was done to personnel; but so hot and accurate was the hostile fire that the gunners had temporarily to leave their guns.

Meanwhile, the Middlesex Yeomanry had worked down the west bank and succeeded in getting a squadron across at Mak Fath Allah ford. This squadron charged the guns and put them out of action.

The enemy holding the ford at Mak Abu Naj now commenced to withdraw and came under heavy machine gun and automatic rifle fire, suffering very severely and abandoning an enormous quantity of warlike stores.

It had been a very hot day, the going bad, and the horses had been without water since leaving Beisan; the Brigade therefore went into bivouac at 17:00 hours.

An officer's patrol of about 1 troop had been sent out into the mountains to the west to try and gain touch with the XX Corps cavalry regiment (Worcestershire Yeomanry) somewhere in the neighbourhood of Kh Atuf. The patrol reported itself to the O.C. the corps cavalry regiment at 06:00 hours on 24th, and succeeded in getting back again to its own brigade. It covered altogether 50 miles of most difficult country and was frequently held up by elements of Turkish VIII Army. This long distance patrol was probably the most difficult of the very limited number carried out in Palestine.

September 24
The report continues:
> On 24th, 11th Cavalry Brigade moved down both sides of the Jordan with the object of mopping up the retreating

Turkish Army, which was retiring on Beisan, apparently ignorant of the fact that our cavalry had been in possession of the place since the 20th.

Almost immediately on leaving bivouac the Middlesex Yeomanry came in contact with a hostile advance guard about 1,200 strong, supported by numerous machine guns, which was marching down the Wadi el Maleh [probably a Wadi running eastwards from the Jude An Mts down to the ford at Makel Sherar]. Hants Battery and one section machine guns were quickly pushed forward and dealt most severely with the advance guard, which was diverted from its line of march and forced back on to the column it was protecting; both the advance guard and the column were thrown into disorder and retired over the Jordan in hopeless rout [probably over the ford Mak el Masudi].

The battery was playing on them at ranges under 8,000 yards, and the machine guns and H.R.s, pushing forward to the very banks of the river, made the ford a veritable shambles. The hostile transport cut their horses out of their traces and, mounting, galloped into the foothills in the utmost disorder. On the west bank alone 4,000 prisoners and 29 machine guns were captured, in addition to many machine guns abandoned.

A further 1,000 prisoners were captured by 10th Cavalry Brigade on the west bank a little farther north. This Brigade was ordered to collect all rifles discarded by the Turks south of Beisan, the estimated number being 8,000.

The C-in-C, in his despatch, in referring to this date, 24 September, states 'the last remnants of the VII and VIII Turkish Armies had been collected. As armies they had ceased to exist, and but few had escaped.'

Comments
(a) It might have been thought that the C-in-C, having succeeded

in placing three cavalry divisions at vital points on the enemy's lines of retreat, would have been content to allow them to consolidate their positions there and await the arrival of the enemy's columns. But he was no believer in passive action; the retreating enemy, hotly pursued from the south, found themselves simultaneously heavily attacked from the north, and had no chance whatever to recover.

(b) Soldiers who were not present in this campaign may well find it hard to believe that such an appalling disaster could have happened to these two Turkish armies if they had only continued to fight. But there is a limit beyond which no troops can struggle, and this limit was probably reached by these Turks. Those British soldiers who took part in the retreats of August 1914, and March 1918, will no doubt understand. Let them cast their memories back and imagine, for instance, what would have happened if, on the night and day following the Battle of Le Cateau, Von Marwitz's Cavalry Corps had been standing astride all the lines of retreat of the British Army, with Von Kluck's Army in close pursuit.

(c) It will again be noticed that, on practically every occasion, cavalry leaders, from divisional commanders down to squadron commanders, chose the mounted form of attack. Time and morale effect were two vital factors; the mounted form of attack has no equal in morale effect and it obtains a definite decision, either success or failure, in the quickest possible time.

But it will be seen that leaders did not forget the urgent necessity of supporting fire; in the first place to help their mounted attack to get in and, in the case of failure, to get out again.

25 September

All Palestine west of Jordan having been cleared, Semakh, at the south end of Lake Tiberias, remained the only place in this area known to be still held. It was decided to capture it; very few troops were available, and the 4th A.L.H. Brigade of Ausdiv – very weak because of large detachments taken from it – was ordered to march from Mule on 24 September, via Beisan, and capture Semakh at dawn on 25 September. The action was remarkable for the great dash and determination with which the operation was carried out. The following account is an extract from the official report of the Brigade Commander, Brigadier-General W. Grant, D.S.O.:

On 24th September 1918, the 4th Cavalry Division were at Beisan with one Regiment [Central Indian Horse] holding Jisr el Mejamie. A patrol of Indian Cavalry had been fired on and driven back near Semakh on the 23rd; and a Squadron of the C.I.H., which made a reconnaissance towards the village on September 24, had met with machine gun fire and had also been shelled by a field gun and forced to retire.

The 4th A.L.H. Brigade [less 4th A.L.H. Regiment and two squadrons of the 12th L.H. Regiment] left Mule at 0830for the purpose of relieving part of the 3rd A.L.H. Brigade, which was holding an outpost line between Mule and Beisan. Before completing the relief, instructions were received from Ausdiv to continue the march to Beisan, which was reached by the Brigade at 1845. Information was received here that it was reported that the Turks were holding Semakh for the purpose of covering the removal of the large dump of stores and supplies that had been accumulated there. The 4th A.L.H. Brigade [less 4th A.L.H. Regiment and two squadrons 12th A.L.H. Regiment] was ordered to capture Semakh at dawn on 25th, and then push up the Yarmuk valley and protect the railway bridges between there and Deraa.

The Brigade bivouacked at Beisan till 1630 and then proceeded to Jisr Mejamie, where it arrived at 2100. One Squadron (less one troop) of the 12th A.L.H. Regiment, which had marched from Lejjun, rejoined at midnight. The C.I.H. supplied the information that the place was held and that the village and station buildings were on a plain about

2½ miles wide and extending for three miles south of the village [see Plate XVI]. It was stated that there was no cover of any sort on approaching the place, except that there were some undulations in the ground about 8,000 yards to the south-east. A resident of the Jewish village situated a mile away from Semakh, who had just come in, gave the information that the place was held by about 120 Turks and Germans – the latter not in uniform – and also that there were not more than four machine guns. It was also known that the enemy had one field gun, as it had been used against the Squadron of the C.I.H. that afternoon.

A message was received here from Ausdiv at Mule that the 15th A.L.H. Regiment was marching from Jenin to reinforce the Brigade, but that they would not arrive before daylight. It was left to the discretion of the G.O.C. whether he attacked at dawn or waited until reinforced by the 15th A.L.H. Regiment.

In view of the information received, the G.O.C. decided that he had sufficient force to capture the place, and that there would be less casualties if the place were rushed just before dawn, than if the attack were delivered in daylight. The question of time was of particular importance as the principal role assigned to the Brigade was the protection of the Yarmuk valley bridges and tunnels.

Orders were issued that the 11th A.L.H. Regiment were to attack, mounted, from the south-east just before dawn, under the covering fire of the machine guns, and the 12th A.L.H. Regiment (less five troops) would be held as a reserve.

Jisr Mejamie is six miles south of Semakh and there were two bridges to cross at the Jordan and Yarmuk rivers respectively; so two hours was allowed for the march. Dawn being expected at 0450, the Brigade marched from Jisr Mejamie at 0230. A British Officer and three Indians were provided by the C.I.H. as guides. A Squadron was also sent by that Regiment along the road on the west bank of the Jordan to act as a flank guard.

After crossing the bridge over the Yarmuk river, the Brigade deployed into column of squadrons, each in line of troop columns, and moved parallel to the road east of the railway line [Plate XVI]. The 11th A.L.H. Regiment, with one section of machine guns attached, were leading with one squadron (C) as advance guard, followed by Brigade Headquarters, Signal Troop, Machine Gun Squadron and 12th A.L.H. Regiment.

On approaching Semakh, the Machine Gun Squadron was ordered to support the 11th A.L.H. Regiment.

At 0425, when quite dark, intense hostile machine gun and rifle fire was opened along the whole front. The four advanced machine guns immediately came into action frontally, while the 11th A.L.H. Regiment swung off to the right so as to charge from south-easterly direction. As soon as the 11th A.L.H. Regiment had cleared their front, the eight reserve machine guns also came into action in line with the advanced guns. The machine gun squadron had then six guns in action on each side of the railway line and distributed intense scathing fire on the enemy's line.

A and B Squadrons of the 11th A.L.H. Regiment charged mounted with drawn swords, in two lines of half squadrons, with about 200 yards distance between lines. As they charged they yelled, which enabled the machine gunners to know their whereabouts and when to cease their fire, as it was still quite dark. These two squadrons broke right through the enemy's line and rode on to the east side of the railway buildings; two troops swung round the west of the railway buildings and entered the village. The railway buildings and the village were found to be strongly held, so the two squadrons dismounted, left their horses in a wadi near the pump house and attacked on foot. In the meantime C Squadron of the 11th A.L.H. Regiment, which had formed the advance guard, detached one troop to act as escort to the machine guns, and the remainder moved to protect the right rear of the two charging squadrons, and took up a position on Hill 877, watching the railway to Deraa and the road to Sumra. At 0510 they were sent to support the other squadrons in the village. C Squadron of the 12th A.L.H. Regiment was sent in on the left flank to the west of the village and took part in clearing the latter and the attack on the railway buildings.

It was apparent to our machine gun squadron that the most effective enemy fire was coming from machine guns and automatic rifles firing south along the railway towards Jisr Mejamie.

Six guns on the left were detailed to keep down the enemy's fire on their immediate and left fronts, and the six guns on the right to search the road, railway line, and railway station. When the 11th A.L.H. Regiment reached the latter, our machine gun fire was concentrated on two enemy machine guns and one automatic rifle on the railway line and they were soon put out of action. The machine guns were then advanced, one detachment covering the advance of the other, and eight guns took up a position on the west of the village and covering Lake Tiberias and the beach front. The other four machine guns were then galloped through the village to the support of B Squadron of the 11th Regiment, who were engaged with an enemy field gun and machine guns about 500 yards to the east of the engine shed. These were then silenced. When dawn appeared, about 0450, the enemy had taken up a stand in the village and the station buildings. He was fighting in a most determined manner with automatic rifles and bombs, besides rifles, and here most of our casualties occurred. The fighting ceased at 0530, when all the garrison of the railway buildings had been killed.

When the enemy's fire first started, it passed over the heads of the advancing troops, and fell amongst the remainder of the Brigade, which then moved eastwards to a point of cover just south of Hill 877.

Several of our casualties, including one officer, were caused through the treacherous use of the white flag. In one case a man walked up to, and was shot within, two yards of the white flag by an enemy standing just behind the man who held the flag.

Of the two motor-boats at Semakh, one escaped and the other was fired on by a Hotchkiss rifle and burst into flames and eventually sank. A Turkish officer swam ashore from the burning boat and was captured.

The bearer division of the cavalry Field Ambulance with camel *cacolets* had followed the Brigade from Jisr Mejamie. The ambulance wagons and all other wheels, except machine gun limbers, were left behind until daylight and then moved to Semakh.

The enemy had about 100 killed; in addition the captured included:
Germans   7 Officers, 143 O.R.
Turks   16 Officers, 198 O.R.
             Total 364

One field gun and 200 rounds
Seven machine guns and three automatic rifles

Our casualties were :
Killed   3 Officers, 14 O.R.
Wounded   7 Officers, 54 O.R.
             Total 78

Our casualties mostly occurred in the fighting on foot in the village and at the station buildings, where we were at a disadvantage owing to the lack of bombs.

It is considered that, if the attack had been delivered in daylight, the casualties would have been much heavier. As it was, most of the fire went over the heads of the attacking troops. This may have been partly due to the fact that the plain was covered with a dense growth of thistles three feet high, but the darkness was the predominant factor.

The element of surprise, which was hoped for – was absent, as the enemy anticipated our attack and was fully prepared for it.

The prisoners gave information that Liman von Sanders had been there two days previously and had ordered them to defend the place to the last and had threatened to shoot anyone who bolted. This, in addition to a very liberal supply of arak [a native spirit] accounted for the stiff fight put up by the enemy.

The casualties incurred in this action, when compared with every other action fought in the pursuit, were very heavy; and this fact cannot be ignored. But it must be remembered that, in this pursuit, the policy was to run big risks in order to obtain quick decisions, and 4th A.L.H. Brigade had the misfortune to run up against very determined opposition.

Seldom, if ever, has a cavalry formation had the courage to make a mounted attack, over unseen country, in the dark. The attack, successful though costly, was skilfully handed and showed a most brilliant spirit.

Australian and New Zealand Mounted Division.
Once VII and VIII Armies ceased to exist, all eyes turned eastwards over Jordan towards Turkish IV Army; its left had been on the Dead Sea and its right in touch with Turkish VII Army, and it was faced by Chaytor's Force

Major-General Sir E. W. C. Chaytor, K.C.M.G., the Commander of ANZAC Mounted Division, had been specially detailed for this operation to command a mixed force, designated Chaytor's Force and constituted as follows:
ANZAC Mounted Division
20th Indian Infantry Brigade(I.S. Infantry)
Composite Infantry Brigade (two battalions Royal Fusiliers and two battalions W.I. Regiment)
a group of artillery.
The force amounted to 4,000 sabres, 6,500 bayonets and 42 guns. The original role of Chaytor's Force, at the opening of the attack on 19 September, was to form a defensive flank to guard the crossings over Jordan east of Jericho and to be prepared, on receipt of orders, to cooperate in the general advance and seize the crossing at Jisr ed Damie.

It will be seen that ANZAC Mounted Division had been withdrawn from Descorps and was not employed with the other three cavalry divisions in the pursuit up the maritime plain. Its role at first was primarily defensive, although it would undoubtedly have its share of forward movement if the Turks retired all along the line.

Many in ANZAC Division felt disappointed that the role chosen for them should have been primarily a defensive one, while the other cavalry divisions were massed for the main effort. Any pursuit which they could hope for would be difficult, tedious and slow because of the mountains east of Jordan, and gave little promise of dashing exploits. Many must have wondered why the C-in-C selected their division for this task. As the three mounted divisions detailed for the main pursuit were armed with the *arme blanche*, whereas ANZAC Division had elected to remain mounted riflemen, it was thought by some that the C-in-C must consider the armament of a mounted rifleman inferior to that of a cavalryman for a pursuit. This may have been the C-in-C's reason, but, as far as the writer knows, he has never said so. Even if this was one reason, there may well have been another –

ANZAC Division had fought through the campaign since its beginning in April 1916. In the Sinai Peninsula, throughout 1917, and during the first half of 1918, this Division had always been where things were hardest and conditions of life most difficult and rough. Certainly no other mounted division could hope to excel the ANZAC Mounted Division in the extremely difficult work which lay ahead over Jordan in the rough mountains of Moab, and it may well have been for this reason that the C-in-C detailed ANZAC Mounted Division to the eastern flank.

The Retreat of Turkish IV Army
The situation in the Jordan valley on 19 September was as follows:
Chaytor's force held the bridgeheads covering the crossings over Jordan from the Dead Sea northwards to the junction of the Wadi Mellaha with the Jordan; the line there ran along the Mellaha to the strong hill of El Musallabeh; then turning slightly south into the mountains to join up with the right of XX Corps.

IV Turkish Army was entrenched across the valley north of El Musallabeh; thence via Um es Shert ford to the foothills at El Haud; thence the main entrenchments followed the foothills southwards covering the main road to Es Salt and the various mountain tracks to the south of it.

During 19 and 20 September, Chaytor's Force confined itself to vigorous patrolling to ensure that the enemy made no move back without their knowledge. This difficult work was very well carried out.

On the morning of 21 September it was found that the enemy resistance was weakening in front of El Musallabeh. The N.Z.M.R. Brigade supported by the 1st Battalion W.I. Regiment moved forward and sent patrols up the roads leading from the Jude An Mountains down into the Jordan valley. The Turks, however, still clung to their trenches covering Um es Shert ford, and there was no sign of any withdrawal from the main position north and south of Shunet Nimrin.

Throughout 22 September, Chaytor's Force continued to press the enemy. In the early morning Um es Shert ford was captured and later the N.Z.M.R. Brigade captured El Makhruk and so closed the last practical line of retreat of Turkish VII Army; the Commander of the Turkish 53rd Division and 500 prisoners were captured here.

By evening the important crossing at Jisr ed Damie was seized by the New Zealanders, though the enemy still held onto the ford at Mafid Jozele. On the east side of Jordan the Turkish outposts were driven in, and by evening the 2nd A.L.H. Brigade was facing the main Turkish position in the foothills at Shunet Nimrin.

Early in the night it became clear that a general retirement of Turkish IV Army had begun, and orders were issued for the force to follow them vigorously; the New Zealanders by the Jisr ed Damie ford supported by the West Indians; the 2nd A.L.H. Brigade by the main Shunet Nimrin-Es Salt road with the 20th Indian Infantry Brigade in support.

23 September
ANZAC Mounted Division spent the day toiling up the Moab Mountains in rear of the Turks. The New Zealanders found a Turkish rearguard in position in the mountains astride the Jisred Damie-Es Salt track with machine guns and barbed wire. This position was outflanked and rushed by the Canterbury Mounted Rifles; and at 19:00 they took Es Salt with 812 prisoners and 3 guns.

Orders were received from G.H.Q. to cut the retreat of the enemy northwards from Amman, and to join with Feisal's Arabs.

The whole of 24 September was occupied in concentrating the force on top of the hills. Reconnaissances were pushed forward to Amman, and met opposition. That night a party of Auckland Mounted Rifles cut the railway line near Kalaatel Zerka.

25 September

At 06:00 the mounted troops marched on Amman; 2nd A.L.H. Brigade from Ain el Sir; N.Z.M.R. Brigade, followed by 1st A.L.H. Brigade, moving just north of the Es Salt-Amman road. If Amman was lightly held the mounted troops were to push in; if strongly held they were to await the arrival of the infantry.

The enemy were found in position holding the ridges west of the town in a series of localities defended with machine guns; their guns in the rear opened as the troops advanced. The mounted troops pressed forward, galloping round the flanks of the defended localities, and the garrisons surrendered easily. The citadel and town and railway station were captured in quick succession; all resistance ceased at 14:30 hours; 2,500 prisoners, 13 guns and 40 machine guns had been captured.

The capture of Amman and the retreat of the greater part of Turkish IV Army northwards from Amman towards Deraa completely cut off the retreat of the Turkish II Corps which had been stationed at Maan, 120 miles south of Amman on the Hedjaz railway, and which was known to be retiring northwards on Amman.

26 and 27 September

The 2nd A.L.H. Brigade, reconnoitring southwards, located the advancing Turkish II Corps near Ziza station.

1st A.L.H. Brigade pushed northwards and in cooperation with an aeroplane had a successful action. The aeroplane located the enemy in the Wadi el Hammam, and dropped a message on the Light Horse. The aeroplane then returned over the Wadi and drove the enemy back into it with machine gun fire. The Light Horse made a frontal attack with one squadron; another, sweeping round the enemy's right, charged it. The enemy broke and surrendered, 453 prisoners and 3 machine guns being taken.

Water reconnaissances were then pushed on to Mafrak station, but none was found.

28 September
Turkish II Corps was now concentrated near Kastal; it numbered about 6,000, and had three trains on the railway line. It was being watched from the north by 2nd A.L.H. Brigade, and the Arab forces were all round it. The entire water supply to the North was in British hands and escape was impossible. A message was, therefore, dropped on the Turkish Corps Headquarters, which ran as follows:

> To the Commander,
> Turkish Force, Kastal.
> Surrender your force at Kastal. We hold all water you can reach. You cannot march northward now. If you surrender put a large white flag on the station buildings. If you do not surrender you will be bombed by our aeroplanes.

29 September
No answer was returned and preparations were made to bomb this force; but at 11:45 hours the Commander opened negotiations with 5th A.L.H. Regiment, which was picqueting the force on the north. He said he was willing to surrender, but if he put up a white flag as requested the Arabs, who were all round him, would rush him at once. To prevent this 2nd A.L.H. Brigade went forward to accept the Turkish surrender. The Brigade had a great deal of trouble with the Arabs, who numbered several thousand; in particular they made two attempts to rush the Turkish hospital. The Light Horse were finally forced to turn a Hotchkiss gun on to them, and drive them off. Eventually the Arabs dispersed and disappeared and the Turkish surrender was taken.

This ended the operations of the ANZAC Mounted Division; it was unable to do more. A large proportion of Turkish IV Army had escaped northwards to Deraa, but they had been harried in retreat and were in an exhausted condition. ANZAC Mounted Division could not pursue any further for two reasons. Firstly, reconnaissances had discovered no water between Amman and Deraa; to follow the Turks into that area would merely be to share with them the agony of thirst and its consequences, and quite possible disaster. Secondly, almost immediately Turkish II Corps was taken, malaria broke out and nearly 6,000 (out of 11,000) of Chaytor's Force went down within a month.

ANZAC Mounted Division can be well satisfied with its share in the victory; it was in pursuit of one-third of the entire Turkish forces; its work lay in the roughest country in all Palestine; and it captured 10,822 prisoners, 57guns and 147 machine guns.

The Pursuit to Damascus(Map C)
The total defeat of the VII and VIII Turkish Armies, and the retreat of the IV Turkish Army had removed any serious obstacle to an advance on Damascus. 55,000 Turks had been captured, but 45,000 Turks and Germans still remained, either in Damascus or retreating on it; of these latter, the remnants of IV Army, retreating through Deraa, formed the largest part. It is true that these units were in a state of disorganisation, but, given time, they could have pulled themselves together and could have formed a force capable of delaying any further advance.

The C-in-C therefore, on 25 September, ordered the Desert Mounted Corps to pursue to Damascus, to occupy the city, and to intercept the retreat of the remnants of IV Turkish Army.

Descorps was to advance on Damascus in two columns; Ausdiv and Fivecav from Nazareth, via Tiberias, Jisr Benat, Yakub Bridge, Kuneitra and Sasa; Fourcav from Beisan via Jisr Mejamie, Irbid, Deraa and thence north (a distance of 120 miles), in cooperation with Feisal's Arabs, who were already operating against Deraa from the eastward.

26. PHASE V PART 2
(Ref. Map C, and Plate XVI.)

Advance on Damascus.
As previously stated, the C-in-C had ordered Descorps to pursue to Damascus, to occupy the city, and to intercept the Turkish IV Army, which was retreating from Amman through Deraa to Damascus.

On 26 September, Fourcav concentrated at Beisan, with one Brigade at Jisr Mejamie and patrols out eastward searching for the allied Arabs.

Ausdiv concentrated at Tiberias with patrols to Safed; Fivecav moved up from the coast to Kefr Kenna, close behind Ausdiv.

27 September 27 (see Plate XVI)
At 06:00, Ausdiv left Tiberias, followed by Fivecav. All went well until the Jordan was reached, and here the bridge at Jisr Benat Yakub was found to be destroyed, and the opposite bank held by Turks and Germans with field guns, machine guns and rifles. Ausdiv was faced with a very difficult task; the enemy's position completely commanded the river; a turning movement by the north would be cramped for room, as the southern end of Lake Huleh is only 1½ miles north of the bridge; and to the south of the bridge the river is unfordable, and the country, east of the river, only just passable, owing to the huge slabs of lava rock

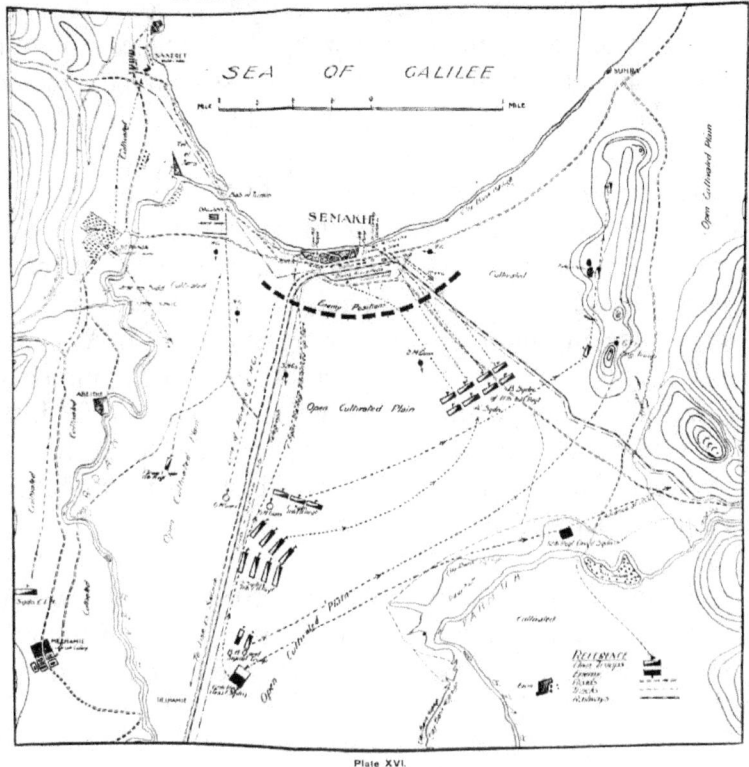

PALESTINE—MAP SHOWING DISPOSITION OF TROOPS DURING PERIOD OF OPERATIONS AGAINST SEMAKH BY THE 4th AUSTRALIAN L.H. BRIGADE, ON SEPTEMBER 25, 1918.

Plate XVI.

which cover the glacis sloping down to the river.

East of Jordan the road runs as if in a defile, owing to the almost impassable nature of the ground to north and south of it; and it rises over 8,500 feet before Kuneitra, 18 miles away, is reached.

The situation was an anxious one; time was a vital factor if Turkish IV Army was to be intercepted at Damascus; and it was obvious that the enemy in position east of Jordan was holding an ideal rearguard position, and that many more equally suitable positions existed between it and Kuneitra.

A frontal attack would have been costly, and the G.O.C. Ausdiv decided to try and turn both flanks and so manoeuvre the enemy out of his position.

The 3rd A.L.H. Brigade was ordered to try and cross the river at the south end of Lake Huleh; the 5th A.L.H. Brigade, to hold the enemy in front with one regiment, and to cross with the remainder about 8 miles to the south, where a ford had been reported.

Both brigades were energetically opposed and did not succeed in crossing for many hours; the leading regiment of 3rd A.L.H. Brigade got across a few men at a time under cover of the massed fire of the remainder of the Brigade, including the other two Regiments, the machine gun squadron, and the R.H.A. battery. The 5th A.L.H. Brigade, a few miles to the south, turned the southern flank of the position; although they found no ford, they were able to effect a crossing, as they were outside the reach of effective opposition. In this case, therefore, it was the mobility of the cavalry, which defeated the defending infantry.

Owing to the rough country east of Jordan, Ausdiv was not concentrated at Deir el Saras until well after dawn the following day, 28 September, and most of the troops had been struggling all night amongst the rocks.

The enemy, estimated at 1,000 strong, succeeded in escaping in motor-lorries; they left 70 prisoners and four field guns in our hands. A delay of nearly 24 hours had been forced upon Ausdiv, a delay which might have been much greater but for the splendid determination of the Australian Light Horse to force a crossing.

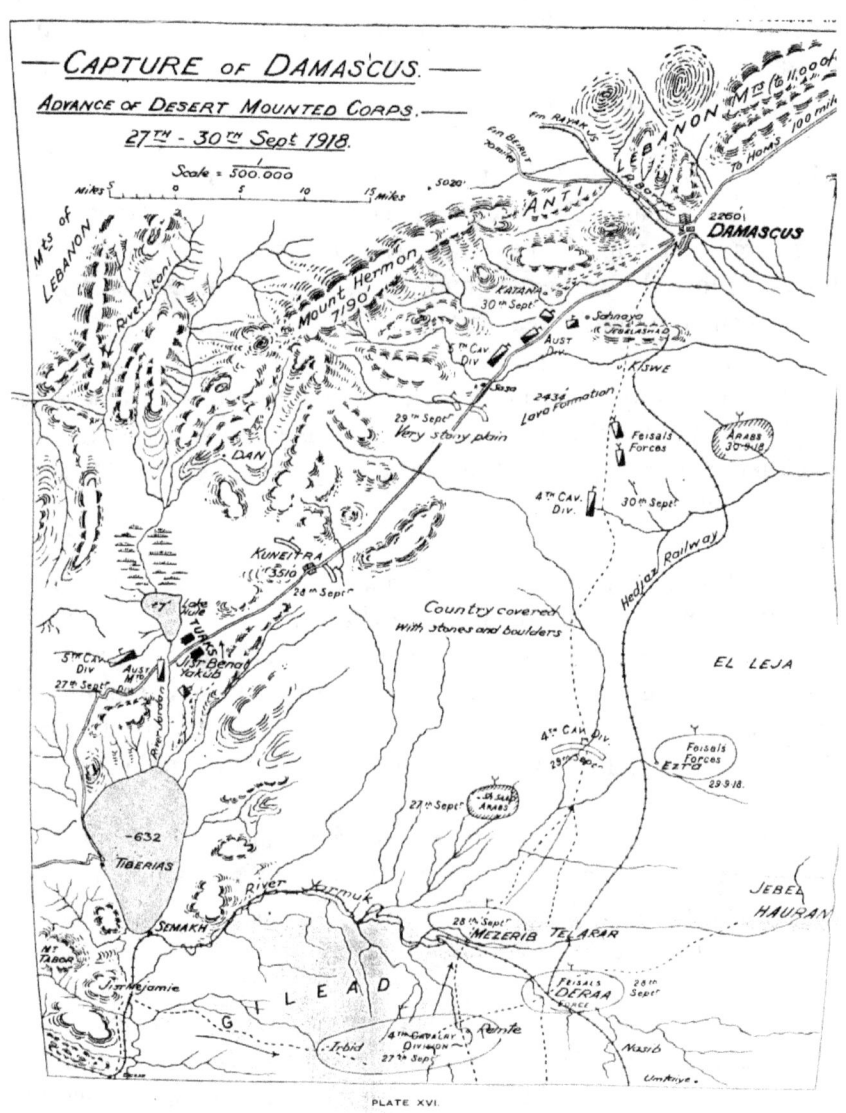

PLATE XVI.

29 September
Early on this day Descorps Head Quarters, Ausdiv and Fivecav were concentrated at Kuneitra; Australian engineers had repaired the Jordan bridge and all the transport was across. The intelligence showed that we were on the far side of all the main obstacles to success, for from Kuneitra a great plain stretched away to Damascus.

Much time had been lost; it was felt that great efforts must now be made to reach Damascus, if Turkish IV Army was to be intercepted. It was decided that Ausdiv should march at 1700 hours, followed by Fivecav, and it was hoped that Damascus, 37 miles distant, might be reached early next morning.

Earlier in the day an armoured car reconnaissance had disclosed the fact that a hostile force, with guns, was in position astride the road about four miles south of Sasa; and in spite of this fact, the night march was ordered.

At 20:00 hours, the 3rd A.L.H. Brigade was held up by machine gun fire between the Wadi Mughaniye and Sasa. They were ordered to clear the enemy away. The operation proved very difficult owing to the masses of lava deposits making it impossible for mounted men to move across country in the dark; the enemy's right flank was protected by an impenetrable bog.

An attack was made in the dark, and at 03:00 hours on 30 September, the enemy was driven from his position by 3rd A.L.H. Brigade, leaving 2 field guns, 7 machine guns and 25 prisoners in our hands.

The experience of this night seems to show that it is unwise to march cavalry through the night if opposition is to be expected; cavalry are not well able to carry out an attack on a position during darkness. In this case the 3rd A.L.H. Brigade fought for many hours through the night, while the remainder of Ausdiv and Fivecav lay down on the road holding their horses and listening to the fight in front. As a result no one in two divisions got any real sleep and little progress was made.

It is easy now to say that it would have been wiser to have postponed the hour of march from Kuneitra until such time as would have ensured the advance guard coming up against the enemy's known position soon after dawn next morning, instead of, as occurred, early in the night.

30 September
To make up for the delay, the pursuit was pushed with great speed; the way seemed open to Damascus, still 20 miles distant. During the morning a contact aeroplane dropped a message on Ausdiv Headquarters to say that about 2,500 Turks were in position on the ridge Jebel el Aswad, a narrow ridge which extends westwards as far as the village of Kaukab on the main Damascus-Kuneitra road.

General Hodgson decided to operate with the whole of Ausdiv in order to reduce delay to a minimum. He ordered the only two regiments of the 4th A.L.H. Brigade which were present, under Lt-Col Bourchier, to attack frontally against the enemy's right at Kaukab, supported by the fire of 19th Brigade R.H.A.; while the 5th and 3rd A.L.H. Brigades were to manoeuvre round the enemy's right, directing their advance on Katana.

Under support from very heavy fire from the Horse Artillery, and assisted by the movement of the two brigades past the enemy's right, Colonel Bourchier's force very quickly completed all preliminary arrangements and made a mounted attack straight at the ridge. The enemy did not wait; large numbers fled into the woods behind the position, to be captured later on; but they left 72 prisoners and 12 machine guns in Col Bourchier's hands.

On this occasion the unusual sight could be seen of an entire cavalry division (less one regiment) manoeuvring in two wings in comparatively close formation across an open plain against an enemy in position, with the R.H.A. in action supporting the advance; both wings of the division being within full view of each other, and the Divisional Commander riding forward with his staff between the two wings and controlling them by gallopers. Such a manoeuvre had been visualised in our training manuals, but has seldom actually occurred in modern war; it is not likely to occur often, if ever, in the future, unless the enemy's air forces are first driven from the battle area, as was the case on this occasion.

Meanwhile, a hostile column of 2,000 had been reported by contact aeroplane to be moving from Kiswe towards Damascus (Plate XVI.). The G.O.C. Fivecav sent 14th Cavalry Brigade to intercept this force. This brigade cut the enemy column in half, capturing the bulk of the leading portion, including the remnants of 3rd Turkish Cavalry Division, with Divisional Commander and staff. The Brigade then pushed on and bivouacked for the night in the southern outskirts of Damascus.

The rear half of the column cut in two by 14th Cavalry Brigade broke back and moved up the West Zabirani towards Khan Shiha. The remainder of Fivecav was sent to deal with this and captured 1,000 prisoners, heading the remainder off towards Fourcav, the guns of which Division were seen, just before dusk, to be firing from the direction of Khiara towards Kiswe. Thus, at this hour, the junction of the two widely separated columns of Descorps may be said to have been effected; and also the Arab forces from the east had established touch with Fourcav.

Fourcav had carried out a pursuit of 140 miles in six days; it had met difficult country throughout, and had carried its supplies with it on wheels. The following is an extract from Descorps' report on the march of Fourcav:

> September 26. Fourcav. was moving via Jisr Mejamie and Irbid on Deraa. The road was found very difficult and bad. The leading Brigade (10th Cavalry Brigade) met with opposition en route, but made Irbid by nightfall.
>
> September 27. 10th Cavalry Brigade still met with

opposition and some good work by the Dorset Yeomanry in a charge resulted in 200 prisoners and 20 machine guns. Touch was gained with the Arab Forces to the east.

September 28. Deraa was entered without opposition. It was found in a general state of confusion, having been heavily bombed by our aeroplanes and looted by Bedouins.

September 29. Fourcav., with the Arab Forces on the right flank, reached Ezra (Dilli) Station, and contacted the retreating Turkish IV. Army.

September 30. The Division followed up the retiring Turks, firing into and breaking up their columns, and on 31 October arrived at Zerakiye, getting in touch with the remainder of Descorps.

Ausdiv
After breaking down the opposition at Kaukab, about noon September 30, Ausdiv pressed on through Katana; its task was to get astride the enemy's lines of retreat from Damascus along the Beirut and Homs roads (Plate XVI). 5th A.L.H. Brigade followed by 3rd A.L.H. Brigade found the hills and gardens about El Mezze strongly held and 16 machine guns were located firing from long-prepared positions. Two alternatives presented themselves: the first, to charge mounted along the narrow plain, only a few hundred yards broad, which runs south-west from El Mezze (Map C); the second, to turn to the left and scramble on foot up the hills to the west of El Mezze, and so reach the Barada Gorge from the heights above and to the south of it.

It was decided not to run the risk of the heavy casualties, which might be expected if a mounted attack was made into such a confined space: this is one of the few occasions in this pursuit when the British cavalry declined the mounted attack when the surface of the ground was suitable for it.

The dismounted cavalry working into the hills made little

progress; fortunately, about 13:00 hours, Notts Battalion R.H.A. arrived and quickly came into action against the enemy's machine guns; the effect was almost instantaneous; the machine guns ceased firing, and the crews abandoned their guns and fled; such is the effect of even weak artillery upon demoralised troops. Few better examples could be found to show the necessity of a mobile artillery, even though weak in shell power, with a cavalry formation.

Scrambling over the hills, 5th A.L.H. Brigade, led by the *Régiment Mixte de Cavalerie* (Commandant Lebon), reached the southern heights overlooking the Barada Gorge just before dusk.

It was seen that a huge crowd of fugitives (now believed to have consisted of 14,000 troops and the belongings of Turkish officers, including their wives), and masses of transport were struggling to escape through the gorge. Machine guns we returned on to the head of the column and the defile was turned into a veritable shambles; railway trains and every conceivable kind of transport were wrecked. There was no way of escape for those in front, and those in rear fled back to Damascus; 4,000 of these were captured by 14th A.L.H. Regiment.

The next morning, October 1, the 3rd A.L.H. Brigade succeeded in getting astride the Damascus-Homs road, and the large force in Damascus and all that remained of Turkish IV Army were trapped; 13,000 of these were rounded up by Ausdiv during this day. It is believed that at least 22,000 (including sick) were taken at, or in the vicinity of, Damascus.

With the capture of this city, the triumph of General Allenby's army was complete.

On 26 September, when Descorps started out on the second stage of its pursuit, some 45,000 Turks and Germans were still in Damascus or retreating on it. It is true that these troops were in a state of disorganisation, but, given time, the enemy could have formed a force capable of delaying any further advance. The destruction of Turkish IV Army and the capture of an additional 20,000 prisoners prevented any possibility of this. The remnants of the Turkish armies in Palestine and Syria, numbering some 17,000 men, of whom only 4,000 were effectives, fled northwards, a mass of individuals without organisation, without transport, and without any of the accessories required to enable it to act even on the defensive.

The prisoners captured by Descorps and passed through the Corps cages between the dates 19 September and 22 October numbered 2,417 officers and 46,409 other ranks, of which 158 Officers and 1,703 other ranks were Germans. These do not include large numbers evacuated direct to hospitals.

The battle casualties of Descorps (3 cavalry divisions) during the operations were very light, amounting to:

	British Officers	Indian Officers	British O.R.	Indian O.R.
Killed	11	5	51	58
Wounded	36	12	200	117
Missing	1		15	27
Total	48	17	266	202

The sick rate of the Corps, however, had been exceptionally high, principally due to malaria. As a result, Fourcav was unable to march when called on later to follow Fivecav northwards towards Aleppo.

27. EXPLOITING SUCCESS

Although the enemy's field armies had practically ceased to exist, General Allenby was determined to exploit his success and to advance to the line Rayak-Beirut (see Plate XVII). This would provide a port, with a road and railway leading inland to Rayak and Damascus.

One move forward led to another, and as a result, Fivecav was called upon to make, and successfully accomplished, a most remarkable march, which only ended at Muslimie Junction, north of Aleppo.

This account of the doings of Descorps would be incomplete, however, without some statement as to the task accomplished by Fivecav. The following is, more or less, an extract from the C-in-C's despatch (see Plate XVII).

Descorps, leaving Ausdiv at Damascus, moved on Rayak on 5 October. No opposition was encountered; on the aerodrome were found the remains of 80 aeroplanes, which had been burnt by the enemy before he retired.

In the meantime the 7th (Meerut) Division had marched from Haifa to Beirut, arriving on October 8. Ships of the French Navy had already entered the harbour.

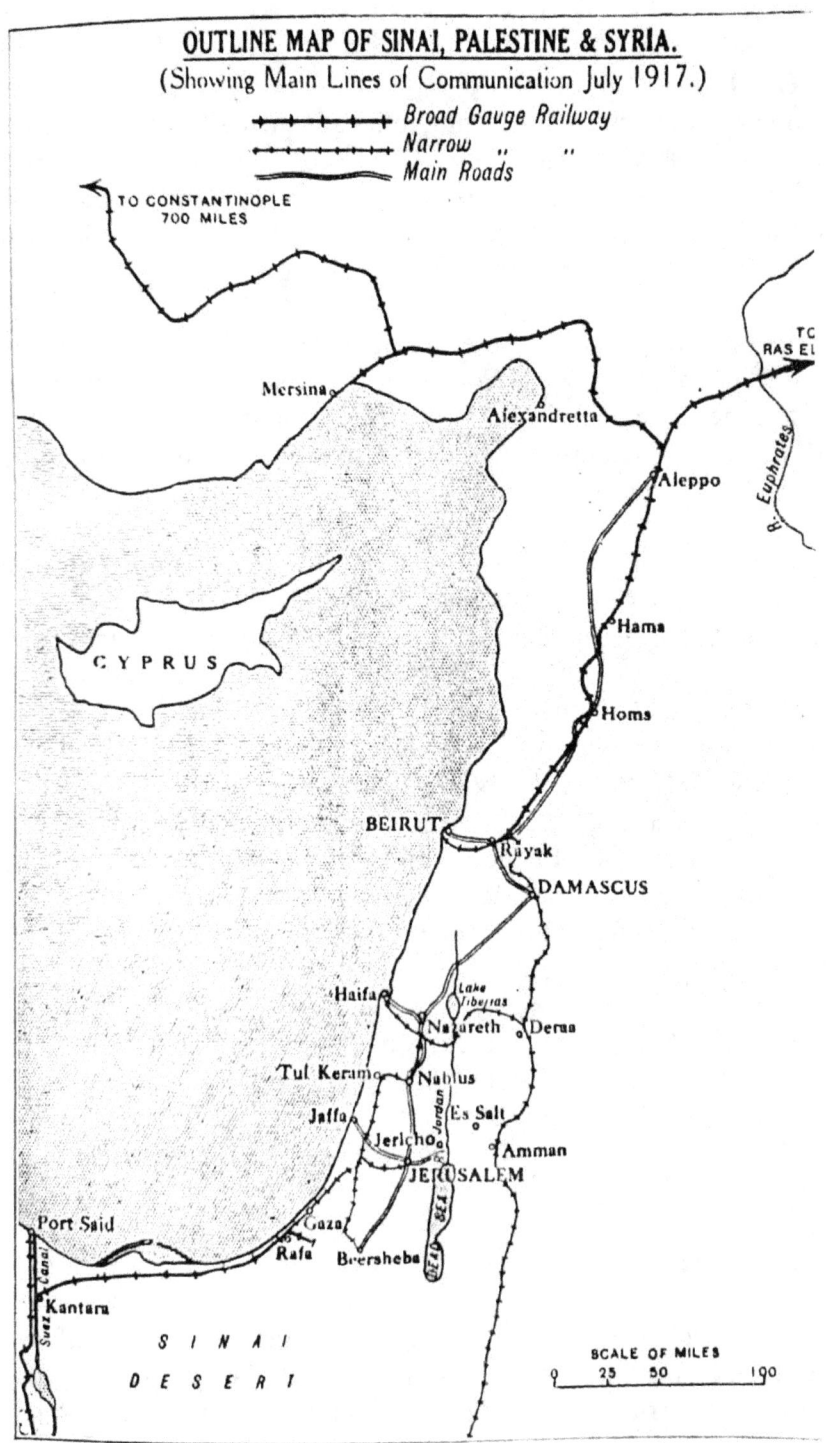

9 October
Descorps was ordered to continue its advance and occupy Homs, leaving Ausdiv at Damascus, XXI Corps was to advance along the coast from Beirut for 50 miles to Tripoli. Fivecav, preceded by a column of armoured cars, reached Homs on 15 October, having marched over 80 miles since leaving Rayak.

Tripoli, on the coast (50 miles north of Beirut), had been occupied on 18 October by XXI Corps cavalry regiment and armoured cars; they were followed by one Brigade of 7th (Meerut) Division. The occupation of Tripoli provided a shorter route by which to supply Fivecav at Homs.

Having secured Homs and Tripoli, the C-in-C determined to seize Aleppo quickly. Fivecav and the armoured cars alone were available. Ausdiv, at Damascus, was over 100 miles distant from Homs, and could not be brought up in time. Fourcav, near Rayak, was much-reduced in strength by sickness, and needed a rest to reorganise. Time was of importance, and the C-in-C judged that Fivecav would be strong enough for the purpose. The information available indicated the presence of some 20,000 Turks and Germans at Aleppo; of these, only some 8,000 were combatants and they were demoralised; moreover, reports from all sources showed that considerable numbers were leaving the town daily by rail for the north.

On 20 October, the armoured cars under command of G.O.C. Fivecav had reached Hama without opposition. They consisted of Nos 2, 11 and 12 L.A.M. Batteries and Nos 1 (Australian), 2 and 7 Light Car patrols, (Ford vans carrying one or two machine guns and crew).

On 21 October Fivecav marched from Homs.

On 22 October the armoured cars reached a village halfway between Homs and Aleppo, just as the enemy's rearguard left the village in lorries. A German armoured car, a lorry and some prisoners were captured.

The enemy was not encountered again till 24 October, when a body of cavalry was dispersed 10 miles south of Aleppo. Five miles further on, the armoured cars were checked by strong Turkish rearguards, and had to remain in observation until the cavalry came up.

On the afternoon of 25 October, the armoured cars were joined by 15th (I.S.) Cavalry Brigade; that evening a detachment of the Arab Army reached the eastern outskirts of Aleppo, and during the night forced their way in, inflicting heavy casualties on the enemy.

Early on the morning of 26 October the armoured cars and 15th Cavalry Brigade, moving round the west side of the town, gained touch with the enemy. The Turkish rearguard consisted of some 2,500 infantry, 150 cavalry, and eight guns. The Mysore Lancers and two squadrons of Jodhpur Lancers attacked the enemy's left, covered by the fire of the armoured cars, the M.G. squadron, and two dismounted squadrons of Jodhpur Lancers. The Mysore and the Jodhpur Lancers charged most gallantly. A number of Turks were speared, and many threw down their arms, only to pick them up again when the cavalry had passed through and their weakness had become apparent. The squadrons were not strong enough to complete the victory, and were withdrawn till a larger force could be assembled. That night the Turkish rearguard withdrew to a position 20 miles north of Aleppo. Fivecav remained in observation astride the roads leading north from Aleppo, and occupied Muslimie railway junction; it was too weak to continue the advance to Alexandretta till the arrival of Ausdiv, which had already left Damascus to join it. Before the latter could arrive the Armistice between the Allies and Turkey had been concluded, and came into force at noon on 31 October.

Fivecav had covered 500 miles between 19 September and 26 October, and during this period had lost only 21 percent of its horses.

So ended this great achievement of Desert Mounted Corps. Cavalry history repeated itself a century and more after Jena; and we cavalry soldiers can be quite confident, provided we ally ourselves to modern developments, that history will repeat itself again.